JN254433

2018／第21号

音韻研究
Phonological Studies

日本音韻論学会 編
The Phonological Society of Japan

開拓社

目次 / **Table of Contents**

講演 / Lectures

発表要旨 / Abstracts

巻頭言 / FOREWORD

巻頭言：日本音韻論学会のこれから

　日本音韻論学会では、一昨年の 2016 年に『現代音韻論の動向：日本音韻論学会 20 周年記念論文集』を発刊しました。同時期に、学会ロゴの選定、英語ホームページ作成、20 周年記念シンポジウム開催、20 周年記念パーティーの開催なども行いました。学会の設立が 1997 年ですから、その設立 20 周年記念を行うのは 2017 年ではないかと思われた方もいらっしゃるかもしれません。しかし、年祝いの行事は伝統的に「満年齢」ではなく「数え年」で行なっていたこと、田端前会長の任期最終年度にやりたかったこと、事業報告を記念すべき『音韻研究』第 20 号で果たしたかったこと、などの理由から 2016 年に行ったというわけであります。

　さて、この巻頭言は慣例に従って、歴代会長の就任と退任のご挨拶の時期に、みなさまへメッセージをお送りするスペースとして与えられたものです。例の『現代音韻論の動向』では「日本音韻論学会の昔と今」というテーマで学会の経緯や動向について副会長として書かせていただきましたが、ここでは「日本音韻論学会のこれから」を占いたいと思います。「昔と今」を受けての「これから」です。

　その「占い」に関して示唆的なのが、今年度の音韻論フォーラム 2017 に招聘され、この『音韻研究』第 21 号にも所収されている Elan Dresher 氏と Keren Rice 氏のご研究です。トロント学派のお二人です。今回のご講演を聞いていて、「当たり前を疑うこと」という当たり前なテーゼを改めて思い知らされました。テクニカルに重要な細部はさておき、根本のところで特に印象深かったのが、次の 2 つの論点です。つまり、1 つは、音韻素性が普遍的・生得的で、かつそれ以上分解不可能なプリミティブだという「常識」に対し、言語ごとの学習で形成される「創発的な特性(emergent property)」であるというお二人の主張。もう 1 つは、有標性階層が普遍的・生得的で、これにより言語の可能・不可能なパターンが説明できるという「常識」に対し、最も有標な舌背音が挿入や中和に現れるなどの「不可能な多様性」から、これも言語ごとの学習で形成されるべきであるという Rice 氏の主張。前者はすでに Dresher (2009) *The Contrastive Hierarchy in Phonology* (CUP)で体系的に打ち出されていましたし、Mielke (2008) *The Emergence of Distinctive Features* (OUP)も同じ流れにありました。また、後者についても、早くから Hume and Tserdanelis (2002) "Labial Unmarkedness in Sri Lankan Portuguese Creole" (*Phonology*19) や Blevins (2004) *Evolutionary Phonology* (CUP)などがこの流れにありました。最近でも Samuels (ed.) (2017) *Beyond Markedness in Formal Phonology* (John Benjamins)はこの流れに追い打ちをかけます。

　もちろん時代を問わず「本流」に対する「傍流」は常にあるわけで、アンチテーゼの存在は今に始まったものではありませんが、その「傍流」が「本流」を凌駕する勢いを時代とともに持つようになるというところがポイントです。そして、最近の「言語の起源と進化」を考える進化言語学の潮流では、音韻素性や有標性（階層どころか概念そのもの）が普遍的・生得的なプリミティブであることは、完全に否定されます。人間言語がある種の固有性を持つとしても、進化が近縁他種との連続性のもとで漸進的に（ほんの少しずつ）生ずるものだとすれば、他種にない人間固有の普遍的・生得的なプリミティブが豊かすぎるというのは、想定上あり得ないからです。思うに、人間言語の固有性は、人間固有の生得的な実体としてではなく、ある程度他種と共通する基盤の「使い方」にこそあるのではないでしょうか。その「使い方」は、学習や認知の能力など普遍文法の外にあるものに他なりません。

　さて、時代とともに後発の「傍流」が「本流」を凌駕する（くらいの勢いを見せる）現象もまた、

今に始まったことでもありません。そもそも 20 世紀後半以降の音韻論は、構造主義・相対主義音韻論 → SPE 流生成音韻論 → 自然音韻論 → 原理とパラメータの非線状音韻論 → 最適性理論 → 実験・コーパス音韻論、といった潮流で流れてきました。その背景で、音韻論以外の文法理論も、アメリカ構造主義言語学 → 生成文法標準理論 → 生成意味論 → 解釈意味論・原理とパラメータのアプローチ → 認知言語学（認知意味論・認知文法） → ミニマリストプログラム → 実験・コーパス統語論、のような変遷を経験しました。矢印は勢いのある「傍流」の発生を意味します。いずれの領域でも、大雑把にザックリいうと、これらは「機能主義」と「形式主義」の拮抗、または「定量・実証主義」と「定質・思弁主義」の相克として、特徴付けられるのではないかと思います。そうした振り幅の中で、最近では「機能主義」「定量・実証主義」が文字通り「幅を利かせている」といってよいでしょう。

　こうした変遷の中で、私たちは一体、何を信じて研究生活を送ったらよいのでしょうか。拠り所となる真実とは何なのでしょうか。「私たち」というのは、研究上のアイデンティティ確立を模索する若い研究者だけでなく、ずっと研究を続けてきた中堅以上の研究者も含みます。時代精神によってプラットフォームが変遷する以上、アイデンティティの問い直し作業がどの研究者にも常に迫られるからです。一生続きます。その作業の中で、過去の非常識が現在の常識に、現在の常識が未来の非常識になることを覚悟しなければなりません。蛇足ですが、日常生活でもこの覚悟の必要性を最近痛感しました。雷が鳴り始めた時にどう危険を回避するかについて、「木の下へ避難する」「金具は身に付けない」というのが、私の子供の頃（昭和 40 年代）の常識でした。しかし、『池上彰のニュース そうだったのか!! #59』（2017 年 9 月 16 日放送、テレビ朝日）によると、今の常識では「木の高さから 45 度下方で待つ」「金具を身に付けても付けなくても同確率で落ちる」そうです。雷鳴と雨に打たれながら「45 度下方」を探す覚悟はありますか？

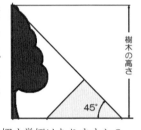

　結局、拠り所が変遷する以上、採るべき道は次のようなものでしょう。つまり、真実は二者択一ではなく二者両立にあるものと想定して、バランスよく方法論に精通する努力を怠らないこと（当然、「二者」を「多者」に置き換えても構いません）。もっと言えば、健全なアカデミズムとは、認め合い学び合う懐の深さにこそあるということ。逆に、盲信・不信を動機とした枠組み依存や、その動機からくる縄張り主義は、自らの命取りとなるでしょう。拠り所をなくした時に損するのは自分なのですから。むしろ、「45 度下方」のように、不安であっても拠り所からある程度の距離をおくのが得策でしょう。

　もちろん学会としても、形式主義・思弁主義か機能主義・実証主義かの枠組みや、理論系・実験系・記述系などの方法論、そして対象言語も問わず歓迎されるべきです。外国語学、国語学、日本語学、方言学、歴史言語学、社会言語学、心理言語学、一般言語学など様々な専門領域が含まれます。特定の主義主張に閉じこもらずに広くアンテナを張ってこそ、専門分野や背景を越えて「音」をめぐり互いに啓発し合うことができ、ひいては音韻研究の真の発展に繋がるわけで、ここが大事です。本学会が枠組みや方法論や対象言語を問わないことは、この『音韻研究』第 21 号を見ても明らかでしょう。

　以上、音韻研究の経緯と在り方を鑑みた本学会の今後の精神に関する私見をもって、会長の巻頭言としました。この任期中は東京オリンピックの開催などもあり波乱含みですが、学会はみなさまの研究例会・音韻論フォーラムのご投稿とご参加、および機関紙『音韻研究』へのご投稿で成り立っております。この 4 年間（もちろんそれ以降も）どうかよろしくご協力のほどお願い申し上げます。

2017 年 10 月　　　　　　　　　　　　　　　　　　　　　日本音韻論学会　会長

　　　　　　　　　　　　　　　　　　　　　　　　　　　田 中 伸 一

論文 / PAPERS

Is Syllabification Necessary in Tokyo Japanese? Syllables as Non-lexical Units[*]

Akitsugu Nogita
Kokushikan University

ABSTRACT.   This study attempts to support Labrune's (2012) analysis that the Tokyo Japanese phonological hierarchy lacks the syllable node by discussing various problems of the syllable-based analyses for pitch accent patterns and other phenomena. Syllable is a sonority unit while mora, or *haku* 'beat', is a timing unit. Based on these definitions, I argue that syllable does not have a role in distinguishing lexical items, and I demonstrate that many phenomena can be explained better without involving syllable. It would be safer to only state that phonetically syllable-like behaviours could be observed in certain places of a word in certain conditions.

Keywords: syllable-less analysis, sonority peak, mora, Japanese syllable structure, Labrune (2012)

1. Background
1.1 Introduction
Accounts of syllable in Tokyo Japanese (henceforth Japanese) differ. On one hand, various studies (e.g. Kawahara 2016; Tanaka 2013) provide evidence that syllable does exist in Japanese. On the other hand, Labrune (2012) argues that foot is directly linked to mora without syllable in the phonological hierarchy. In my opinion, the traditional view that syllable exists in the Japanese phonological hierarchy sounds too strong; it would be better rephrased that "phonetically syllable-like behaviors are occasionally observed in Japanese" or that "a combination of multiple morae could behave like one unit in certain places of a word in certain conditions." In this study, I support Labrune's syllable-less analysis by pointing out several problems of the traditional syllable-based view, and argue that syllable is a unit with a *sonority peak,* while mora in Japanese is a (psychological) *timing* unit (cf. Tanaka 2008), therefore these can be independent of each other. Thus, syllable in Japanese is a *non-lexical* unit and is absent in the phonological hierarchy. More specifically, 1) syllable does not have a role in distinguishing lexical items, and 2) it is not necessary to parse every mora into a syllable. In other words, syllable in Japanese is a phonetic artefact that arises at the post-lexical level.

There was an incident that triggered my argument. As a native speaker of Tokyo Japanese and an English-as-a-second-language learner, it was not until learning Mandarin (which is a syllable-dominant language and has both stress and pitch contrasts) as my third language that I was finally able to "feel" syllable, stress, and foot in English. Before learning Mandarin, I was deaf to these entities, although I had learned the theories. At that time, I used to follow the traditional syllable-based view when analysing Japanese sounds. After I became able to recognize syllable by hearing, I started to have a whole different view.

1.2 Definition of terms
Before discussing the details, I will define some of the terms used in this paper.
(1) Syllable – A unit with one sonority peak
(2) Mora – A unit originally used to measure syllable weight (Kubozono 1998). In this study I define mora as a (psychological) timing unit (cf. Tanaka 2008). In this sense, the general Japanese term *haku* 'beat' may be more appropriate or less confusing.
(3) Unsyllabified segment – A segment not incorporated into a syllable
(4) Non-lexical – Lacking a role to distinguish lexical items: for example, in Japanese, native Japanese speakers are aware of the phonetic difference between [oɾe] (with a flap 'r') and [ore] (with a trill 'r') and these two forms can change registers or can be used in different social settings; but both still represent the same lexical item /ore/ (first person for males).

There is also a crucial term *foot*, but in this paper I will not discuss it. I tentatively regard *foot* as a combination of two morae, in accordance with Kubozono and Honma (2002).

2. Two tiers, timing tier and sonority tier

In the most common analysis, the so-called special/dependent morae, /Q/ (moraic obstruent), /N/ (moraic nasal), /R/ (the second half of a long vowel), and /J/ (the second half of a diphthong) are combined with the preceding independent mora /V/, /CV/ or /CGV/ (V = vowel, C = consonant, G = glide) making a two-mora syllable, such as a /CVN/ syllable. Three-mora syllables arguably exist when there are two consecutive dependent morae, such as /CVJN/ as in /waJN/ 'wine' (Kubozono 1994:9). While the syllable node is placed above the mora node and below the foot node in the phonological hierarchy in the traditional view (e.g. Tanaka 2013), I propose that there should be two independent tiers – a timing tier and a sonority tier. The former is used to distinguish lexical items while the latter is not. Note that the sonority tier constructed with syllables is generally not necessary, but one can use it when syllable-like behaviours are observed (as in mora-note assignment in lyrics as discussed in §3.3). For instance, the word /haNtai/ 'opposition,' realized as [hantai], is syllabified as [han. tai] (period = syllable boundary) in a common analysis, as shown on the left side in Figure 1.

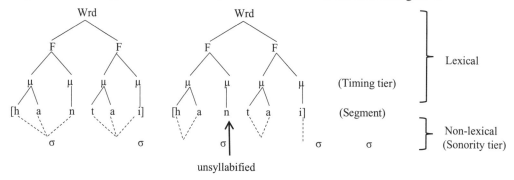

Figure 1 *The phonological hierarchy with timing (lexical) and sonority (non-lexical) tiers*
F = foot, μ = mora, σ = syllable

/haNtai/ can also be realized as [ha. n. ta. i] in slower speech, with more weight on [n] and an amplitude dip between [a] and [i]. In this case, [n] can be unsyllabified, and [a] and [i] may belong to different syllables, as shown on the right side in Figure 1. This means that the syllable structure can vary depending on the phonetic realization, but the lexical item and the mora structure stay the same. This suggests that syllable is non-lexical, and is independent from the mora and foot nodes, which is the reason that I propose two tiers.

Some linguists (e.g. Kondo 2000) regard morae with devoiced/deleted high vowels as non-syllabic.[1] Including such morae, /gakuɕiki/ 'scholarship', for example, often realized as [gakuɕki] with its first [i] devoiced/deleted, can be analyzed as a three-syllable word [ga. kuɕ. ki] based on its three sonority peaks, as shown on the left side in Figure 2. However, it can also be realized as [ga. ku. ɕ. ki] in slower speech, with more weight on [ɕ], which can be regarded as unsyllabified, as shown on the right side in Figure 2. Although it is not shown in Figure 2, [gakɕki] is also a possible realization, which can be analyzed as two syllables, like [gak. ɕki], or as three syllables, like [gak. ɕ. ki] if [ɕ] is regarded as another sonority peak; or [ɕ] can also be unsyllabfied. Again, the syllable structure varies depending on the phonetic realization, but it does not change the lexical item or the mora and foot structures.

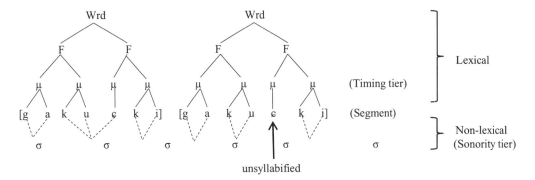

Figure 2 *The phonological hierarchy with two tiers, with high vowel deletion involved*
F = foot, μ = mora, σ = syllable

3. Problems of the traditional syllable-based view

In this section, I discuss what the traditional syllable-based view overlooks.

3.1 A lack of rhyme constituent

According to Kubozono (1998), there is no evidence that a rhyme constituent exists in Japanese. Kubozono (1998) mentions that mispronunciation is one of the pieces of evidence: for example, /teQkiN koNkuɾiRto/ ([tekkiŋ koNkuɾi:to]) 'reinforced concrete' was mispronounced as [kokkin teŋkuɾi:to], in which the morae /te/ and /ko/ were switched, rather than as *[koŋkin tekkuɾi:to], in which the so-called syllables /teQ/ and /koN/ were switched. In other words, the connections between /te/ and /Q/ in /teQ/, as well as between /ko/ and /N/ in /koN/, are loose. If there is no rhyme constituent, there is no need to attach a so-called dependent mora (i.e., /R/, /J/, /N/, /Q/) to an independent mora (i.e., /V/, /CV/, /CjV/). Nevertheless, transcription like /teQ. kiN. koN. ku. riR. to/ (period = syllable boundary in the traditional view), for example, is fairly common in Japanese phonology papers. One of the problems of the syllable-based analysis is a lack of explanation for the discrepancy between the claim of necessity of syllable – a dependent mora is attached to its preceding independent mora – and that of a lack of rhyme – a dependent mora is not attached to its preceding independent mora.

Note that /Q/ alone is unpronounceable, so it is possible to regard /(C)(j)VQ/ as one unit, depending on the purpose. However, as will be discussed in §4.2, in Matsuzaki's (1996) experiment, /Q/ was recognized as a separate unit from the preceding mora about half of the time by native Japanese speakers. Besides, the degree of independency of morae varies, as mentioned in Tanaka (2008) and Labrune (2012). So it is questionable to routinely combine these four morae, /R/, /J/, /N/, and /Q/, with the preceding mora.

3.2 Pitch accent and syllable

Syllable is commonly referred to in order to explain pitch accent patterns. Since this topic is too big to discuss in one section, I will mention only a few points here. The fundamental question is whether /ko ↓ i/ (↓ = pitch downstep, ↑ = pitch upstep) 'romantic emotion', for example, should really be analyzed as one syllable while /ko ↑ i/ in /ko ↑ i ↓ taroR/ 'Koitaro (a person's name)' (Tateishi 2017:532) should be analyzed as two syllables only because of their pitch patterns. I consider that syllabification needs to be based on sonority, not pitch patterns. Compare the Mandarin one-syllable words *hài* 'harm' (falling tone) and *hái* 'still' (rising tone), for example. As seen in the aforementioned /haNtai/ and /gakuɕiki/, if a speaker smoothly connects /ko/ and /i/, like [koi͡], it may sound like one syllable, regardless of its pitch; whereas if a speaker pronounces it more slowly with an amplitude dip between [ko] and [i], it may sound like two syllables, regardless of its pitch. Again, whether /koi/ realizes as [koi] or [ko. i] does not affect the meaning of the word or the mora structure.

However, if this were stress, it would be a different story since stress only falls on a syllable nucleus; [kói] (acute accent = stress) may sound like one syllable (i.e., [kój]), while [koí] could sound like two syllables. Japanese pitch nucleus often seems treated as equivalent to stress, but these differ in many ways: stress may involve phonological neutralization (e.g. vowel neutralization in unstressed syllables in English, and tone neutralization in unstressed syllables in Mandarin), and it also involves duration and rhythmic patterns; but Japanese pitch accent lacks these characteristics. In addition, stress and pitch contrasts can coexist, as seen in Mandarin. In the traditional view, there seems a presupposition that a pitch nucleus must fall on a syllable nucleus just as stress does, but this presupposition would need to be reconsidered.

With that said, in Japanese loanwords, it is well-attested that a pitch accent nucleus shifts from the default third last mora (-3) to the fourth last mora (-4) when the third last mora is a dependent mora (i.e., /R/, /J/, /N/, /Q/) since dependent morae tend to avoid pitch nuclei: for example, /su. ku. **ra** ↓ N̲. bu. ɾu/ (-4) (↓ = pitch downstep, bold = pitch nucleus, period = syllable boundary in the traditional view) 'scramble' instead of the default */su. ku. ɾa N̲. ↓ bu. ɾu/ (-3) (Tanaka 2013:74). The common argument is that this leftward shift is the evidence that /ɾa N/, in this case, behaves like one unit (i.e., syllable). As well, if the final mora is a dependent mora, there are variations between '-3' and '-4', such as /a. re. **ru** ↓ gi R̲/ (-3) or /a. **re**. ↓ ɾu. gi R̲/ (-4) for 'allergy' and /e. ne. **ru** ↓ gi R̲/ (-3) or /e. **ne**. ↓ ɾu. gi R̲/ (-4) for 'energy' (Tanaka 2013: 74). It seems that the third last *syllable*, rather than mora, tends to bear a pitch nucleus (Tanaka 2013). However, the problem is that this analysis does not explain why the pitch nucleus does not shift to the fourth last mora (i.e., the third last *syllable*) when the second last mora is a dependent mora, as in /ko. ɾe. su. te. **ro** ↓ R̲. ɾu/ (not */ko. ɾe. su. **te**. ↓ ɾo R̲. ɾu/ 'cholesterol' (Sakamoto 2005:5); according to Sakamoto (2005), when the second last mora is a dependent mora, the pitch nucleus predominantly falls on the default third last mora (i.e., the second last *syllable*) in both real and nonsense words. The same goes for the case in which both the last and third last morae are dependent morae, the pitch nucleus predominantly falls on the fourth last mora (i.e., the second last *syllable*), instead of the fifth last mora (i.e., the third last *syllable*), as in /a. so. ɕi. e ↓ R̲. ɕo N̲/ (not */a. so. **ɕi**. ↓ e R̲. ɕo N̲/) 'association' (Sakamoto 2005:5). This means that syllabifying every mora causes a problem. On the other hand, there is also a generalization that the *syllable* that contains the third last mora (instead of the third last syllable) bears a pitch nucleus (c.f., Kubozono and Honma 2002), but in this case, why is only the third last dependent mora incorporated into a syllable while other dependent morae as in /ko ɾe su te ɾo R̲ ɾu/ and /a so ɕi e R ɕo N̲/ are ignored?[2]

To solve these problems, I suggest that the case with the third last mora being a dependent mora and the case with the last mora being a dependent mora need to be regarded as two different phenomena. In the case with the last mora being a dependent mora, as will be discussed in §3.3, I argue that a low-ranked mora based on Labrune's (2012) scale[3] tends to be weakened and to become extrametrical (cf. Tanaka 2013) or invisible (cf. Giriko 2006) in the final position, so in some cases the final mora may not count. This simple extrametricality/invisibility analysis without involving syllable can sufficiently explain the variation between /a re **ru** ↓ gi R̲/ (-3, default) and /a **re** ↓ ɾu gi R̲/ (-4, R is extrametrical). As for the case with the third last mora being a dependent mora, due to the page limitation I plan to discuss the details in my next paper but briefly, I focus on tone rather than pitch accent nucleus, which often seems confused with stress; I adopt Backley and Nasukawa's (2013) theory that low tone (rather than high tone) functions as the marked tonal property in Japanese. In this theory, the default pitch pattern in loanwords is expressed that the low tone starts at the second last mora (i.e,. /-HLL/) (H = high, L = low). Based on this, I explain that the underlying rightmost high tone tends to become low due to anticipatory assimilation when it is on a dependent mora; in other words, the low tone begins one mora earlier. For example, in /su ku ɾa N̲ b̲u̲ ɾu/, the underlying /LHHHLL/ becomes [LHHLLL] due to anticipatory assimilation. Likewise, /ko ɾe su te ɾo R̲ ɾu/ (the second last mora is a dependent mora but the third last mora is not) stays with /LHHHHLL/ with no assimilation, and /a so ɕi e R̲ ɕo N/ (the last and third last morae are dependent morae) shows /LHHHHLL/ becoming [LHHHLLL]. Due to the page limit, I need to wait for my next paper to phonetically explain why this assimilation occurs, but this analysis, which does not involve syllable, can solve the above mentioned problems.[4]

3.3 How to deal with discrepancies between the numbers of morae and musical notes

In lyrics of Japanese songs, the basic rule is one mora is assigned to one musical note. Previous studies show that when the number of morae and the number of notes do not match, a combination of an independent mora and a dependent mora (e.g. /hoN/) is more likely to be assigned to one note than a combination of two independent morae (e.g. /kami/) (Kubozono 2008; Tanaka 2008). For example, according to Kawahara (2016:184), in the three-note chanting phrases in baseball games, the four-mora names of players like /i tɕi ɾo R/ and /da R wi N/ are assigned to /i - tɕi - ɾoR/ and /da - R - wiN/ (hyphen = division based on musical notes), in which /ɾoR/ and /wiN/ behave like one unit. In the traditional view, this is one of the pieces of evidence that Japanese has syllable. The problem is that Kawahara (2016:184) also shows the examples /na ga ɕi ma/ and /sa N ta na/ divided into /na - gaɕi - ma/ and /sa - Nta - na/, in which /gaɕi/ and /Nta/, a unit with two sonority peaks, are assigned to one note, but there are no explanations for this; /sa N ta na/ divided into /sa - Nta - na/ instead of /saN - ta - na/ is particularly problematic for the traditional syllable-based view.

An alternative explanation is that again, a low-ranked mora based on the aforementioned Labrune's (2012) scale[3] tends to be extrametrical in the final position. For example, the utterance-final elongated polite copula /desu/ (phonetically [des]) typically realizes as [de::::::s], rather than [desu::::::] or [des::::::], which means that [des] indeed phonetically behaves like one syllable with coda-like extrametrical [s], meaning that phonetically syllable-like behaviours could be observed in the final position. Likewise, /R/ in /i tɕi ɾo R/ and /N/ in /da R wi N/ would be susceptible to extrametricality/invisibility (Giriko 2006), so it is understandable that the last two morae are likely to be assigned to one musical note. Besides, when two morae must be pronounced quickly in order to be assigned to one musical note, a two-mora unit with one sonority peak (e.g. /hoN/) is easier to pronounce than that with two sonority peaks (e.g. /kami/) since for the latter, singers must quickly open and close their mouth twice. Thus, it is natural that a two-mora unit with one sonority peak (e.g. /hoN/) tends to be preferred in such situations. This means that syllable is indeed active at a certain phonetic level. However, as seen in the aforementioned /na - gaɕi - ma/ and /sa - Nta - na/, two-mora units with two sonority peaks can also be assigned to one note. In chanting or songs, mora-to-note assignment would depend on composers' sense of music. So it can be explained that any two-mora combination can potentially be assigned to one note but preferred combinations should musically sound good and/or be easy to pronounce. Again, no matter whether /na ga ɕi ma/, for example, is assigned to [naga - ɕi - ma], [na - gaɕi - ma], or [na - ga - ɕima], the meaning of the word does not change since mora-to-note assignment occurs at the non-lexical level. Given these data, mora-note assignment patterns can only demonstrate syllable at some phonetic level but are not sufficient evidence that the syllable exists in the Japanese phonological hierarchy.

3.4 Independency from foot

As mentioned above, I do not go into *foot* in this paper, but depending on the definition of foot, another problem of the traditional syllable-based view is that there can be discrepancies between syllable boundaries and foot boundaries. If foot is defined as a combination of two morae, in accordance with Kubozono and Honma (2002), foot and syllable boundaries do not always match. For example, in word formation, /po. ke. mo N/ 'Pokemon' is made from the first two morae of both /po. ke Q. to/ 'pocket' and /mo N. su. ta R/ 'monster', and so is /ma. za. ko N/ 'mother's boy' from /ma. za R/ 'mother' and /ko N. pu. re Q. ku. su/ 'complex' (Kubozono and Honma 2002:77). In these cases, the syllables /keQ/ in /po. keQ. to/ and /zaR/ in /ma. zaR/ are broken apart into morae, and the foot boundaries and syllable boundaries do not match: i.e., /(po. ke) (Q. to)/ and /(ma. za) R/ (bracket = foot boundary, period = syllable boundary). Likewise, Minusa's (2009) analysis shows the case where foot and syllable boundaries do not match, as in /(gu. ru) (R. pu)/ 'group' and /(a N). (ba. ra) (N. su)/ 'unbalance' (95-96); Fujikawa (2013) mentions that such analyses are problematic. However, the syllable-less analysis does not need to deal with such issues. Or, if syllable and foot are in different tiers as shown in Figure 1 and 2, such issues can be solved, even when one wants to divide words into syllables.

4. Other issues to note
4.1 Unsyllabified consonants

Syllabification is not relevant in some languages, so not all segments need to be incorporated into a syllable in human languages. For example, in the word *scílksq't* in Moses-Columbia Salish (spoken on the west coast of North America), only the underlined *cíl* is considered a syllable; the rest are unsyllabified (Czaykowska-Higgins and Willett 1997:385).[5] Likewise, Fujikawa (2013) analyzes word-initial /N/ occurring in recent Japanese loanwords, such as /Ndʑamena/ 'N'Djamena' (103) as independent without being part of a syllable. Unsyllabified consonants also occur in Japanese English-as-a-second-language (ESL) learners' interlanguage. In Nogita and Fan's (2012) study, in which lower-intermediate Japanese ESL learners pronounced English words syllable by syllable with a pause, some participants syllabified the word *subject*, for example, as [sʌ. bᵊ. dʒɪ. kʰ. tʰ]. While they pronounced full vowels for [sʌ] and [dʒɪ], they did not insert a full vowel after every consonant, meaning that they were aware that [b], [k], and [t] were not followed by a vowel; after the release of [b] there was a short vocalic sound but this was too short for a full vowel. However, they put weight on these consonants assuming that these alone were independent prosodic units. Guo and Nogita (2013) analyze these as unsyllabified consonants, as shown in Figure 3.[6]

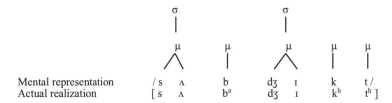

Figure 3 Unsyllabified consonants in 'subject' by Japanese ESL learners' interlanguage

As seen in these data, there are cases where syllabification is not required, implying that the so-called special/dependent morae /N, R, Q, J/ do not need to be attached to the preceding mora.

4.2 Awareness of dependent morae

In Matsuzaki's (1996) experiment, native Japanese speakers heard sound stimuli of four mora Japanese words with the dependent morae /R, Q, N, J/, such as [de pa : to] (/de pa R to/) 'department store,' [ɾo bo t to] (/ɾo bo Q to/) 'robot,' [dʑi ɾe m ma] (/dʑi ɾe N ma/) 'dilemma,' and [do ɾa i bu] (/do ɾa J bu/) 'drive,' and were asked to express each word as shapes like ⬭⬭⬭⬭ , ⬭⬭⬭, ⬭⬭⬭, ⬭⬭⬭, ⬭⬭, ⬭⬭, ⬭⬭, and ⬭. The results showed that bimoraic units were categorized as one unit in the following consistency order: /CVR/ (88%) > /CVQ/ (56%) > /CVN/ (45%) > /CVJ/ (37%) (C = consonant, V = vowel). This apparently showed their syllable awareness. However, if sonority peak has a lexical role, words like [dʑi ɾe m ma] (/dʑi ɾe N ma/), for example, should be assigned to ⬭⬭⬭ (or even ⬭⬭⬭) nearly 100% of the time since other syllabification patterns would make a different lexical item. In other words, Matsuzaki's results seem only to show their *phonetic* awareness. Note that /CVR/ being recognized as one unit as frequently as 88% of the time indicates a tight connection of /CV/ and /R/; or in other words, a long vowel tends to be recognized as one unit. However, this is not sufficient evidence of syllable existing in the phonological hierarchy. Moreover, one of the reviewers commented that s/he does not think that Matsuzaki's results necessarily show syllabic awareness, but that the participants just showed a certain hierarchy between morae when the participants were explicitly asked to operate certain distinctions which might otherwise be artificial to them, and might have felt obliged not to always select the same item in the list.

4.3 Perceived numbers of syllables

At the Phonology Forum in 2017, I pronounced different phonetic realizations of /haNtai/, /gakuɕiki/, /aɕita/, and /koi/ to demonstrate different syllabification patterns, and when I discussed this with a few native English speaking phonologists, they said that they perceived different numbers of syllables depending on the phonetic realization, as I had expected (e.g. [hantai] → 2, [ha n ta i] → 4, [aɕita] → 3, [aɕta] → 2, [koi] → 1, [ko i] → 2, and so forth).[7] Although more formal and extensive experiments are needed, this can also indicate that syllable structures do not have a lexical role. Besides, when I demonstrated these to Japanese phonologists, they commented that [aɕta] in Tokyo Japanese certainly has only two sonority peaks but there are still three syllables. In other words, the number of sonority peaks (or vowels) and the number of syllables do not match. This implies that the definition of syllable in the traditional syllable-based view needs to be clarified.

5. Conclusion

I argue that, in Tokyo Japanese, syllable, or a unit based on a sonority peak, does not have a role in distinguishing lexical items. In fact, both [o. tɕi. ai] and [o. tɕi. a. i], for instance, are the correct forms of /oteiai/ (surname). In addition, syllabifying all the morae causes various problems in analyses of pitch accent and other issues as discussed above. Therefore, I propose that the syllable should not be placed above the mora node in the phonological hierarchy. It is safer to only state that phonetically syllable-like behaviors could be observed – or a combination of multiple morae could behave like one unit – in certain places of a word in certain conditions in Japanese. Finally, I may appear to criticize eminent linguists' theories but this present study would not have been possible without their extensive data collection and analyses which I am respectful of.

Notes

* This paper is a revised version of my presentation at the Phonology Forum 2017. I would like to thank the audience and reviewers for their insightful comments, which helped me greatly improve my argument.
[1] In Japanese, short high vowels /i/ and /u/ between voiceless consonants are typically devoiced or deleted, as known as High Vowel Devoicing/Deletion.
[2] There is also an analysis analogous to the Latin stress analysis (Tanaka 2008), which appears to solve the problems mentioned here, but its own problem will be discussed in my future papers. As another noticeable problem, it is known that initial mora lowering as a word boundary marker does not occur when the second mora is a dependent mora (e.g. /CV R/ → HH rather than *LH). This phenomenon is traditionally explained by the syllable-based analysis. However, as Tateishi (2017) points out, initial mora lowering still occurs in /CV Q/, which cannot be explained by the syllable-based analysis. This will also be discussed in my future papers.
[3] Labrune (2012:141) proposes a scale of the relative capacity of tone-bearing units from the most likely tone-

bearing to the least likely tone-bearing, instead of the traditional independent-dependent mora dichotomy:
Ca > Co, Ce > Cu, Ci > a > o, e > i, u, CV$_{devoiced}$, CV$_{epenthetic}$ > R > N > Q

[4] I have recorded native Tokyo Japanese speakers pronouncing nonsense compound words, and found that occasionally the rightmost high tone on /CV/ became low. This phenomenon also cannot be explained by the traditional syllable analysis. My anticipatory tone assimilation analysis better explains this.

[5] Based on my perceptual impression, unsyllabified consonants in the Salish languages almost sound like Japanese morae with High Vowel Devoicing/Deletion.

[6] Alternatively, Goad and Kang (2003) analyze such ESL learners' consonant productions as onset-nucleus (ON) sharing syllables, or vowel-less syllables. Still, these syllables are distinguished from syllables with a full vowel.

[7] I also discussed this with a Mandarin speaking phonologist but her syllabification patterns were somewhat different from those of English speaking phonologists (e.g. [hantai] → 2, [ha n ta i] → 2, [aɕita] → 3, [aɕta] → 3). It would be worth examining how speakers of different languages syllabify Japanese words.

References

Backley, Phillip and Kuniya Nasukawa. 2013. The role of L in the pitch accent system of Tokyo Japanese. *Phonological Studies* 16.37–44.

Czaykowska-Higgins, Ewa and Marie Louise Willett. 1997. Simple syllables in Nxaʔamxcín. *International Journal of American Linguistics* 63(3).385–411.

Fujikawa, Naoya. 2013. Morae, syllables and feet in Tokyo Japanese phonology. *Ariake: Kumamoto University Linguistic Papers* 12.79–112.

Giriko, Mikio. 2006. Invisibility of moraic nasal in Japanese. *Journal of the Phonetic Society of Japan* 10(2).61–71.

Goad, Heather and Hyun-Sook Kang. 2003. Word-final syllabification in L2 acquisition with emphasis on Korean learners of English. In *Proceedings of the 6th Generative Approaches to Second Language Acquisition Conference* 122–129.

Guo, Xiaoqian and Akutsugu Nogita. 2013. Lexical schwa and inserted schwa produced by Mandarin Chinese EAL learners. *Working Papers of the Linguistics Circle of the University of Victoria* 23(1).81–109.

Kawahara, Shigeto. 2016. Japanese has syllables: a reply to Labrune. *Phonology* 33(1).169–194.

Kondo, Mariko. 2000. Vowel devoicing and syllable structure in Japanese. *Japanese/Korean Linguistics* 9.125–138.

Kubozono, Haruo. 1994. On syllable weight in Japanese. *Studies in the Japanese Language* 178.7–17.

Kubozono, Haruo. 1998. On the universality of mora and syllable (<Features> Theories of syllable and mora). *Journal of the Phonetic Society of Japan* 2(1).5–15.

Kubozono, Haruo. 2008. /ai/-/au/ asymmetry: A phonetic account. *Asymmetries in phonology: An East-Asian perspective*, ed. by Haruo Kubozono, 147–163. Tokyo: Kuroshio Shuppan.

Kubozono, Haruo and Takeru Honma. 2002. *Onsetsu to mōra*. Tokyo: Kenkyūsha.

Labrune, Laurence. 2012. Questioning the universality of the syllable: Evidence from Japanese. *Phonology* 29(01).113–152.

Matsuzaki, Hiroshi. 1996. Native speakers' perception of Japanese speech segmentation. *Journal of the Department of Japanese, Tohoku University* 6.81–92.

Minusa, Tomoyuki. 2009. An OT analysis of loanword accentuation in Tokyo Japanese. *Ibunka no Shosō* 30.89–100.

Nogita, Akitsugu and Yanan Fan. 2012. Not vowel epenthesis: Mandarin and Japanese ESL learners' production of English consonant clusters. *Working Papers of the Linguistics Circle of the University of Victoria* 22(1).1–26.

Sakamoto, Kiyoe. 2005. Gairaigo no onsetsukōzō to akusento. *Ronshū* 1.1–24

Tanaka, Shin'ichi. 2008. *Rizumu/akusento no yure to on'in/keitai kōzō*. Tokyo: Kuroshio Shuppan.

Tanaka, Shin-ichi. 2013. Review of Labrune, Laurence (2012). *Journal of the Phonetic Society of Japan* 17(1).70–80.

Tateishi, Koichi. 2017. More arguments against Japanese as a mora language. *34th West Coast Conference on Formal Linguistics* 529–535.

On the Perception of the Geminated Elided Pronoun *l'* in Parisian French

Céleste Guillemot
International Christian University

ABSTRACT. This paper reports the experimental investigation of a diachronically recent change in Parisian French. Previous studies (Carvalho 2002, Tranel 1987) affirm that the elided form *l'* of the pronouns *le* and *la* are geminated by French native speakers from Paris. Namely, they claim that gemination is contrastive in some cases and therefore is undergoing a phonologization process. The current paper presents a preliminary study of this phenomenon and discusses its reality in native perception. Results show that although French native speakers are able to identify categorically consonant length in contrastive environments, they were unable to do so in the case of gemination of the elided pronoun.

Keywords: French phonology, perceptual experiment, gemination, elided pronoun, phonologization

1. Introduction

Graphic double consonants occur very frequently in French orthography but do not always reflect the actual pronunciations: In many cases a double consonant in the spelling only has the phonetic value of a singleton (e.g. *année* [ane] 'year'). Some double consonants may optionally be realized as geminates, but are not lexically contrastive. French is therefore usually described as having no consonant quantity contrast. If that is mostly true at the phonological level, geminate consonants often emerge at the phonetic level in identical consonant sequences across word/morphemes boundaries, or resulting from schwa deletion processes (see section 2.). This paper reports a preliminary study on the perception of the singleton/geminate contrast by French native speakers in a particular case of gemination: gemination of the elided pronoun *l'*.

2. Gemination in French

French (which has the same Latin origins as Italian) used to have a consonantal length contrast but underwent a degemination process from the 7th or 8th century. (Klein 1963; Posner 1996) This process occurred only in Western Romance languages, which already underwent a lenition process on intervocalic singletons (e.g. from Meisenburg 2006: latin *sapere* 'to know' > [saber]). On the other hand, in the case of Eastern Romance languages that didn't undergo such a process, the consonant quantity contrast was retained which explains why gemination does occur in modern Italian.

In modern French, the consonant quantity contrast is not lexically distinctive. Graphic double consonants are found in abundance in French orthography, yet they seldom indicate anything concerning the actual pronunciation, nor represent identical consonant sequences as illustrated in (1). (1a) and (1b) have graphic double consonants but are never geminated while in (1c) /m/ is variably geminated.

(1) a. *année*   [ane]   'year'
     b. *appelle*   [apɛl]   'calls'
     c. *sommaire* [sɔmɛʀ]~[sɔmmɛʀ] 'summary'

Out of the twenty consonant letters in the alphabet, only seven can never be double consonants in the spelling: h, j, k, q, v, w, x. Orthographic rules account for the pronunciation of some of the ll, ss, cc and gg sequences in intervocalic position, which is respectively [j], [s], [ks] and [gʒ]. In other cases, the double consonant is either pronounced as a singleton or as a geminate. Whether a double consonant is pronounced as geminated or not depends on various intralinguistic and extralinguistic factors such as morpho-phonological environment, etymology, speech style, or speaker. In general, sonorants (/m/=51%, /l/=35%, /n/=25%, /r/=23%) show a higher propensity to be realized as geminates than fricatives or obstruents (Walter 1976:438). They also constitute the only consonant type that can be pronounced as geminated without any stylistic effect (Tranel 1987): Indeed, gemination in French is often associated with an educated pronunciation (Walter 1976; Tranel 1987). It is also well known for being a characteristic of meridional French, and observed less frequently in the Northern part of France in general (Martinet 1945).

Putting aside graphic double consonants, which are mainly related to stylistic effects, phonetic gemination in French emerges mainly in two cases: when gemination is induced by a schwa-deletion, or at a morpheme boundary. The phonological process of schwa-deletion in French leads to the emergence of a variety of obligatory non-underlying (phonetic) geminates. As shown in (2), a schwa deleted between two identical consonants word-internally or at word boundaries generates identical consonant sequences.

(2) *netteté*   → [nɛtte]   'neatness'
    maman   → [mmã]   'mom'
    coupe pas → [kuppa]   'it doesn't cut'

Morphologically induced geminates occur principally during the process of affixation of the negative prefix in- to words beginning with /n/, /m/, /l/ and /r/ (3). This results in identical consonant sequences at morpheme boundaries through regressive assimilation. For most words following this structure, both the geminated and the singleton pronunciation are listed in the dictionary.

(3) *in + lisible* → *illisible*   [il(l)izibl̩] 'illegible'
    in + mortel → *immortel*   [im(m)ɔʀtɛl] 'immortal'
    in + réel   → *irréel*   [iʀ(ʀ)eɛl] 'unreal'

Finally, according to Tranel (1987:149), the distinction between the imperfect and conditional forms of the verbs *courir* 'to run' and *mourir* 'to die' is made based on the consonantal length as illustrated in (4). This is one of the rare cases where gemination is semantically distinctive in French. Furthermore, it is the only word-internal double consonant case where gemination is systematic (Martinet 1945; Walter 1976; Tranel 1987). In this case, gemination occurs within the word because of the concatenation of an -r ending stem and a conditional ending beginning with r-. The same contrast appears in -er verbs with –r ending stems (e.g. *declarer* 'to declare', *déchirer* 'to tear') because of a schwa-deletion process (Meisenburg 2006) as in (4).

(4)

Verb	Imperfect form	Conditional form
courir	*il courait* / cour+ait [kuʀɛ]	*il courrait* / cour+rait [kuʀʀɛ]
mourir	*il mourait*/ mour+ait [muʀɛ]	*Il mourrait*/ mour+rait [muʀʀɛ]
déclarer	*il déclarait*/déclar+ait [deklaʀɛ]	*il declarerait*/ déclar+erait [deklaʀʀɛ]

3. The elided pronoun *l'*

Elision in French refers to the process of dropping the final vowel of a word when it precedes a vowel-initial word, or a word beginning with a mute h. It is indicated with an apostrophe in the spelling. This paper discusses the case of the elision of the pronouns *le* and *la* before a verb beginning with a vowel or a mute h. An example of the elision process discussed here is given in (5) below.

(5) *On a vu le film.*   →   On l'a vu.
     'We saw the movie.'   'We saw it.'

Some previous studies have been observing the emergence of the elided pronoun *l'* pronounced as geminated in particular in the Paris region. Typical examples of this phenomenon are given in (6).

(6) *Je l'ai fait*   'I did it'   [ʒəlɛfɛ]~[ʒəllɛfɛ]
     On l'a vu   'we did it'   [õlavy]~[õllavy]
     Je l'avais dit   'I said it'   [ʒəlavedi]~[ʒəllavedi]

In a 1945 linguistic survey (Martinet 1945), participants are asked about their pronunciation of the elided pronoun in the sentence *Je l'ai dit* 'I said it'. Martinet's (1945) results show that the national mean percentage of gemination is 23%, and a higher propensity for the pronoun to be geminated is observed in the northwestern part of France. Specifically, in the region of Paris, a geminated pronunciation of the pronoun was observed for more than 50% of the participants and was also more frequent among young people. Martinet's (1945) survey provides very interesting data, and although it suffers from some methodological issues related to the time of data collection, it suggests that this linguistic change might have been already active in the first-half of the 20th century.

Carvalho (2002:164) analyzes this phenomenon as a generalization of the gemination of the elided pronoun in *il l'a dit* [illadi] 'he said it'. He affirms that this phenomenon corresponds to a diachronically recent phonologization of the geminate consonant in French, a change initiated by the educated pronunciation of sonorants in words such as *sommet* [sɔmme] 'peak' or illustre [illystr] 'illustrious'. In his analysis, the morpheme boundary moves so that the geminate consonant is taken as the object elided pronoun itself (7).

(7)   *il l'a dit*   →   /il + l + a + di/→   /i + ll + a + di/

According to Carvalho (2002:163) this strategy is used in order to satisfy two constraints:

LIAISON: A floating C is attached to the following segment only when it is a
                vowel (otherwise it may be deleted: e.g. *il mange* 'he eats'/ilmãʒ/ is
                often realized as [imãʒ]).
DISTINCTION: All relevant distinction has to be preserved.

(8)

il l'a dit	LIAISON	DISTINCTION
iladi	*!	
→ illadi		*

As illustrated in (8), following these constraints the third person pronoun *il* should be realized as /i/ in order to satisfy LIAISON. However, it would then violate DISTINCTION because the output of *il l'a dit* 'he said it' would be [iladi] and the distinction with *il a dit* 'he said' [iladi] would be lost. Gemination of the elided pronoun emerges in the output in order to retain the distinction between the two expressions. For Carvalho (2002:164) if the elided pronoun is realized as a geminate consonant, then the geminate itself is homo-morphemic as shown in (7) and therefore spreads to the whole paradigm as in (9).

(9)

je l'ai dit	/ʒə	↑	e	di/	=	[ʒə l:edi]	
tu l'as dit	/ty		a	di/	=	[tyl:adi]	
il l'a dit	/I	ll	a/õ	di/	=	[il:adi]	
nous l'avons dit	/nu		avõ	di/	=	[nul:avõdi]	
vous l'avez dit	/vu	↓	ave	di/	=	[vul:avedi]	

From Carvalho (2002:165)

Tranel (1987:151) also notes some cases of gemination of the elided personal pronoun *l'*. He proposes two contrastive environments: Where the elided personal pronoun contrasts with its non-elided form before a verb with an initial consonant (10), and where the elided personal pronoun contrasts with the elided definite *le* or *la* (11).

(10) *Tu l'apprendras*   'you will learn it'   [tyllaprãdra]
      Tu la prendras   'you will take it'   [tylaprãdra]

(11) *Nous voulons l'envoyer* 'we want to send it' [nuvulõllãvwaje]
      Nous voulons l'envoyé   'we want the envoy'   [nuvulõlãvwaje]

The gemination of the elided pronoun is investigated experimentally in Meisenburg (2006) where both perception and production of geminates in French are studied. The results show that although the elided pronoun is often pronounced as a geminated /l/ for the third person, results are non-consistent for the generalization to the first person, even in emphatic contexts. Moreover, there was no relevant data for perception in this study.

4. Methodology

The present study questions the reality of this specific case of phonologization of geminates for French native speakers. If the gemination of the elided pronoun is contrastive, then it should be reflected in native speakers' perception. Namely, in a minimal pair, native speakers should be able to discriminate the singleton from the geminate. The experiment in this study investigates and compares the perception of both positional (phonetic) geminates and the case of phonemic gemination discussed above for the same consonant /l/.

14 participants took part in a listening experiment: 6 men and 8 women from 19 to 58 years old who are all native speakers of French from Paris. The listening task was presented to the participants using a computer with the software Praat (Boersma and Weenik 1992-) and headphones. They were asked to identify the stimuli they heard as singleton or geminate by clicking the word(s) on the screen.

The stimuli were French sentences with minimal pairs illustrating the singleton/geminate contrast are shown in (12).

(12) a. *Une belle âme* [ynbelam] 'A beautiful soul'   **vs.**
         Une belle lame [ynbellam] 'A beautiful blade'.
      b. *Il a dit* [iladi] 'he said'   **vs.**   *Il l'a dit* [illadi] 'he said it'
      c. *Je la prends* [zelaprã] 'I take it' **vs.** *Je l'apprend* [jellaprã] 'I learn it'

The stimuli (a) in (12a) constitute a case of positional gemination: an identical consonant sequence that emerges as a word boundary through schwa-deletion. The gemination in the output is only phonetic. Stimuli (b) in (12b) is also a case of surface gemination where an identical consonant sequence appears at a word boundary. In stimuli (c) the elided pronoun in isolation is geminated and contrasts with the non-elided pronoun "*la*" (12c).

Both the geminate and the singleton stimuli were recorded from a male native speaker from Paris using a unidirectional headset microphone (Senheiser PC USB 8) and Praat (Boersma and Weenik 1992-). The sampling frequency was 44,1 kHz and quantization was

16 bits. In order to create a gating experiment, geminate stimuli were modified using Praat by cutting the duration of the constriction at zero crossings by 3ms decrements from the geminate to the singleton duration. As a result, (a), (b), and (c) have each 7 stimuli: the geminate and the singleton stimulus, and 5 stimuli with a modified constriction duration. The research project itself investigates many other types of geminates in French and as such the other stimuli were included as fillers for a total of 98 stimuli. The stimuli's sound files were used in a two-way forced choice identification task using a Praat MFC Experiment script where they were presented to the participants in a random order.

Statistical analyses were conducted to verify the statistical significance of the results of the experiment. Distributional skews were tested by a logistic regression analysis using R (R Development Core Team 2008).

5. Results and analysis

(13)   a.   b.

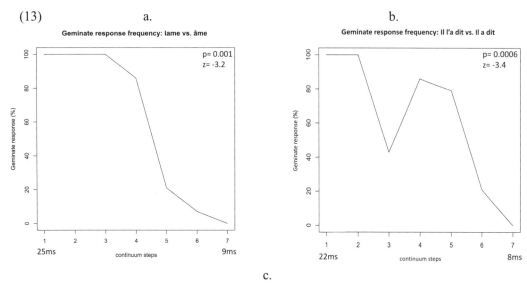

c.

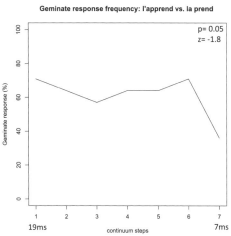

The three line graphs in (13) represent the percentage of geminate response (vertical axis) as a function of the constriction duration of the stimuli for (a) on the left, (b) in the middle and (c) on the right. The horizontal axis represents the 3ms continuum steps in decreasing order so that 1 is the non-modified geminate stimuli and 7 the non-modified singleton stimuli. Absolute duration of the geminate and singleton stimuli are indicated on each graph under the horizontal axis.

5.1. Stimuli (a)

In the case of stimuli (a) *une belle âme* [ynbelam] 'a beautiful soul' vs. *une belle lame* [ynbellam] 'a beautiful blade', both the non-modified geminate and singleton stimuli (step 1 and 7) were identified accurately by all participants. The singleton/geminate ratio of the stimuli was of around 2.77. The line graph on the left shows a clear categorical perception of the singleton/geminate contrast, with a perceptual boundary located between 16 and 13ms (step 4 and 5). The test by logistic regression showed that the effect of constriction duration on the percentage of geminate identification is statistically significant (p= 0.001, z=-3.2).

5.2. Stimuli (b)

For stimuli (b) *il a dit* [iladi] 'he said' vs. *il l'a dit* [illadi] 'he said it', similarily to (a), identification of the non-modified stimuli had a 100% accuracy rate. The singleton/geminate ratio of stimuli (b) was about 2.75. No conclusion can be made from the observation of the line graph in the middle about native speakers' perception of the consonantal length contrast: The line graph shows a categorical perception except for step 3. This may be due to a manipulation error and should be investigated further in future experiments. The statistical test showed however that the constriction duration and the percentage of geminate identification are significantly correlated (p=0.0006, z=-3.4).

5.3. Stimuli (c)

The results for stimuli (c): *je la prends* [zelaprã] 'I take it' *vs. je l'apprend* [jellaprã] 'I learn it'*,* show a different pattern than in (a) and (b). The singleton/geminate ratio was about 2.71. Here non-modified stimuli were not identified accurately by the participants: the geminate non-modified stimulus was identified as geminated in 71% of the responses, and the non-modified singleton stimulus was identified as singleton in 64% of the responses. Moreover, the line graph on the right shows a perception that is not linear nor categorical as the stimuli don't seem to be identified by the participants. Statistical tests show no significant correlation between constriction duration and geminate identification (p=0.05, z=-1.8)

5.4. Analysis

The results of the experiment above show that in the case of stimuli (a) and (b) which are cases of surface gemination, participants use duration as an identification cue to accurately distinguish the geminate and the singleton stimuli. Statistical testing by logistic regression shows that consonantal length identification is significantly correlated with constriction duration. However, the results for stimuli (c) show a different tendency: The identification of non-modified stimuli was lower than for (a) and (b), and no correlation between identification and constriction duration was observed. This suggests that the native speakers who took part in the experiment were unable to identify and distinguish geminate and singleton stimuli from each other based on constriction duration. Although the consonantal length contrast in stimuli (c) should allow a semantic distinction (only *je l'apprend* is subject to gemination), it appears that at least in terms of perception, native speakers do not make – and may not be aware of – this distinction: In (c) native speakers are unable to distinguish *je l'apprends* 'I learn it' from *je la prends* 'I take it'.

The present result provides evidence against the phenomenon of phonologization of the consonantal length contrast in the case of the elided pronoun *l'* for native speakers of Parisian French described in previous studies (Carvalho 2002; Tranel 1987). Although all participants were native speakers from Paris, the results didn't indicate a significant role of consonant constriction duration. Further investigation is needed, especially in terms of production, in order to determine whether participants usually pronounce the elided pronoun as geminated.

6. Conclusion

French is often described as being a language without a consonantal length contrast. Indeed, in most cases, the distinction between a long and short consonant emerges at the phonetical level only as the result of identical consonant sequences across morpheme; word boundaries, or schwa deletion (positional gemination). It has been mentioned in previous studies that a recent phenomenon of phonologization of the consonantal length contrast was observed in French for the elided pronoun *l'*. The present study provides an experimental investigation of the perceptual reality for native speakers of geminate consonants in French, and compares the perception of positional gemination and the geminated elided pronoun. The results of the listening experiment show that while the participants were able to identify accurately, and rather categorically, the geminate and singleton stimuli for phonetic gemination (stimuli a and b), this was not the case for the gemination of the elided pronoun *l'* (stimulus c). Similarly, a statistically significant correlation between constriction duration and geminate identification was observed for (a) and (b) while it was non-significant for (c). This provides a piece of evidence against the affirmation about phonologization of the consonantal length contrast in Carvalho (2002) and Tranel (1987) which is consistent with the experimental results of Meisenburg (2006)

The current paper reports a preliminary experimental study on the nature of gemination in French, a topic which needs further investigation. Issues such as the nature of perceptual identification cues, length contrast in other gemination types and other consonants will be discussed in future studies.

Acknowledgements

I would like to thank the audience at the Spring meeting of the Phonological Society of Japan for their valuable comments on this project. All remaining errors are mine.

References

Boersma, Paul and David Weenink. 1992-2016. *Praat: doing phonetics by computer*. www.praat.org.

Carvalho, J. Brandão de. 2002. *De la syllabation en termes de contours CV* [On syllabification of CV contours]. Habilitation thesis for research supervising. School for Advanced Studies in the Social Sciences. Paris.

Klein, Hans-Wilhelm. 1963. *Phonetik und Phonologie des Französischen* [French phonetics and phonology]. München: Hueber.

Martinet, André. 1945. *La prononciation du français contemporain* [Pronunciation of contemporary French]. Genève – Paris: Librairie Droz.

Meisenburg, Trudel. 2006. Fake geminates in French: a production and perception study. *Speech Prosody 2006*, ed. by Rüdiger Hoffmann and Hansjörg Mixdorff. Abstract Book and CD-ROM Proceedings. Dresden: TUD Press Verlag der Wissenschaften GmbH.

Posner, Rebecca. 1996. *The Romance languages*. Cambridge: Cambridge University Press.

R Development Core Team. 2008. *R: A language and environment for statistical computing. R Foundation for Statistical Computing*. Vienna, Austria. http://www.R-project.org.

Tranel, Bernard. 1987. *The sounds of French*. New York: Cambridge University Press.

Walter, Henriette. 1976. *La dynamique des phonèmes dans le lexique français contemporain* [Dynamics of phonemes in the French contemporary lexicon]. Paris: France Expansion.

Opacity in Slavic Voicing Assimilation[*]

Naoya Watabe
The University of Tokyo / JSPS

ABSTRACT. This paper focuses on problematic patterns in Slavic voicing assimilation. While /v/ preceding voiceless obstruent consonants emerges as the voiceless [f] like the other voiced obstruents, it fails to trigger voicing on the preceding voiceless consonants. This results in the following two sound patterns: one in which voiceless consonants precede [v], which is observed in many Slavic languages including Russian; the other in which /v/ undergoes progressive devoicing, as observed in Polish. In previous researches, /v/ or [v] have been differentiated from the other voiced obstruents as (semi-)sonorants. Based on this idea, this paper proposes that the failure of the voicing should be attributed to underspecification for [voice] on this consonant. Furthermore, the difference between the Russian and Polish cases can be accounted for by re-ranking faithfulness constraints on [sonorant] and a markedness constraint on the disagreed clusters.

Keywords: Russian, Polish, voicing assimilation, opacity, Optimality Theory, Turbid Representations

1. Introduction

As in many other languages, regressive voicing assimilation within consonant clusters is observed in Slavic languages. For example, as shown in (1), lexically voiced consonants in Russian and Polish change to their voiceless counterparts when they are followed by voiceless consonants, while voiceless consonants change to their voiced counterparts when voiced ones follow. In other words, voiced consonants cannot occur adjacent to voiceless consonants and vice versa.

(1) Voicing assimilation in Slavic languages
  a. Russian[1]

ri**b**-a	'fish'	ri**p**-ka	(dim.)
obra**z**ʲets	'sample'	obra**s**ts-a	(gen. sg.)
no**g**atʲ	'nail'	no**k**tʲ-a	(gen. sg.)
k-anʲ-e	'to Ania'	**g**-daṣ-e	'to Dasha'
s-mam-oi̯	'with mom'	**z**-babuṣk-oi̯	'with gramma'
pro**s**ʲ-it	's/he requests'	pro**z**ʲ-ba	'request'

  b. Polish

ri**b**-a	'fish'	ri**p**-ka	(dim.)
dex	'breath'	t**x**-u	(gen. sg.)
z-mam-õ	'with mom'	**s**-pap-õ	'with dad'
pro**ɕ**-i	's/he requests'	pro**z**-ba	'request'
li**ʈʂ**-i	's/he counts'	li**dʐ**-ba	'number'

It has been documented, however, that while a voiced labial fricative /v/ undergoes devoicing when occurring before voiceless consonants, it fails to trigger voicing on the preceding voiceless consonants (refer to section 2). This paper attempts to account for this pattern by assuming that /v/ is underspecified for voicing.

The remainder of the paper is organized as follows. First, section 2 examines the behavior of /v/ in detail. Next, section 3 reviews previous research on voicing assimilation under the framework of Optimality Theory (OT). Section 4 proposes a refined explanation of the phonological pattern of /v/. Finally, section 5 concludes the discussion.

2. Facts

As shown in (2), like other voiced obstruents, /v/ undergoes regressive devoicing when voiceless consonants follow.

(2) /v/ preceding voiceless consonants
  a. Russian

nʲev-a	'Neva (river)'	nʲef-s̲kʲ-ii̯	(adj.)
vʲesʲ	'all (masc. sg.)'	fs̲ʲ-e	(pl.)
v-moskv-u	'to Moscow'	f-k̲azanʲ	'to Kazan'

  b. Polish

brvʲ-i	'eyebrow (gen. sg.)'	bref-k̲-a	(dim.)
vʲeɕ	'village'	fɕ̲-i	(gen. sg.)
v-lubliɲ-e	'in Lublin'	f-k̲rakovʲ-e	'in Krakow'

As briefly mentioned in the last section, however, this consonant fails to trigger voicing on the preceding voiceless consonants. The failure of regressive voicing results in two patterns. In one pattern, voiceless consonants precede [v], which is observed in Russian and many other Slavic languages. As shown in (3a), voiceless consonants remain voiceless when /v/ follows in the derivation as well as within a word. Several words from Czech and Bulgarian also show the same pattern as given in (3b) and (3c) respectively.

(3) Voiceless+[v]
  a. Russian (see also Padgett 2002)

| k-anʲ-e | 'to Ania' | k-vanʲ-e / *g-vanʲ-e | 'to Vania' |
| zvʲerʲ 'beast' | *vs.* | svʲerx 'above' | |

  b. Czech: svjet   'world'
  c. Bulgarian: tvorʲ-a 'create (1sg)'

In the other pattern, observed in Polish, /v/ undergoes progressive devoicing to avoid disagreement, as shown in (4a). Interestingly, a similar pattern is also applied to /r/, which emerges as a retroflex consonant,[2] as illustrated in (4b).

(4) Progressive devoicing (Polish: see also Gussman 2007:307)
  a. /v/   tserkʲev-n-i 'Orthodox'   tserkf-i / *tserkv-i, *tsergv-i 'church (gen. sg.)'
  b. /r/   pʲur-o   'feather'   pʲuz̨-e (loc. sg.)
                        but
         lustr-o   'mirror'   lusts̨-e / *luzdz̨-e (loc. sg.)

These patterns suggest that the /v/ (and /r/ in Polish) should be differentiated from other voiced obstruents. The next subsection briefly reviews previous research on this topic.

3. Previous research

The patterns of /v/ could be considered phonologically opaque because [v] cannot superficially be differentiated from the other voiced obstruents. This is especially problematic when applying output-based phonological theories, such as OT. In the remainder of this section, this article will review an OT approach to voicing assimilation and consider Padgett's (2002) analysis of /v/'s failure to trigger regressive voicing.

3.1. Voicing assimilation in OT

Assimilation patterns, including voicing assimilation, have been explained by assuming certain markedness constraints on feature-wise disagreements. The following constraint has been assumed for voicing assimilation:

(5) AGREE (voice) (cf. Lombardi 1999; Padgett 2002 among others):
    "Obstruent clusters must agree in [voice]."

Next, we consider directionality, i.e., whether the assimilation is regressive or progressive.

Padgett (2002) proposes that the obstruent faithfulness varies depending on what type of segment follows.[3] If the faithfulness constraint on pre-sonorant obstruents (6a) along with (5) outranks that on pre-obstruent obstruents (6b), then regressive voicing is predicted.

(6) a. FAITH_{PRE-SONORANT} (voice):
  "Consonants in the output must be specified for [voice] in the same manner as in the input <u>if the consonants immediately precede a sonorant</u>."
  b. FAITH_{PRE-OBSTRUENT} (voice):
  "Consonants in the output must be specified for [voice] in the same manner as in the input <u>if the consonants immediately precede an obstruent</u>."

See (7) for an illustration. The first candidate, in which the obstruent cluster does not agree in voicing, violates (5). While the second candidate, in which the preceding consonant in the cluster is devoiced, violates (6b), the third candidate, in which the following consonant preceding a sonorant (i.e. vowel) is voiced, violates (6a). Since (5) and (6a) outrank (6b), the second candidate is selected as the optimal output.

(7) e.g., /rib-k-a/ → [ripka] 'fish (dim.)' (Russian: see also Padgett 2002)

/rib-k-a/	FAITH_{PRE-SONORANT} (voice)	AGREE (voice)	FAITH_{PRE-OBSTRUENT} (voice)
ribka		*W	L
☞ ripka			*
ribga	*W		L

Note that consonants preceding sonorants can undergo voicing and devoicing in Polish. Refer to (8). This suggests that the consonant should be assumed to be faithful only on pre-vocalic obstruents, as described in (9). Meanwhile, (10) demonstrates that, in Polish, unlike in Russian, (9) outranks AGREE (voice) while (6a) is outranked by AGREE (voice).

(8) Voicing assimilation before sonorants in Polish (Gussman 2007:295-296)
  jab**b**wek 'apple (gen. pl.)'   ja**p**w**k**-o   (nom. sg.)
  vʲatr   'wind'   vʲa**dr**#**z**axodni 'westerly wind'

(9) FAITH_{PRE-VOCALIC} (voice):
  "Consonants in the output must be specified for [voice] in the same manner as in the input <u>if the consonants immediately precede a vowel</u>."

(10) e.g., /jabwko/ → [japwko] 'apple' (Polish)

/jabwko/	FAITH_{PRE-VOCALIC} (voice)	AGREE (voice)	FAITH_{PRE-SONORANT} (voice)	FAITH_{PRE-OBSTRUENT} (voice)
jabwko		*W	L	
☞ japwko			*	
jabwgo	*W		L	

In this section, we have explored how voicing assimilation is explained under the OT framework. The next subsection discusses Padgett's (2002) analysis of /v/.

3.2. Problem of /v/: Padgett's (2002) analysis

Many Slavists have noted that /v/ was historically a sonorant /w/ (e.g., Townsend and Janda 1996). Some researchers have extended this assumption to their analyses of the synchronic pattern. However, Padgett (2002) argues that this does not work in the OT framework because the [v] is regarded as an obstruent on the surface regardless of whether it is a sonorant in the input.

Instead, Padgett (2002:15) points out that the Russian [v] "has more formant structure and intensity, and less frication" and is, therefore, phonetically more sonorous than the other obstruents; assuming a semi-sonorant consonant [ʋ]. Voiceless consonants preceding [ʋ] thus avoid voicing due to the faithfulness constraint on pre-sonorant consonants (i.e., FAITH_PRE-SONORANT (voice)). On the other hand, this semi-sonorant consonant undergoes devoicing when a voiceless consonant follows because it is targeted by AGREE (voice). Note that in Padgett's (2002) analysis, [ʋ] is latently specified as [+voice]. This analysis is summarized in (11).

(11) i. /spʲerx/ → [spʲerx] 'above'
ii. /laʋka/ → [lafka] 'bench'   (cf. Padgett 2002)

	FAITH_PRE-SONORANT (voice)	AGREE (voice)	FAITH_PRE-OBSTRUENT (voice)
/spʲerx/			
☞ spʲerx		*	
zpʲerx	*W	L	
sfʲerx	*W	L	
/laʋka/			
laʋka		*W	L
☞ lafka			*
laʋga	*W		L

However, Padgett's analysis would not work in Polish, where /ʋ/ (or /v/) can undergo progressive devoicing for the sake of assimilation; this pattern should violate FAITH_PRE-VOCALIC (voice) (see 10). Note that the regressive devoicing cannot be accounted for regardless of whether the '/v/' is obstruent or semi-sonorant. Consider (12).[4]

(12) e.g., /tserkʋ-i/ [?]→ [tserkfi] 'church (gen. sg.)' (Polish: see 4a)

/tserkʋ-i/	FAITH_PRE-VOCALIC (voice)	AGREE (voice)	FAITH_PRE-SONORANT (voice)	FAITH_PRE-OBSTRUENT (voice)
tserkʋi		*!		
☠ tsergʋi			*	
☻* tserkfi	*!			

With this inconsistency taken into account, the next section refines the OT approach to the patterns of /v/.

4. Proposed account

While the current analysis primarily parallels Padgett's (2002) argument, there is one crucial difference: specification for [voice]. Unlike in Padgett's (2002) analysis, this paper assumes that sonorant consonants are underspecified for [voice]. In 4.1, this section discusses representational issues. Then, subsection 4.2 addresses the difference between the Polish and Russian cases in the current model.

4.1. Underspecification and Turbid representations

First, I will address the inconsistent progressive devoicing of /ʋ/ in Polish. The failure in (12) results from the devoicing of /ʋ/ preceding a vowel. The current analysis thus assumes that sonorant consonants are underspecified for [voice]. Since this consonant cannot violate the faithfulness constraints on [voice], the current ranking (refer to 10, 12) correctly predicts the attested pattern, as demonstrated by (13).

(13) e.g., /tserkv̥-i/ → [tserkfi] 'church (gen. sg.)' (Polish)

/tserkv̥-i/	FAITH_{PRE-VOCALIC} (voice)	AGREE (voice)	FAITH_{PRE-SONORANT} (voice)
tserkv̥i		*!	
tsergv̥i			*!
☞ tserkfi			

However, another problem arises: why do /v̥/ and /r/ emerge as voiced unless they appear adjacent to voiceless consonants? Since these consonants are underspecified for [voice], whether they emerge as voiced or voiceless depends on the markedness hierarchy between voiced and voiceless consonants. For the present, there is no evidence that voiced consonants are less marked than voiceless ones in the languages concerned.[5] It is thus impossible to predict the situation in which voiced consonants are preferred to voiceless ones with other things being equal.

One explanation is that underlying properties are reflected in the outputs even if they are not phonetically realized. Tanaka (2014, 2015) proposes the following representation based on Goldrick's (2001) Turbid Representations (see also van Oostendorp 2008): underlying units (segments, features, etc.) do (phonologically) emerge in the outputs even when deleted, which are represented as <X>. By adopting this approach, the feature-wise representation of the (semi-)sonorants and their alternatives can be assumed, as seen in Table 1.

	Segments		Features	
Input	/v̥/	/r/	[sonorant]	[ ]
Output	[v]	[z]	<[sonorant]>	[+voice]
	[f]	[s̥]	<[sonorant]>	[−voice]

Table 1: *Turbid representations for the consonants concerned*

Note that phonological analyses have for a long time made a representational distinction between obstruent voicing and sonorant voicing (see Ito, Mester and Padgett 1995 for an OT analysis). Moreover, as noted by van Oostendorp (2008) and Tanaka (2014, 2015), preservation of input phonological information has been proposed under the earliest OT framework, Containment Theory[6] (Prince and Smolensky 1993/2004), though most recent OT analyses have been adopted strictly output-oriented framework, Correspondence Theory (McCarthy and Prince 1995). One main problem in the latter approach is that it cannot account for phonological opacity: the above assumed sonorant-origin obstruents, for instance, cannot be distinguished from underlying obstruents under strictly output-based phonology. This paper, therefore, adopts Turbid Representations, assuming the following constraint on sonorant-origin voiceless consonants to eliminate voiceless consonants derived from the (semi-)sonorants:

(14) *[−voice]-<[sonorant]>:
"Consonants specified for [sonorant] in the input (<u>even if not specified in the output</u>) must be voiced in the output."

If this constraint outranks the general markedness constraint on voiced consonants (*[+voice]), underlying sonorants are voiced when they change to obstruents, as demonstrated in (15). Note that the constraint in (14) should be outranked by the constraints relevant to voicing assimilation in order to predict the progressive as well as the regressive devoicing of sonorants. Consider (16). The (semi-)sonorants (/v̥/ or /r/) change to obstruents for the sake of voicing assimilation because AGREE (voice) and FAITH (voice)[7] outrank the constraint detailed in (14).

(15) e.g., /pʲur-e/ → [pʲuʐe] 'feather (loc. sg.)' (see 4b)

/pʲur-e/	*[−voice]-<[sonorant]>	*[+voice]
pʲuʂe	*W	L
☞ pʲuʐe		*

(16) e.g., /lustr-e/ → [lustʂe] 'mirror (loc. sg.)' (see 4b)

/lustr-e/	FAITH_PRE-VOCALIC (voice)	AGREE (voice)	FAITH (voice)	*[−voice]-<[son]>
lustʐe		*W		L
luzdʐe			*W*	L
☞ lustʂe				*

So far, this section has discussed the strict voicing assimilation observed in Polish. The next subsection extends the current approach to Russian, where voiceless consonants precede the semi-sonorant [ʋ].

4.2. Sonorant preservation and variation between Russian and Polish

In Russian, neither regressive voicing nor progressive devoicing occurs when voiceless consonants precede the semi-sonorant [ʋ] (refer to 3). In other words, the semi-sonorant remains even when a disagreement in voicing emerges, unlike in Polish. This suggests that the faithfulness constraint on [sonorant] should outrank AGREE (voice). Note that the semi-sonorant changes to a voiceless obstruent (i.e., [f]) when it precedes voiceless consonants. Hence, the ranking of the faithfulness constraint on [sonorant] should depend on the type of the following segment. The following positional faithfulness constraint can thus be assumed:

(17) FAITH_PRE-SONORANT (sonorant):
"Consonants in the output must be specified for [sonorant] in the same manner as in the input <u>if the consonants immediately precede a sonorant</u>."

While this constraint outranks AGREE (voice), AGREE (voice) outranks the general faithfulness constraint (FAITH (sonorant)). Refer to (18) for a presentation of the ranking argument.

(18) i. /sʋʲerx/   → [sʋʲerx] 'above'
     ii. /nʲeʋ-sk-iɪ̯/ → [nʲef-sk-iɪ̯] 'bench' (see 2)

	FAITH_PRE-SONORANT (sonorant)	AGREE (voice)	FAITH (sonorant)	FAITH (voice)	*[−voice]-<[son]>
i. /sʋʲerx/					
☞ sʋʲerx		*			
zʋʲerx		*8		*W	
zvʲerx	*W	L	*	*	
sfʲerx	*W	L	*		*
ii. /nʲeʋ-sk-iɪ̯/					
nʲeʋskʲiɪ̯		*W	L		
☞ nʲefskʲiɪ̯			*		*
nʲevzgʲiɪ̯			*	*W*	L

When the semi-sonorant is preceded by a voiceless consonant, as shown in (18i), the change to the obstruents (i.e., [v] or [f]) for the sake of voicing assimilation is eliminated by the constraint (17). Since the voicing of the preceding voiceless consonant is eliminated by FAITH (voice), no change in voicing is predicted. In contrast, when the semi-sonorant precedes a voiceless consonant, as demonstrated in (18ii), the sonorant preservation does not violate (17) and is eliminated by AGREE (voice). This consonant is voiceless due to FAITH (voice), which blocks the voicing of voiceless consonants that follow the semi-sonorant.

The discussion thus far suggests that the difference between the Russian and Polish can be attributed to the re-ranking of FAITH$_{PRE-SONORANT}$ (sonorant) and AGREE (voice): unlike in Russian, where AGREE (voice) is dominated by FAITH$_{PRE-SONORANT}$ (sonorant), in Polish, AGREE (voice) should outrank FAITH$_{PRE-SONORANT}$ (sonorant) and FAITH (sonorant), as shown in (19). In other words, the sonorant preservation is defeated by the strict voicing assimilation. The rankings of the constraints for the two patterns are summarized in (20).

(19) i. /tserkʋ-i/ → [tserkfi]   'church (gen. sg.)' (cf. 13)
      ii. /ʋ-krakoʋ-e/ → [fkrakoʋʲe]   'in Krakow'

	AGREE (voice)	FAITH(PRE-SONORANT) (sonorant)	FAITH (voice)	*[−voice]-<[son]>
i. /tserkʋ-i/				
tserkʋ-i	*W	L		
tsergvi		*	*W	L
☞ tserkfi		*		*
ii. /ʋ-krakoʋ-e/				
ʋkrakoʋʲe	*W	L		
☞ fkrakoʋʲe		*		*
vgrakoʋʲe		*	*W	L

(20)   Summary of the constraint rankings

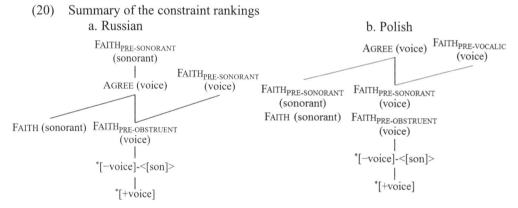

        a. Russian   b. Polish

In Russian, AGREE (voice) is outranked by FAITH$_{PRE-SONORANT}$ (sonorant), which allows voiceless obstruents preceding [ʋ]. In Polish, in contrast, AGREE (voice) is undominated, which results in progressive devoicing of sonorant-origin obstruents.

5. Conclusion

This paper has discussed the inconsistent behavior of /v/ in Slavic voicing assimilation. As proposed in previous research, this consonant should be a sonorant. From observing the Polish pattern, it was argued that the sonorants should be underspecified for [voice], which would not violate the relevant faithfulness constraint. In contrast, this article argues that the difference between the Russian and Polish patterns is accounted for by re-ranking the (positional) faithfulness constraint on [sonorant].

This discussion implies that the phonological or contrastive voicing of obstruents should be differentiated from the phonetic voicing of sonorants or vowels, which may be phonologically inactive. However, because sonorants tend to be voiced by default, there may be a correlation between phonological and phonetic voicing. Future research may provide more insight into this contradiction.

Notes

* This paper is based on my oral presentation in "Phonology Forum 2017" at Tokyo Metropolitan University on August 25, 2017. I am deeply grateful to many attendants who commented on my presentation. I am also indebted to the anonymous reviewers for many helpful comments. This work was supported by JSPS KAKENHI Grant Number 15J03345. All the errors are mine.
[1] Reduction of unstressed vowels is observed in Russian. For the sake of simplicity, this process is not described in this paper.
[2] This process is triggered by front vowels and regarded as a kind of palatalization.
[3] Since this paper adopts Containment Theory (see 4.1) unlike Padgett (2002), the faithfulness constraints are tentatively assumed as FAITH.
[4] Since the ranking has been given above, a combination tableau is not used here and in (13).
[5] As Vaux and Samuels (2005) claim, the markedness hierarchy between voiced and voiceless consonants cannot be determined without considering aspiration. Aspiration in Russian and Polish needs to be discussed in future research.
[6] Turbid representations make a distinction between underlying phonological specification (*Projection*) and surface realization (*Pronunciation*), which has not been clearly addressed in earlier Containment Theory research.
[7] In the following discussion, the positional faithfulness constraints on [voice] are unified into FAITH (voice) because only underlying obstruent consonants would violate it within clusters including the semi-sonorant.
[8] Voiced obstruents preceding the semi-sonorant still violate AGREE (voice) because the semi-sonorant is not specified for [+voice]. Note that the other sonorants are not affected by this constraint.

References

Goldrick, Matthew. 2001. Turbid output representations and the unity of opacity. *Proceedings of the North East Linguistics Society* 30.231–245.

Gussman, Edmund. 2007. *The phonology of Polish*. Oxford: Oxford University Press.

Ito, Junko, Armin Mester, and Jay Padgett. 1995. Licensing and underspecification in Optimality Theory. *Linguistic Inquiry* 26.571–613.

Lombardi, Linda. 1999. Positional faithfulness and voicing assimilation in Optimality Theory. *Natural Language and Linguistic Theory* 17.267–302.

McCarthy, John J. and Alan S. Prince. 1995. Faithfulness and reduplicative identity. *Papers in Optimality Theory*, ed. by Jill N. Beckman, Laura W. Dickey and Suzanne Urbanczyk, 249–384. Amherst: GLSA, University of Massachusetts.

Padgett, Jaye. 2002. Russian voicing assimilation, final devoicing, and the problem of [v]. ROA-528.

Prince, Alan and Paul Smolensky. 1993/2004. *Optimality Theory: constraint interaction in generative grammar.* New York: Blackwell.

Tanaka, Shin-ichi. 2014. Turbid representations for opacity: the underlying and surface representations for voiced obstruents in Japanese and English. *Papers from the Thirty-First National Conference of the English Linguistic Society of Japan* (JELS 31).193–199.

Tanaka, Shin-ichi. 2015. Yūseisei no tsuyosa kara mita nihongo no futōmei genshō: nigori no hyōji ni yoru tōmeika. *Nihongo kenkyū to sono kanōsei* ed. by Takashi Masuoka, 26–51. Tokyo: Kaitakusha.

Townsend, Charles E. and Laura A. Janda. 1996. *Common and comparative Slavic: phonology and inflection.* Columbus: Slavica Publishers.

van Oostendorp, Marc. 2008. Incomplete devoicing in formal phonology. *Lingua* 118.1362–1374.

Vaux, Bert and Bridget Samuels. 2005. Laryngeal markedness and aspiration. *Phonology* 22.395–436.

The Learnability of the Accentuation of Sino-Japanese Words and Loanwords: The Hidden Structure Problem[*]

Motong Li
Osaka University

ABSTRACT. This paper analyzes the learnability of dominant accentual patterns of Sino-Japanese words and loanwords using the constraint ranking proposed by Li (2017) as the target grammar. Convergence results of computational simulations vary across algorithms and levels of inputs. Learning in the face of hidden structure, learners of Robust Interpretive Parsing (RIP; Tesar and Smolensky 2000) did not converge, indicating the failure to make full use of available probabilistic information. Instead, two novel parsing strategies proposed by Jarosz (2013) help to solve related problems of RIP, yielding significant improvements in performance even with the relatively complex target grammar.

Keywords: learnability, hidden structure, Gradual Learning Algorithm, Robust Interpretive Parsing, Expected Interpretive Parsing

1. Introduction

Learnability deals with the problem of how learners approach, and eventually converge to the target grammar. In Optimality Theory (OT; Prince and Smolensky 1993/2004) particularly, learnability asks how learners equipped with an initial constraint ranking update each constraint position until the final ranking matches the adult one. Compared to general OT work that focuses on the construction of the adult grammar, learnability is less studied, and less accountable when there are hidden structures like feet that need to be parsed (e.g. whether [σσ'σ] should be parsed into iambic /(σσ')σ/ or trochaic /σ(σ'σ)/). Depending on the data and the algorithm, the attempt to disambiguate sometimes fails, bringing inconsistency to the whole OT analysis.

Taking several combinations of learning and parsing algorithms into consideration, this paper conducts a computational study on the learnability of dominant accentual patterns observed in Sino-Japanese words and loanwords. The main purpose here is to examine the convergence rate of different algorithms with or without the intervention of the hidden structure problem, and to present various learning patterns into which the results can be classified.

2. Multi-level representation

Apoussidou (2007), which studied the learnability of metrical phonology in detail, used a three-level phonological representation for the hidden structure problem. As shown in (1), these three levels, Underlying Form (UF), Surface Form (SF) and Overt Form (OF), are represented by vertical bars, slashes and brackets respectively.

(1) Three-level phonological representation (Apoussidou 2007)
    UF |σσσ| Syllables only
    SF   /(σ'σ)σ/   Syllables, foot structures and the stress
    OF   [σ'σσ]   Syllables and the stress

UF only consists of syllables, and can be extracted trivially from SF and OF in Apoussidou's analyses of grammatical stress in Latin and Pintupi. SF, which is the output level of general OT analyses, contains the full structural description, namely syllables, foot structures and the stress. Compared to SF, OF lacks the hidden foot structures but has the remaining overt information, and is hence more realistic considering the process of perception. Ambiguity emerges when OF is parsed into SF for learners to obtain the foot structure.

3. Target grammar and dominant accentual patterns

Based on Ito and Mester (2016) which conducted a thorough OT analysis of loanwords, Li (2017) proposed a constraint ranking that accounts for dominant accentual patterns of both Sino-Japanese words and loanwords simultaneously, as presented in (2).

(2) Constraint hierarchy as the target grammar[1] (Li 2017)

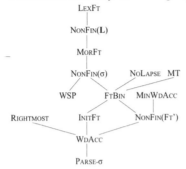

Dominant accentual patterns of the two lexical strata are shown in 0, with foot structure optimally specified (L: light syllable; H: heavy syllable; #: morpheme boundary; +: lexeme boundary; boldface: foothead).

(3) Dominant accentual patterns (Li 2017)
a. Sino-Japanese words and loanwords

(**L'**)	(**L'L**)	(**H'**)

b. Sino-Japanese words

(**L'**)#L	(**L**)#(**LL**)	(**L'L**)#L	(**H'**)#L	(**L**)#(**H**)
(**H**)#(**LL**)	(**LL**)#(**H**)	(**H**)#(**H**)	(**LL**)#(**LL**)	

c. Loanwords

(**L'L**)L	(**H'**)L	(**L'**)H	(**LL**)(**LL**)	(**H**)(**LL**)
L(**H'**)L	(**LL**)(**L'L**)L	(**LL**)L(**L'L**)L	(**H'**)H	(**H**)L(**L'L**)L
(**H**)(**L'**)H	L(**L'L**)H	L(**H'**)H	L(**H**)(**LL**)	(**L'L**)H
(**H**)+(**H**)	(**LL**)+(**L**)	(**LL**)+(**H**)	(**H**)(**H'**)L	(**LL**)(**LL**) (**L'L**)L

In order to explain the different accentual distribution in these lexical strata, the analysis in Li (2017) highly relied on constraints such as quantity-sensitive NONFIN(**L**) and morpho-phonological LEXFT and MORFT, which all referred to the foot structure in particular ways. The complexity of foot specification makes it even harder to parse the hidden structure as expected in an ambiguous condition.

4. Algorithms

This section briefly introduces two learning algorithms, Error-Driven Constraint Demotion (EDCD; Tesar and Smolensky 2000) and Gradual Learning Algorithm (GLA; Boersma 1997, 1999; Boersma and Hayes 2001), and the parsing algorithm Robust Interpretive Parsing (RIP; Tesar and Smolensky 2000), which are all widely used in learnability-related literature.

4.1 EDCD

EDCD is a learning algorithm based on original OT which has discrete ranks. This algorithm assumes that, given a set of grammatical structural descriptions as inputs and a constraint hierarchy H_{start} as the initial grammar, learners use their current grammar H to select the optimal candidate, and compare it with the real data. If the current optimal output *loser* does not match the real data *winner*, then the deciding constraints that favor the *loser* should be minimally demoted below constraints that favor the *winner*, resulting in a new constraint hierarchy H_{new}. Learners will use H_{new} to update their current grammar and apply it to the next input. This learning process will not stop until all optimal outputs produced by the learner's grammar match the real data.

4.2 GLA

GLA is based on stochastic OT (Boersma 1997, 1999; Boersma and Hayes 2001), which is aimed at modeling free grammatical variation and speech errors that are frequently seen during the early learning stage. Unlike the discrete ranking in original OT, the ranking in stochastic OT is continuous, with each constraint numerically assigned a ranking value. At evaluation time, the evaluator adds a Gaussian random variable (mean = 0, standard deviation = *evaluation noise*) to each constraint to temporally randomize their current ranking value.

An example from Boersma and Hayes (2001) is shown in (4). Constraints C_2 and C_3 have their own distribution of ranking values. At evaluation time, it is possible to choose the selection points within the range of these two constraints. Generally as in (4a), selection point $\cdot_2$ is ranked higher than $\cdot_3$, resulting in $C_2 \gg C_3$ with high probability, but if $\cdot_2$ and $\cdot_3$ are randomized as in (4b), then C_3 would outrank C_2.

(4) Stochastic evaluation (Boersma and Hayes, 2001)
   a. Common result: $C_2 \gg C_3$

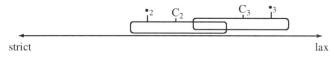

   strict   lax
   b. Rare result: $C_3 \gg C_2$

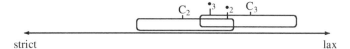

   strict   lax

Unlike EDCD, whose update rule only permits minimal demotion, GLA often demotes constraints that favor the *loser* and promotes constraints that favor the *winner* symmetrically. The range of demotion and promotion is decided by the parameter *plasticity* (ε). If ε is set to 1, then the ranking value should be added or subtracted by 1 regarding whether the constraint favor the *winner* or the *loser*. As reported in Boersma (2003), GLA performs better than EDCD when the problem of hidden structures gets involved[2].

4.3 RIP

RIP is a representative parsing algorithm in OT for learners to build hidden structures from overt information. An example from Apoussidou (2007) is shown in (5). Compared to general OT work whose input level is often UF, the input level of RIP is OF, which means that overt information like stress or accent is incorporated in it.   Candidates in RIP are repre-sented in SF, but all restricted to those whose OF is identical to the input. Learners then pick one candidate ☞RIP as optimal based on their current grammar (ALLFT-L) ALLFT-R) TROCHAIC) IAMBIC in (5)), and interpret it as the *winner* for the current data.

(5) RIP in OT (Apoussidou 2007)

OF: [σσ'σ]	ALLFT-L	ALLFT-R	TROCHAIC	IAMBIC
a. /σ(σ')σ/ [σσ'σ]	*!	*		
☞RIP b. /(σσ') σ/ [σσ'σ]		*	*	
c. /σ(σ'σ)/ [σσ'σ]	*!			*

Next, as shown in (6), learners do general OT evaluation with UF as the input and an unlimited candidate set, pick one candidate ☞VP as optimal, and compare it with ☞RIP. If ☞VP and ☞RIP are different from each other, then the update rule based on EDCD (TROCHAIC demoted below IAMBIC) or GLA (TROCHAIC demoted and IAMBIC promoted numerically) is applied. If they match each other, then the current learning step ends and the algorithm moves to another datum.

(6) Error detection, given underlying form (Apoussidou 2007)

UF: |σσσ|	ALLFT-L	ALLFT-R	TROCHAIC	IAMBIC
a. |σσσ| /σ(σ')σ/ [σσ'σ]	*!	*		
☞RIP b. |σσσ| /(σσ')σ/ [σσ'σ]		*	*!	
c. |σσσ| /σ(σ'σ)/ [σσ'σ]	*!			*
☞VP d. |σσσ| /(σ'σ)σ/ [σ'σσ]		*		*
e. |σσσ| /σ(σσ')/ [σσσ']	*!		*	
f. |σσσ| /(σ')σσ/ [σ'σσ]		**!		
g. |σσσ| /σσ(σ')/ [σσσ']	*!*			

In the next two sections, computational simulations are carried out to examine the convergence rate in different situations where the input level (SF or OF) and the learning algorithm (EDCD or GLA) are taken into consideration.

5. Simulations: without parsing

This section conducts simulations with SF as the input level, which means the *winners'* optimal foot structures are known to learners without parsing. Training data are shown in 0 with full structural description. Praat (version 6.0.19; Boersma and Weenink 2016) is used to carry out all simulations in this paper.

5.1 EDCD

The parameter settings for EDCD learners are specified in (7). The update rule and the initial ε mean that ranking values of deciding constraints that favor the *loser* are minimally demoted below constraints that favor the *winner* by one. Due to the discreteness of original OT, the value of ε here does not affect the actual ranking. Because variation of ranking values is not allowed in EDCD, evaluation noise is set to 0. The number of ε assigned 1 indicates that ε is kept to 1 during the whole learning process. Replications per ε set to 1,000 stipulates that 1,000 learning steps are carried out for the current ε. After 1,000 learning steps, the result is counted as one simulation for one learner. Twenty learners are simulated here, and the initial ranking values of constraints are all set to 100. After the whole learning process, 100,000 SF data are randomly generated based on the learner's final grammar, and are compared with the actual OF data shown in 0 to calculate the accuracy rate without considering the foot structure. The algorithm is considered to have converged successfully only if the learner's accuracy rate is 100%.

(7) parameter settings for EDCD learners

Update rule	Evaluation noise	Initial ε	Number of ε	Replications per ε
EDCD	0	1	1	1,000

As a result, all EDCD learners converged to the target grammar (convergence rate = 100%), the effect of which was proven in Tesar and Smolensky (2000). Learners' final rankings can be classified into two patterns. Ten learners belong to the first pattern, Linguist Analysis (P_{LA}), which is identical to the target constraint hierarchy shown in (2). Figure 1 presents the ranking dynamics of this pattern. From this we can see that the learning process effectively stops at about the 125th learning step, after which ranking values do not change anymore.

The second pattern, Crucial Ties (P_{CT}; 10 learners), treats two or more constraints with tied ranks as one constraint and counts their violation marks jointly. An example for learners whose INITFT and WDACC ranked equally is given in 0. The unaccented (8a) and ante-penultimate-mora-accented (8b) violate WDACC and INITFT respectively. Because of the equal rank of these two constraints, violation marks here are canceled out, bringing the competition to the final-rank PARSE-σ. However, as pointed out by Apoussidou (2007) and McCarthy (2008), the strategy of crucial ties does not have enough evidence to prove itself valid. Turning back to 0, it is implausible to consider that not parsing the initial syllable into a foot is as disadvantageous as not having an accent.

(8) Crucial Ties: WDACC and INITFT

|LLLL| (/amerika/ 'America')	LEXFT	MT	MINWDACC	NOLAPSE	RIGHTMOST	NONFIN(L)	MORFT	NONFIN(σ)	FTBIN	NONFIN(FT')	WSP	INITFT	WDACC	PARSE-σ
☞ a. /(LL)(LL)/													*	
b. /L(L'L)L/												*		*!*

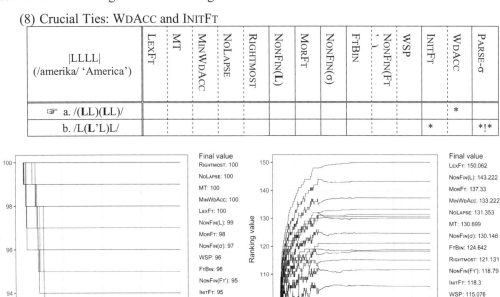

Figure 1 EDCD, P_{LA}, without parsing   **Figure 2** GLA, P_{LA}, without parsing

5.2 GLA

The parameter settings for GLA learners are specified in 0. The update rule set to *Symmetrical all* means that constraints that favor the *loser* are demoted, and constraints that favor the *winner* are promoted symmetrically. In order to make use of stochastic knowledge, evaluation noise is assigned a value of 2. The number of ε is set to 4 and each of them are used 10,000 times (40,000 times in total). To model different learning speeds in different learning stages, the decrement of ε is set to 0.1, which means that the first ε is 1, the second

0.1, the third 0.01, and the forth 0.001. Other parameter settings are the same as those in Section 5.1.

(9) parameter settings for EDCD learners

Update rule	Evaluation noise	Initial ε	Number of ε	Replications per ε	ε decrement
Symmetric all	2	1	4	10,000	0.1

GLA learners also learned the target grammar successfully (convergence rate = 100%), and they all belong to P_{LA}. The ranking dynamics of one representative learner are shown in Figure 2, where constraint demotion and promotion can both be observed. In the early learning stage, ε has a big value and learning errors occur frequently, which makes the ranking dynamics fluctuate greatly. But as learning proceeds, ε becomes smaller and learning errors decrease, resulting in near-stable ranking values.

6. Simulations: parsing with RIP

This section runs simulations with OF as the input level, which is more realistic considering the process of perception. In order to get a full structural description for the input, learners must make use of their parsing algorithm, at the risk of wrongly guessing a hidden structure that does not match the expected one. Here EDCD and GLA learners are equipped with RIP, with the same training data (foot structure removed) and parameter settings as in Section 5. Basic statistics of the accuracy rate of these two algorithms are given in 0.

(10) Descriptive statistics of EDCD/RIP and GLA/RIP

Algorithm	N	Mean	SD	Median	Min	Max
EDCD/RIP	20	0.89	0.15	0.98	0.5	0.98
GLA/RIP	20	0.92	0.01	0.92	0.92	0.94

Compared to the guaranteed convergence illustrated in Section 5, neither EDCD/RIP nor GLA/RIP learners converged to the target grammar. A statistical difference was not found between these two algorithms (Mann-Whitney U test, $U = 157.5$, $p = .245$).

6.1 EDCD/RIP

Results of EDCD/RIP learners can be classified into two patterns. The first pattern, $P_{NF(F')/IF\uparrow}$, has twelve learners with the reversed partial ranking NONFIN(FT'), INITFT ≫ FTBIN. The linear ranking of this pattern is shown in 0, with |LLLH| as its input. (11b) and (11c) have identical violation marks, hence the chance for each of them to be selected as optimal is nearly fifty-fifty. When (11c) is randomly chosen, the accuracy rate decreases because the OF of (11c) does not match the real data.

(11) $P_{NF(F')/IF\uparrow}$: antepenultimate- and pre-antepenultimate-mora accentuation

|LLLH| (/are'ruɡi:/ 'allergy')	INITFT	LEXFT	MT	MINWDACC	NONFIN(FT')	NOLAPSE	RIGHTMOST	NONFIN(L)	MORFT	NONFIN(σ)	WSP	FTBIN	WDACC	PARSE-σ
a. /L(L'L)H/	*!										*			**
☞ b. /(L)(L'L)H/											*	*		*
☞ c. /(LL)(L')H/											*	*		*

The remaining eight learners belong to P_{SLUMP}, whose ranking values of several constraints fall sharply. Accuracy rates of this pattern vary greatly, with a minimum of 50%. The ranking dynamics of one representative learner are shown in Figure 3, where the slump of FTBIN, PARSE-σ, RIGHTMOST and WDACC can be clearly observed. Due to the lowest rank of WDACC, words consisting of three or more moras will be output without an accent in this ranking, which cannot reflect the accented part in the real data correctly.

6.2 GLA/RIP

Most of the GLA/RIP learners have the reversed partial ranking MORFT ≫ NONFIN(L) and INITFT, NONFIN(FT') ≫ FTBIN ($P_{MF/NF(F')/IF\uparrow}$). This pattern also gives |LLLH| two optimal candidates, and wrongly outputs |H#L| (/kyu:'#yo/ 'salary') and |LL#L| (/ko'ku#chi/ 'notification') as /(**H**)#(**L**)/ and /(**LL**)#(**L**)/ without an accent. The ranking dynamics of this pattern are shown in Figure 4, where a fluctuating rise of WDACC and RIGHTMOST can be observed, with the ε decrement set to 0 (the result is the same as the ε decrement set to 0.1).

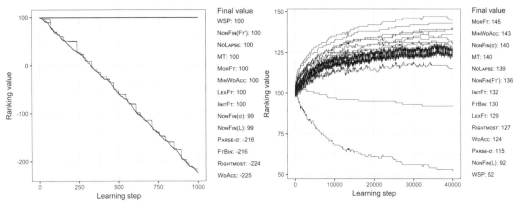

Figure 3 EDCD/RIP, P_{SLUMP} **Figure 4** GLA/RIP, $P_{MF/NF(F')/IF\uparrow}$ (ε decrement = 0)

7. Reexamination of RIP

The convergence failure of EDCD/RIP and GLA/RIP learners can be partly attributable to the parsing algorithm. This section introduces Jarosz (2013), which gave a detailed re-examination of RIP and proposed two alternatives, Resampling Robust Interpretive Parsing (RRIP) and Expected Interpretive Parsing (EIP).

7.1 RRIP

In order to highlight the problem of RIP, the algorithm of RIP reformulated by Jarosz (2013) is shown in 0, which does not affect the behavior of the original parsing algorithm.

(12) Reformulated RIP for GLA (Jarosz 2013)
  1. Initialize Stochastic Grammar: G_0
  2. Iterate over d in D:
     a. Sample $G' \sim G_i$
     b. Input = uf(d)
     c. Output = Optimize$_{G'}$(Input)
     d. If overt(Output) ≠ d:
        i. Parse = RIP$_{G'}$(d)
        ii. G_{i+1} = Update(G_i, Parse, Output)

Jarosz stated that "[F]rom the reformulation it is clear that parsing is only relevant in case the selected grammar G' generates an error…What is odd about this use of interpretive parsing in the stochastic setting, then, is that the learner nonetheless uses the known-to-be-incorrect G' for interpretive parsing." In order to solve this problem, Jarosz added a simple modification to RIP, as shown in 0, with step 1 to 2c identical to those in 0. The difference between RRIP and RIP is that if G' generates an error, the learner simply resamples another grammar G″ and uses it for interpretive parsing. This helps the learner reference its stochastic grammatical knowledge, the advantage of which is confirmed using simulations in Section 8.1.

(13) RRIP for GLA (Jarosz 2013)
 …
 2d. If overt(Output) ≠ d:
    i. Sample G″ ~ G_i
    ii. Parse = RIP$_{G″}$(d)
    iii. G_{i+1} = Update(G_i, Parse, Output)

7.2 EIP

The second problem pointed out by Jarosz (2013), the parsing-production mismatch, is exemplified in 0. Given the assumed ranking values, ALLFT-L ≫ ALLFT-R ≫ TROCHAIC ≫ IAMBIC and ALLFT-R ≫ ALLFT-L ≫ TROCHAIC ≫ IAMBIC will be generated stochastically with equal probability, resulting in (14a) and (14c) being output as optimal nearly 50% of the time. TROCHAIC ≫ IAMBIC is fully activated to disfavor (14b) and (14d).

(14) The parsing-production mismatch (Jarosz 2013)

|LLL|	ALLFT-L 300	ALLFT-R 300	TROCHAIC 200	IAMBIC 100
a. /(L'L)L/		*		*
b. /(LL')L/		*	*	
c. /L(L'L)/	*			*
d. /L(LL')/	*		*	

However, if the learner hears [LL'L] and has to parse it with its current grammar, then candidates for RIP are restricted to (14b) and (14c) whose OF is identical to the real datum. This time, which candidate will be selected as the optimal SF depends in whole on the relative rank of ALLFT-R and ALLFT-L, leaving TROCHAIC and IAMBIC inactivated. In Jarosz's words, "[A]ccording to the learner's current grammar, /(LL')L/ is the only possible parse of [LL'L], but RIP fails to reflect this categorical restriction imposed by the grammar."

In order to solve this problem, Jarosz proposed EIP, as shown in 0. With step 1 to 2c unchanged, when an error is detected, EIP repeatedly resamples new grammars from the current one until the OF of the output matches the real datum d.

(15) EIP for GLA (Jarosz 2013)
 …
 2d. If overt(Output) ≠ d:
    i. Parse ~ P(parse | G_i, d)
    ii. G_{i+1} = Update(G_i, Parse, Output)

8. Simulations: parsing with RRIP and EIP

Based on Jarosz's proposition, this section conducts simulations using the novel parsing strategies RRIP and EIP. Because these algorithms require stochastic knowledge, the learning algorithm here is restricted to GLA. Training data and other parameter settings are the same as in Section 6. Basic statistics of the accuracy rate are given in 0, which includes the above-mentioned results of GLA/RIP for comparison.

(16) Descriptive statistics of GLA/RIP, GLA/RRIP and GLA/EIP

Algorithm	N	Mean	SD	Median	Min	Max
GLA/RIP	20	0.92	0.01	0.92	0.92	0.94
GLA/RRIP	20	0.94	0.02	0.94	0.94	1
GLA/EIP	20	1	0	1	1	1

A statistical difference is found between these three algorithms (Kruskal-Wallis H test, H = 48.627, p < .001), and the result for Bonferroni-corrected pairwise comparisons is significant (Mann-Whitney U test, p < .001 for all three pairs).

8.1 GLA/RRIP

Three patterns are observed in GLA/RRIP learners. Two learners belong to P_{LA}, converging to the target grammar successfully. The second pattern ($P_{MF/NF(F')\uparrow}$; 17 learners) has the reversed partial ranking MORFT $\gg$ NONFIN(L) and NONFIN(FT') $\gg$ FTBIN, which wrongly parses |H#L| and |LL#L| into /(**H**)#(**L**)/ and /(LL)#(**L**)/ with WDACC and RIGHTMOST fluctuating relentlessly as presented in Figure 4. The last learner has the third pattern $P_{FB\uparrow}$ where FTBIN outranks NONFIN(σ), NOLAPSE and MT, parsing |LH| (/ri'bon/ 'ribbon') and |HLH| (/rande'bu:/ 'rendezvous') into /(**LH**)/ and /(**H**'L)H/ with a trimoraic foot.

To summarize, although two learners fortunately acquired the target grammar relying on their random resampling strategy, the fact that 90% of the learners failed to reach the goal still calls the validity of RRIP into question.

8.2 GLA/EIP

As shown in 0, all GLA/EIP learners successfully converged with their outputs all matching the real data in the OF level. Twelve learners are classified into P_{LA}, and the remaining eight learners belong to the pattern $P_{NF(F')\uparrow}$ with NONFIN(FT') outranking FTBIN. The ranking dynamics of $P_{NF(F')\uparrow}$ are shown in Figure 5, with the ε

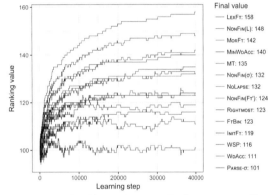

Figure 5 GLA/EIP, $P_{NF(F')}\uparrow$ (ε decrement = 0)

decrement set to 0. The only difference between $P_{NF(F')\uparrow}$ and P_{LA} is the output of |LL| (/me'mo/ 'note'). In P_{LA}, |LL| is parsed into /(**L**'L)/ with a bimoraic foot structure due to the effect of FTBIN, while in $P_{NF(F')\uparrow}$ /(**L**')L/ is output as optimal, leaving the word-final mora unparsed to avoid violating NONFIN(FT'), as shown in 0. However, because these two outputs have the same OF [L'L], learners of these two patterns can communicate without any hindrance. Hence the result of $P_{NF(F')\uparrow}$ is also counted as converged. Moreover, the final value of NONFIN(FT') and FTBIN in $P_{NF(F')\uparrow}$ are almost identical, so it is highly probable for $P_{NF(F')\uparrow}$ to shift to P_{LA} as learning proceeds.

(17) $P_{NF(F')\uparrow}$: monomoraic-foot /(**L**')L/ as optimal

|LL| (/me'mo/ 'note')	LEXFT	NONFIN(L)	MORFT	MINWDACC	MT	NOLAPSE	NONFIN(σ)	NONFIN(FT')	RIGHTMOST	FTBIN	INITFT	WSP	WDACC	PARSE-σ
☞ a. /(**L**')L/										*				*
b. /(**L**'L)/								*!						

Final value (Figure 5 legend):
LEXFT: 158
NONFIN(L): 148
MORFT: 142
MINWDACC: 140
MT: 135
NONFIN(σ): 132
NOLAPSE: 132
NONFIN(FT'): 124
RIGHTMOST: 123
FTBIN: 123
INITFT: 119
WSP: 116
WDACC: 111
PARSE-σ: 101

9. Conclusions

This study carried out several computational simulations to examine the learnability of dominant accentual patterns of Sino-Japanese words and loanwords. With a full structural description incorporated in the input level of perception, both EDCD and GLA learners converged efficiently. However, under more realistic conditions, the ambiguity of hidden structures cannot be effectively tackled by RIP. RRIP and EIP proposed by Jarosz (2013) were introduced to overcome the problem of RIP. Finally, GLA/EIP learners all successfully converged, showing that EIP can take full advantage of probabilistic information even in the face of an intricate target grammar. Future work will mainly cover the examination of different parameter settings and update rules, and the simultaneous learning-parsing algorithm for both the lexicon and the grammar.

Notes

* This paper is a revised version of a presentation at the Phonology Spring Meeting 2017, Keio University, on 23 June 2017. I really appreciate the participants who gave feedback to me, as well as two anonymous reviewers who commented on this paper.

[1] Definitions of constraints used in this paper are given below. LEXFT and NONFIN(L) were introduced in Li (2017), while other constraints were defined or referenced in Ito and Mester (2016).
LEXFT: Every lexeme minimally projects its own foot; MORFT: Every lexical morpheme minimally projects its own foot; MT: Feet are (H), (LL), and (L); NONFIN(σ): Word-final syllables are not footheads; NONFIN(L): Word-final light syllables are not footheads; NOLAPSE: Syllables are maximally parsed into feet; MINWDACC: A minimal prosodic word contains a prominence peak; RIGHTMOST: Violated by any foot following the head foot within the prosodic word; WSP: Heavy syllables are footheads; FTBIN: Feet are minimally binary at some level of analysis (mora, syllable); IINTFT: A prosodic word begins with a foot; NONFIN(FT'): Violated by any head foot that is final in its PrWd; WDACC: A prosodic word contains a prominence peak; PARSE-σ: All syllables are parsed into feet.

[2] Tesar and Smolensky (2000) prepared 124 target grammars for their EDCD/RIP simulation, and only 75 of them were learned successfully (convergence rate = 60%). Using the same data set as Tesar and Smolensky (2000), Boersma (2003) reported that GLA/RIP converged on 70% of the target grammars.

References

Apoussidou, Diana. 2007. *The learnability of metrical phonology*. Ph.D. dissertation, University of Amsterdam.

Boersma, Paul. 1997. How we learn variation, optionality, and probability. *Proceedings of the Institute of Phonetic Sciences of the University of Amsterdam* 21.43–58.

Boersma, Paul. 1999. Optimality-Theoretic learning in the Praat program. *IFA proceedings* 23.17–35.

Boersma, Paul. 2003. Bruce Tesar and Paul Smolensky (2000). Learnability in Optimality Theory. Cambridge, Mass.: MIT Press. Pp. vii+ 140. *Phonology* 20.3.436–446.

Boersma, Paul and Bruce Hayes. 2001. Empirical Tests of the Gradual Learning Algorithm. *Linguistic inquiry* 32.1.45–86.

Boersma, Paul. and David Weenink. 2016. Praat: doing phonetics by computer [Computer program] Version 6.0.19. Online: http://www.praat.org/.

Ito, Junko and Armin Mester. 2016. Unaccentedness in Japanese. *Linguistic Inquiry* 47.3:471–526.

Jarosz, Gaja. 2013. Learning with hidden structure in Optimality Theory and Harmonic Grammar: Beyond Robust Interpretive Parsing. *Phonology* 30.1.27–71.

Li, Motong. 2017. The distribution of dominant accentual patterns in Sino-Japanese words: A comparison with loanwords. *Phonological Studies* 20.11–20.

McCarthy, John J. 2008. *Doing Optimality Theory: Applying theory to data*. Malden, MA: Wiley-Blackwell.

Prince, Alan and Paul Smolensky. 1993/2004. *Optimality Theory: Constraint interaction in generative grammar*. Malden, MA & Oxford, UK: Blackwell.

Tesar, Bruce and Paul Smolensky. 2000. *Learnability in Optimality Theory*. Cambridge, MA: The MIT Press.

|H| and |L| Have Unequal Status[*]

Kuniya Nasukawa   Phillip Backley
Tohoku Gakuin University   Tohoku Gakuin University

ABSTRACT. In Element Theory, the elements |H| and |L| are often regarded as forming a natural pair since they both refer to laryngeal properties and both have a similar distribution. This paper, however, challenges this view by arguing that |H| and |L| do not have equal status within the element set, and do not in fact show the same distributional patterns. The asymmetry between the two elements is discussed in terms of their intrinsic phonological properties and their roles in the hierarchically organized melodic structure employed in Precedence-free Phonology (Nasukawa 2014, 2016; Nasukawa and Backley 2017). The discussion also defends the claim that the asymmetric distribution of |H| and |L| is a natural result of creating an optimal structure for expressing melodic contrasts based on the size of carrier signal modulations between the C and V domains.

Keywords: Laryngeal elements, asymmetric relations, Precedence-free Phonology, modulated carrier signal

1. Introduction

Element Theory (Kaye, Lowenstamm and Vergnaud 1985; Harris 1990, 1994, 2005, 2009; Harris and Lindsey 1995, 2000; Nasukawa 2005a; Nasukawa and Backley 2005; Backley and Nasukawa 2009a; Backley 2011) is an approach to segmental representation which uses monovalent primes called 'elements' as the basic units of segmental structure. Most versions of Element Theory use the six elements |A I U ? H L|, which are present in all languages. Elements are to be understood as mental objects which encode lexical contrasts. They are also active in dynamic phonological processes such as assimilation and lenition.

Besides existing as units of mental representation, elements also relate to the physical world. For the purposes of spoken communication, each element is associated with a unique acoustic signature (Harris and Lindsey 1995; Nasukawa and Backley 2008), which listeners can perceive in the speech signal. In this respect elements differ from traditional features, which are speaker-oriented—they refer to properties of speech production and/or articulation. Element Theory assumes there is a direct mapping between the mental unit 'element' and its acoustic realization. The acoustic patterns associated with the six elements are as follows.

(1) a. Vowel elements

|A|	'mAss'	central spectral energy mass (F1-F2 convergence)
|I|	'dIp'	low F1 with high spectral peak (F2-F3 convergence)
|U|	'rUmp'	low spectral peak (lowering of all formants)

    b. Consonant elements

|?|	'edge'	abrupt and sustained drop in overall amplitude
|H|	'noise'	high-frequency aperiodic energy
|L|	'murmur'	broad resonance peak at lower end of the frequency range

In principle, any element may occur either in vowels or consonants. However, the intrinsic properties of an element affect the type of segment in which it typically appears: |A I U| naturally belong in vowels whereas |? H L| show an affinity with consonants. Based on this distributional tendency, the element set divides into the two sub-groups in (1): the vowel elements |A I U| represent core (resonance) properties while the consonant elements |? H L| represent peripheral (edge) properties.

Here we focus on the consonant elements, and particularly, on |H| and |L|. (Note that the |?| element is not relevant to the present discussion, as it is solely concerned with the representation of occlusion in oral/nasal/glottal stops.) These two elements are often seen as a natural pair because, although they have opposite values, they tend to refer to similar properties and have a similar distribution. Moreover, it is usually assumed that |H| and |L| represent not just opposite values but equal and opposite values, so that if either one is present in an expression then the other is usually absent. In this paper, however, we challenge this assumption by arguing that |H| and |L| do not have equal status, and consequently, do not have the same distribution. We highlight an asymmetry between |H| and |L| in terms of their intrinsic phonological properties and their roles in melodic structure.

The discussion is organized as follows. Section 2 shows how element-based approaches exploit the head/dependent status of |H| and |L| in segmental representations. It also illustrates how |H| and |L| do not always have equal and opposite values, by introducing evidence that they have an asymmetrical relation, i.e. there are some contexts where only one of them can appear. Then in section 3 we consider why |H| and |L| behave asymmetrically, using a Precedence-free Phonology (or PfP) approach which incorporates aspects of Element Theory and Dependency-government Phonology. PfP is designed to boost restrictiveness by limiting representational redundancy. This move also helps to bring phonology into line with other linguistic components in the grammar (Nasukawa 2014, 2016; Nasukawa and Backley 2017).

2. |H| and |L|
2.1 The head/dependent status of |H| and |L|
In Element Theory (Harris 1994; Nasukawa 2005a; Cyran 2010; Backley 2011; Kula 2012), |H| represents 'noise' or voicelessness in consonants and devoicing in vowels, while |L| represents nasality in consonants and vowels. (2) summarizes the phonetic realization of the laryngeal-source elements.

(2)

	realization in consonants		realization in vowels	
	basic	*salient*	*basic*	*salient*
|H|	noise/voicelessness	aspiration	devoicing	high tone
|L|	nasality	obstruent voicing	nasality	low tone

But as (2) shows, when these elements appear in their salient or 'strong' form they encode other properties too. The phonetically salient form of |H| represents aspiration (positive VOT) in consonants and high tone in vowels, while a salient |L| is realized as obstruent voicing (negative VOT) in consonants and low tone in vowels.

The difference between a basic and a salient realization of an element is captured by headedness. When elements combine, they do so asymmetrically by forming head-dependent relations. Then, when a head-dependent structure is phonetically realized, the relative salience of the head and the dependent elements is reflected in the acoustic character of the entire expression. In standard versions of Element Theory (Kaye, Lowenstamm and Vergnaud 1985; Harris 1994; Harris and Lindsey 1995; Cyran 1997; Kula 2012; and others), an element in its headed form is phonetically more salient or exaggerated than when it occurs as a dependent. For example, dependent |H| encodes voicelessness (positive VOT) in consonants, while headed |H| (head elements are underlined) is realized as aspiration—which may be seen as an extended or exaggerated form of voicelessness (Backley and Nasukawa 2009a:58–59).

An alternative way of expressing the difference between the basic and salient realizations of an element is proposed in the element-based approach called Precedence-free Phonology or PfP (Nasukawa 2012, 2014, 2016; Nasukawa and Backley 2017). In PfP, the elements take on a prosodic role in addition to their melodic role. That is, they not only function melodically as units of segmental structure, but they also function prosodically as organizing units. They do this by projecting on to higher prosodic levels and, in effect, taking the place of traditional units of the prosodic hierarchy such as syllable, foot and word.

In contrast to standard models of Government Phonology and Element Theory, PfP considers the most deeply embedded element in an expression to be strong, and therefore, phonetically salient.

Conversely, the element in the ultimate head position of the domain is deemed the least salient. This reflects an underlying principle of PfP, which is embodied in two complementary assumptions:

1. Dependents do not contribute to structural well-formedness (i.e. they are not required in order to make a structure well-formed), but they do contribute significantly to melodic information. The richness of the melodic information they carry is a function of their phonetic salience—in acoustic terms, they involve relatively large modulations of the carrier signal.
2. Heads are important for building structure because (i) they support dependent structure and (ii) they project to higher structural levels. Unlike dependents, however, heads do not carry much melodic information.

As already noted, for example, head |H| is realized as voicelessness so it is responsible for creating the voiced/voiceless contrast in obstruents. On the other hand, dependent |H| is realized as aspiration (i.e. a more salient form of voicelessness), which is not a contrastive property (in Germanic languages, at least). Dependent |H| is therefore located in the most deeply embedded part of the element structure (Nasukawa and Backley 2015, Nasukawa 2017a). Later we show that head-dependency is relevant to the question of whether |H| and |L| have equal or unequal status within the element set.

2.2 |H| and |L| have unequal distribution patterns

Although this point is not specifically discussed in the Element Theory literature, those who work with elements would probably agree that |H| and |L| make a natural pair. Although they have opposing values, |H| and |L| often modify similar kinds of segments and therefore have a similar distribution. In vowels, for example, |H|(igh) and |L|(ow) tone are the contrasting values in many tonal systems, as indicated in (2). And in consonants we use |H|(igh) and |L|(ow) frequency to identify broad categories such as fricatives (with |H|) and nasals (with |L|), where |H| and |L| describe concentrations of acoustic energy at the top and bottom of the spectrum, respectively. Furthermore, it is usually assumed that |H| and |L| have not just opposite values but equal and opposite values. This implies that each one is equally likely to be active in phonological processes, and that if either one is present in an expression then the other is usually absent.

In this section, however, we argue that |H| and |L| do not always have equal status in the grammar, and do not always have the same distribution. Specifically, we highlight the following asymmetry between |H| and |L|: when a dependent (salient) |L| adds contrastive voicing to an expression, a head |H| representing obstruent noise must also be present in the same structure. In other words, contrastive voicing (with dependent |L|) is restricted to obstruents (with head |H|). In the partial structures in (3ab), salient |L| is shown in bold.

(3) a. voiced stops   b. voiced fricatives   c. nasals
    |... ʔ H **L**| |... H **L**| |... ʔ **L**|

Note that the absence of |H| in (3c) causes |L| to be realized as nasality and not obstruent voicing—recall from (2) that head (basic) |L| represents nasality while dependent (salient) |L| represents contrastive voicing. That is, for |L| to be realized as voicing, |H| must also be present, i.e. |L| must be licensed by |H| (Nasukawa 2005ab; Backley and Nasukawa 2009a).

By contrast, specifying dependent (salient) |H| for aspiration does not require the presence of |L|. This is illustrated in (4ab), where salient |H| is shown in bold (Nasukawa 2005a).

(4) a. aspirated stops   b. aspirated fricatives   c. unaspirated stops
    |... ʔ **H**| |... **H**| |... ʔ **H**|

We even find a parallel in vowel systems which have contrastive tone. Typological variation among tonal systems shows us that tonal contrasts are usually represented by |H| alone (Yoshida 1995; Cabrera-Abreu 2000) or by both |H| and |L| (Pierrehumbert 1980; Pierrehumbert and Beckman 1988; Harrison 2005; Kula 2012; et passim). It is much rarer to find systems that employ |L| alone (Backley and Nasukawa 2013).

3. |H| and |L| in Precedence-free Phonology
3.1 An Overview of Precedence-free Phonology

Precedence-free Phonology (PfP) has its roots in Element Theory and Government Phonology. But to limit representational redundancy and to enhance theoretical restrictiveness, the model avoids referring to precedence relations between units. The units in question could be CV units, X slots, Root nodes, or elements, and the exclusion of precedence information applies to all levels of representation.

The only structural units permitted in PfP representations are the monovalent primes known as elements. At the melodic level, elements combine to create complex segmental structures. They also project to successive levels of prosodic structure, where they form head-dependent relations. In their role as prosodic constituents, elements replace familiar prosodic units such as nucleus, mora, rhyme, syllable and foot.

In PfP, a 'nucleus' is represented by one of the vowel elements in (1a) (Nasukawa 2014, 2016; Nasukawa and Backley 2017). This is a parametric choice which determines the phonetic quality of a language's baseline resonance and the identity of its default vowel. For example, English chooses |A| (basic |A| is realized as [ə]), Fijian chooses |I| (giving [ɨ]) and Japanese chooses |U| (giving [ɯ]). By contrast, full vowels have complex structures in which the baseline element takes one or more dependent elements. (5) shows example structures for a language such as English, which has |A| as its baseline element.

(5) a. [ə]   b. [i]   c. [u]   d. [ɑ]

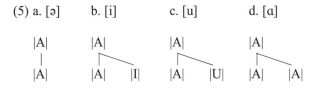

More complex vowel structures are created by introducing further levels of embedding, as illustrated in (6). The mechanism is described more fully in Nasukawa (2017a).

(6) a. [i]   b. [æ]   c. [e]

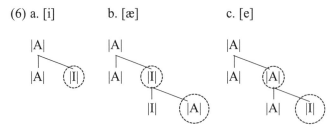

As (5) and (6) illustrate, the phonetic properties of an expression are mostly determined by its dependent elements: listeners perceive the acoustic properties of dependents, which are superimposed on to the background (baseline) resonance. In (6), the elements enclosed in circles are relatively salient; the larger the circle, the bigger an element's contribution to the phonetic outcome of the whole expression. The mapping between head-dependency structure and phonetic exponence is expressed as follows.

(7) The principle of phonetic realization of head-dependency structure
(Nasukawa 2014, 2016, 2017ab; Nasukawa and Backley 2015, 2017)
Dependents, which do not contribute to structural well-formedness, are phonetically more salient in terms of their modulated carrier signal than heads, which are important for building structure.

Thus, the saliency of dependent elements derives from their relatively large modulations of the carrier signal. Following Ohala (1992), Traunmüller (1994, 2005) and Harris (2006, 2009), the energy associated with the carrier signal allows linguistic messages to be heard, while linguistic information itself—with which we identify morphemes/words—is conveyed by carrier signal modulations. Whereas the carrier signal has a schwa-like quality resulting from a structure consisting of non-converging formants, modulations of (i.e. deviations from) this carrier signal are produced by manipulating certain acoustic properties of the signal such as amplitude, spectral shape, periodicity and fundamental frequency (Harris 2009, 2012; Nasukawa 2017ab). In so doing, the properties of dependent elements override the underlying phonetic properties of the baseline (head) element.

Phonetic interpretation therefore depends not only on which elements are present but also on the position of each constituent element in the head-dependency structure. Furthermore, the mechanism just outlined for vowels also applies to consonants. Consonant representations use similar structures which also follow the phonetic realization principle in (7), ensuring that dependents are phonetically more salient than heads (Nasukawa 2016:12–18). However, consonants differ from vowels in that they involve bigger modulations of the carrier signal. And predictably, it is the most obstruent-like consonants which show the biggest modulations of all, which corresponds to their high degree of phonetic salience.

In terms of manipulation of the carrier signal, it is the transition from a vowel to a plosive consonant which produces the most extreme effect, since it involves an abrupt drop in amplitude resulting in a period of silence during the hold phase of the stop. Furthermore, the transition from the hold phase to the stop's release produces an additional burst of aperiodic energy accompanied by place cues in the formant structure. (Note that these place cues are further enhanced if a vowel follows.) Compared with vowel-to-stop transitions, vowel-to-fricative transitions produce less dynamic modulations because both sounds are continuants. And in VC sequences where C is a sonorant, modulation size decreases further because the two sounds are acoustically closer. On this basis, we may generalize that plosives have a maximally modulated carrier signal while vowels involve the smallest modulations.

It may be noted here that the modulated-carrier approach just outlined directly opposes the mainstream view in which phonetic salience is tied to differences in sonority. According to the sonority-based approach, vowels are regarded as being more salient than consonants, with obstruent consonants being the least salient (i.e. the least sonorous) of all.

3.2 The distribution of |H| and |L| in Precedence-free Phonology

Like vowel structures, consonant structures have a parametrically determined choice of baseline element: either |H| or |ʔ|, but not |L|. A bare baseline |H| is realized as [h], as in (8a). But when this baseline |H| takes a second |H| as a dependent, as in (8b), the resulting complex structure is realized as aspiration or positive VOT—an exaggerated form of baseline [h]. On the other hand, the dependent |L| in (8c) is interpreted as obstruent voicing, this being the structure for negative VOT—a more salient form of |L| (Nasukawa 2005a). Besides |H|, the |ʔ| element can also serve as the baseline element in consonants, because like |H| (but unlike |L|) the |ʔ| element is inherently voiceless and therefore produces a significant modulation of the carrier signal. When baseline |ʔ| takes |L| as a dependent, the result is a nasal consonant, as in (8d) (cf. obstruent voicing from |L| as a dependent of baseline |H|).

(8) a. [h]   b. aspiration   c. true voicing   d. nasality

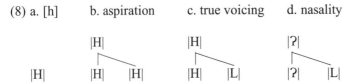

In consonants, then, the asymmetry between |H| and |L| is highlighted by the fact that |H| (but not |L|) is able to function as a baseline (head) element. Moreover, we can infer that |L| typically has no dependents. In other words, |L| prefers to occupy the most deeply embedded position in a complex structure. Having established an asymmetry in the distributional patterns of |H| and |L|, we now consider what the motivation for this might be.

3.3 Why does |L| prefer embedded positions?

To account for the distribution of |L|, we begin by comparing the intrinsic properties of the consonant elements |ʔ H L|. Recall from (1) that |ʔ H N| are naturally associated with consonant properties while |A I U| are primarily associated with vowel properties. Note that this is not an exclusive split, since in principle each element is free to occur in any position.

(9)   Element groupings (Backley and Nasukawa 2009b; Backley 2011)

		c. light	d. dark
a. vocalic	i. aperture		A
	ii. color	I	U
b. non-vocalic	i. source	H	L
	ii. edge	?	

In (9) the elements are further categorized in terms of their acoustic-perceptual properties by dividing them into the two groups 'light' and 'dark' (Backley and Nasukawa 2009b; Backley 2011). |I H ʔ| in (9c) belong to the light group because their acoustic energy is distributed across a wide spectral range; this produces a bright, thin and sometimes sibilant sound. By contrast, |A U L| in (9d) are classified as dark because they have a concentration of acoustic energy at the lower end of the spectrum, giving a warm and mellow sound quality.

Here we focus on the light/dark properties of the non-vocalic elements, where |H| and |ʔ| belong to the light group while |L| is categorized as dark. It is noteworthy that the light elements |H| and |ʔ| are both naturally voiceless, being pronounced individually as the glottal sounds [h] and [ʔ], respectively. Voicelessness is at least partly the reason why |H| and |ʔ| have such a significant effect on the carrier signal, since voicelessness produces such an extreme modulation of the (voiced) baseline resonance. In terms of modulation size, they belong at the opposite end of the scale from vowels. Meanwhile, |L| stands apart from |H| and |ʔ| in being classified as dark; its phonetic realization is characterized by a broad resonance peak near the bottom of the frequency range. This means that the inherent properties of |L| include spontaneous voicing—something it shares with vowels (represented by |A I U|) but not with consonants containing |H| and |ʔ|. In terms of modulation size, |L| shows smaller modulations than either |H| or |ʔ|, since both |L| and the carrier signal have a periodic (resonant) acoustic pattern—recall that the carrier signal is represented by one of the vowel elements in its basic form. By contrast, |H| and |ʔ| are both non-periodic (non-resonant).

In PfP, a syllable-sized (CV) domain has a structure such as the one in (10), in which the C-domain is headed by |H| or |ʔ|. In turn, the C-domain is dominated by a V-domain which comprises vowel elements. The asymmetric dependency relation between a C-head (|H| or |ʔ|) and a V-head (|A|, |I| or |U|) creates the optimal configuration for expressing melodic contrasts because it ensures that the difference in modulation size is maximized between C and V.

(10) The CV unit [gi] in a 'voicing' language (e.g., French)

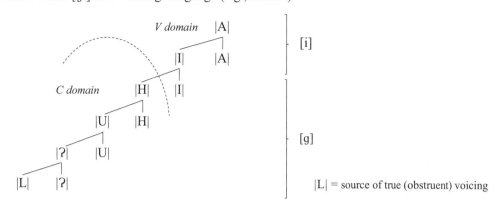

4. Summary

In this paper we have highlighted an asymmetry between the two laryngeal-source elements |H| and |L| in terms of their intrinsic phonological properties and their roles in melodic structure. |H| is inherently voiceless and therefore causes a significant modulation of the carrier signal; furthermore, it can function as a baseline (head) element in the C-domain. By contrast, |L| is inherently voiced and does not cause such a significant modulation of the carrier signal; it prefers to occupy the most deeply embedded position in the hierarchical melodic structure. We have argued that the asymmetry in the distributional patterns of |H| and |L| is a natural result of creating an optimal configuration for expressing melodic contrasts based on the size of carrier signal modulations between the C and V domains.

We hope that further work in this direction will reveal other advantages of adopting a PfP approach to representations.

Notes

* This paper was first presented at the Phonology Forum 2017, Minami-Osaka Campus, Tokyo Metropolitan University, Japan, on 24 August 2017. We thank the participants for their feedback and two anonymous reviewers for their helpful comments on an earlier draft. This work was supported by JSPS KAKENHI Grant Numbers 26284067, 15K02611 (Grant-in-Aid for Scientific Research (B) and (C), Japanese Ministry of Education, Culture, Sports, Science and Technology (MEXT)).

References

Backley, Phillip. 2011. *An introduction to Element Theory*. Edinburgh: Edinburgh University Press.

Backley, Phillip and Kuniya Nasukawa. 2009a. Headship as melodic strength. *Strength relations in phonology*, ed. by Kuniya Nasukawa and Phillip Backley, 47–77. Berlin and New York: Mouton de Gruyter.

Backley, Phillip and Kuniya Nasukawa. 2009b. Representing labials and velars: a single 'dark' element. *Phonological Studies* 12.3–10.

Backley, Phillip and Kuniya Nasukawa. 2013. The role of L in the pitch accent system of Tokyo Japanese. *Phonological Studies* 16.37–44.

Cabrera-Abreu, Mercedes. 2000. *A phonological model for intonation without low tone*. Bloomington: University of Indiana Linguistics Club Publications.

Cyran, Eugeniusz. 1997. *Resonance elements in phonology: A study in Munster Irish*. Lublin: Folium.

Cyran, Eugeniusz. 2010. *Complexity scales and licensing in phonology*. Berlin/New York: Mouton de Gruyter.

Harris, John. 1990. Segmental complexity and phonological government. *Phonology* 7(2).255–300.

Harris, John. 1994. *English sound structure*. Oxford: Blackwell.

Harris, John. 2005. Vowel reduction as information loss. *Headhood, elements, specification and contrastivity*, ed. by Philip Carr, Jacques Durand and Colin J. Ewen, 119–132. Amsterdam: John Benjamins.

Harris, John. 2006. The phonology of being understood: Further arguments against sonority. *Lingua* 116 (10).1483–1494.

Harris, John. 2009. Why final devoicing is weakening. *Strength relations in phonology*, ed. by Kuniya Nasukawa and Phillip Backley, 9–46. Berlin and New York: Mouton de Gruyter.

Harris, John. 2012. Lenition. Intensive lecture series given at the Graduate School of Tohoku Gakuin University.

Harris, John and Geoff Lindsey. 1995. The elements of phonological representation. *Frontiers of phonology: Atoms, structures, derivations*, ed. by Jacques Durand and Francis Katamba, 34–79. Harlow, Essex: Longman.

Harris, John and Geoff Lindsey. 2000. Vowel patterns in mind and sound. *Phonological knowledge: Conceptual and empirical issues*, ed. by Noel Burton-Roberts, Philip Carr and Gerry Docherty, 185–205. Oxford: Oxford University Press.

Harrison, Phil. 2005. Tones and dependency in Yorùbá. *Headhood, elements, specification and contrastivity*, ed. by Philip Carr, Jacques Durand and Colin J. Ewen, 133–166. Amsterdam: John Benjamins.

Kaye, Jonathan D., Jean Lowenstamm and Jean-Roger Vergnaud. 1985. The internal structure of phonological elements: A theory of charm and government. *Phonology Yearbook* 2.305–328.

Kula, Nancy C. 2012. On the representation of tone in Element Theory. *Sound structure and sense: Studies in memory of Edmund Gussmann*, ed. by Eugeniusz Cyran, Henryk Kardela and Bogdan Szymanek, 353–370. Lublin: Wydawnictwo KUL.

Nasukawa, Kuniya. 2005a. *A unified approach to nasality and voicing*. Berlin and New York: Mouton de Gruyter.

Nasukawa, Kuniya. 2005b. The representation of laryngeal-source contrasts in Japanese. *Voicing in Japanese*, ed. by Jeroen van de Weijer, Tetsuo Nishihara and Kensuke Nanjo, 79–99. Berlin and New York: Mouton de Gruyter.

Nasukawa, Kuniya. 2012. Recursion in intra-morphemic phonology. Paper presented at the workshop *Language and the brain: The 9th international conference on the evolution of language*, Kyoto, Japan (13 March 2012).

Nasukawa, Kuniya. 2014. Features and recursive structure. *Nordlyd* 41.1. *Special issue on features*, ed. by Martin Krämer, Sandra-Iulia Ronai and Peter Svenonius, 1–19.

Naukawa, Kuniya. 2016. A precedence-free approach to (de-)palatalisation in Japanese. *Glossa: A Journal of General Linguistics* 1(1).1–21. DOI: http://dx.doi.org/10.5334/gjgl.26.

Nasukawa, Kuniya. 2017a. The phonetic salience of phonological head-dependent structure in a modulated-carrier model of speech. *Beyond markedness in formal phonology*, ed. by Bridget Samuels, 121–152. Amsterdam: John Benjamins.

Nasukawa, Kuniya. 2017b. The relative salience of consonant nasality and true obstruent voicing. *Sonic signatures*, ed. by Geoff Lindsey and Andrew Nevins, 145–162. Amsterdam: John Benjamins.

Nasukawa, Kuniya and Phillip Backley. 2005. Dependency relations in Element Theory: Markedness and complexity. *Proceedings of the Government Phonology workshop. Special issue of Leiden Papers in Linguistics* 2.4, ed. by Nancy Chongo Kula and Jeroen van de Weijer, 77–93. ULCL, Leiden University.

Nasukawa, Kuniya and Phillip Backley. 2008. Affrication as a performance device. *Phonological Studies* 11.35–46.

Nasukawa, Kuniya and Phillip Backley. 2015. Heads and complements in phonology: A case of role reversal? *Phonological Studies* 18.67–74.

Nasukawa, Kuniya and Phillip Backley. 2017. Representing moraicity in Precedence-free Phonology. *Phonological Studies* 20.55–62.

Ohala, John J. 1992. Alternatives to the sonority hierarchy for explaining segmental sequential constraints. *CLS: Papers from the parasession on the syllable*, 319–338.

Pierrehumbert, Janet B. 1980. *The phonology and phonetics of English intonation*. Ph.D. dissertation, Massachusetts Institute of Technology.

Pierrehumbert, Janet B. and Mary E. Beckman. 1988. *Japanese tone structure* (Linguistic Inquiry Monograph 15). Cambridge: MA: MIT Press.

Traunmüller, Hartmut. 1994. Conventional, biological, and environmental factors in speech communication: A modulation theory. *Phonetica* 51.170–183.

Traunmüller, Hartmut. 2005. Speech considered as modulated voice. Ms., Stockholm University.

Yoshida, Yuko Z. 1995. *On pitch accent phenomena in Standard Japanese*. Ph.D. dissertation, School of Oriental and African Studies, University of London.

Glottalization in English Homorganic Glide-Vowel Sequences by Japanese L2 English Learners[*]

Tomomasa Sasa
Iwate Prefectural University

ABSTRACT. While English allows homorganic glide-vowel sequences (a glide-vowel sequence in which both the glide and the following vowel are specified for the same backness and height features), Japanese does not allow them. This fact raises two questions: first, is it possible for Japanese L2 English learners to produce English G-V[ho] sequences? And second, what kind of repair strategy is employed to avoid such sequences if they cannot produce them? To investigate these questions, phonetic recording sessions with 25 Japanese speakers were conducted to test if Japanese L2 learners can produce G-V[ho] sequences. In the first part of the paper, three repair patterns, deletion, vowel shift (lowering) and glottalization, are introduced along with the acoustic analysis of the data. In the latter part, a phonological account of the data using the OT framework is presented to account for the interlanguage grammar of glottalization and deletion. It is demonstrated that the difference between glottalization and deletion can be expressed by the different rankings for DEP and ONSET.

Keywords: second language acquisition, acquisition of phonology, Optimality Theory, Japanese L2 English

1. Introduction

In Japanese, there are restrictions on the co-occurrence of a glide and a vowel (Tsujimura 1996; Vance 2008): [j] can be followed only by three vowels [a u o] and only [a] can follow the glide [w]. In English, there are no such restrictions and sequences such as [j-i] (as in *yield* or *year*) or [w-u] (as in *wool*) are possible. These facts raise the following two questions. First, can Japanese speakers produce English glide-vowel sequences (G-V sequences) that are unattested in Japanese? Second, if they cannot, then, what kind of 'repair strategies' do they employ to avoid such sequences?

In this article, one of the main purposes is to present the results of the phonetic study conducted to investigate these questions above. A phonetic experiment with 25 native Japanese speakers was conducted, and in the presentation of the results, the main focus is placed on homorganic G-V sequences (henceforth abbreviated as G-V[ho]), a G-V sequence in which the glide and the following vowel are specified for the same height and backness specifications. In the experiment, it was observed that the participants employed three repair strategies, glide deletion, vowel shift (lowering), and glottal stop epenthesis or glottal stop epenthesis. Another purpose of this article is to present an Optimality Theoretic (OT: McCarthy and Prince 1995) analysis of the data, with the main focus on two of the attested repair strategies, glottal stop epenthesis and vowel glottalization to formally account for the interlanguage stages of learners.

The organization of this paper is as follows: Section 2 presents the background of this study and the procedures of the phonetic experiment. Section 3 presents the results of the experiment, and the phonological analysis of the data, with emphasis on deletion and glottal stop epenthesis, is presented in Section 4.

2. Phonetic Study
2.1 Background

While English freely allows any G-V sequences, including homorganic G-V sequences such as [j-i], [j-ɪ], [w-u] or [w-ʊ], Japanese exhibits strict restrictions on the sequence of a glide and a vowel. According to Vance (2008:90), in Tokyo Japanese 'a vowel that immediately following /j/ has to be a back vowel' and he also points out that the glide [w] can occur only before the vowel [a]. These facts lead to the question of whether it is possible for native Japanese speakers to produce English G-V sequences that are unattested in Japanese.

Kang (2014) conducted a study in which native Korean speakers produced G-V sequences that are attested in English but unattested in Korean. In Korean, homorganic G-V sequences are not attested as in Japanese, and Kang reports five repair strategies observed among the Korean speakers to avoid G-V[ho] sequences: deletion (/jild/ 'yield'→ [ild]), glottal stop epenthesis or glottalization (/jild/ 'yield'→ [ʔild]), vowel shift (/jild/ 'yield' → [jeld]), glide shift (/jild/ 'yield' → [wild]) and glide vocalization (/jild/ 'yield'→ [i.ild]). Both Japanese and Korean exhibit strict phonotactic constraints on the sequence of a glide and a vowel. Researchers may ask whether Japanese speakers will employ similar repair strategies to avoid such sequences if they fail to produce homorganic G-V sequences. To examine Japanese L2 learner production of G-V[ho] sequences, a phonetic experiment was conducted to investigate the following questions: i) whether Japanese native L2 English learners can produce English G-V[ho] sequences, and ii) what kind of repair Japanese speakers employ should they fail to produce such sequences. For the experiment, the procedures, including the information about the participants, are presented in Section 2.2. The results of the phonetic study are presented in Section 3.

2.2 Experimental Design

Recording sessions were held from November 2016 to February 2017 with 25 native Japanese speakers (However, data from one participant were omitted because of the problems with recording). Recording sessions were held in an anechoic room in Iwate Prefectural University, and speakers were asked to wear a headset microphone which was connected to a Macintosh computer. Sound files were created by the software Audacity, with the sampling frequency of 44.1 kHz, and Praat was used for measurements.

Participants were first to third year students at Iwate Prefectural University at the time of the recording, and they were grouped into two groups based on their TOEIC (Test Of English for International Communication) score: those with the score of 500 and higher are intermediate (n=20), and those with the score below 500 are grouped as basic (n=4). Participants were asked to produce a target word embedded in a carrier sentence, *Say X (target word) again* or *Say X please*. Participants were asked to read each sentence once, and there are 24 tokens for a single item. Two versions of the word/sentence lists, with different sentence orders and different fillers, were prepared and in each, the order of the sentences was fixed. Participants were given the word/sentence list randomly.

There were 60 words on the word list: four words contained a G-V[ho] sequence with [w] (such as *wool, wood*) and five words contained a G-V[ho] sequence with [j] (*year, yield*). Twelve words contained a sequence of [w] followed by the vowel [i e o], unattested sequences in Japanese. Three words contained a sequence of [j] followed by a high back vowel and seven words contained a [j] followed by a mid vowel. There were also words containing a glide followed by a low vowel (attested in Japanese), and there were six words that contained a complex onset with a glide (such as *cute* or *quick*). There were also 13 words that begin with a vowel and six words that functioned as a filler or distracter.

3. Results
3.1 Overview of the Results: G-V[ho] with [j]

The table in (1) presents the number of occurrences of three repair patters along with the accurate pronunciation of the words, *year* and *yield*. For *yield* the number of occurrences outnumbers the number of the participants (n=20 for intermediate, and n=4 for basic): for the pronunciation of *yield,* some speakers employed two repair strategies. For example, two speakers, F13 and M8, both intermediate, employed both glottalization and vowel shift and produced this word as [ʔeld]. Such cases are counted both in glottalization and in vowel shift.

(1) Results (sequences with [j]: numbers indicate the number of occurrences)

	year		*yield*		Total
	Inter	Basic	Inter	Basic	
a) correct ([jiər], [jild])	5	0	4	1	10
b) deletion ([iər], [ild])	5	2	2	2	11
c) clottalization ([ʔiər], [ʔild])	10	2	14	1	27
d) vowel shift ([jeər], [jeld])	0	0	3	1	4

As seen in (1), there were ten tokens of accurate production of the G-V[ho] sequences with [j]. There were also speakers who produced the G-V[ho] sequences with [w] accurately. Therefore, it can be concluded that it is not impossible for native Japanese speakers to produce English G-V[ho] sequences both with [j] and with [w].[1]

The results in (1) also shows that the majority of the participants failed to produce G-V[ho] sequences with [j]. One of the errors, or repair strategies, employed by some of the speakers is vowel shift (Kang 2014). According to Kang (2014), this is one of the repair strategies employed by Korean L2 English learners and in vowel shift the high vowel /i/ is lowered to a mid vowel [e] to avoid the /j-i/ sequence.

A similar phenomenon was observed in this study: for example, in one participant's (Male Speaker 5, intermediate) production of *yield,* the first formant of the vowel was 482.7 Hz while that of the word *inn* was 241 Hz. It is true that more data need to be collected to draw a conclusion safely, but the results obtained from this study suggest that one of the attested repair strategies employed by Japanese speakers is to lower a high vowel to a mid vowel, so that they can avoid G-V[ho] sequences.

3.2 Deletion and Glottalization

There are two more repair strategies employed by Japanese L2 speakers observed in this study: they are deletion and glottal stop epenthesis.

(2) Glottalization   (M10's *yield*)   (3) Glide Deletion (M14's *year*)

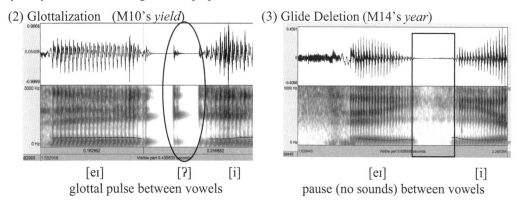

    [eɪ]   [ʔ]   [i]   [eɪ]   [i]
glottal pulse between vowels   pause (no sounds) between vowels

Figire (2) presents glottalization (data from Male Speaker 10: M10, intermediate), and (3) presents glide deletion by Male Speaker 14 (M14, basic). In (3), there are no sounds observed between the vowels [eɪ] and [i] in the sequence, *say year (please)* and thus it is possible to say that this speaker deletes the homorganic glide [j] before the vowel [i]. (2) presents the sequence of *say yield please* by M10: in (2), two glottal pulses are observed between two vowels.

Figure (4), a more detailed figure of (3), reveals that these glottal pulses are followed by irregular pitch periods.

(4) Glottalization (a closer look at (3))

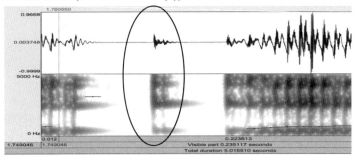

According to Dilley et al. (1996:429), this is a typical pattern observed in the glottalization of the following vowel and we can conclude that this speaker epenthesizes a glottal stop between two vowels in place of a homorganic glide [j].

To summarize the results. First, it is possible for Japanese L2 English speakers to produce G-V[ho] sequences: as in (1), there were 10 tokens of accurate production of the /j-i/ sequences. Second, in the majority of the cases, however, G-V[ho] sequences are avoided, and attested repair strategies include deletion and glottalization.

4. Phonological Analysis

In Section 4, two cases of the attested repair strategies, deletion and glottalization, are phonologically analyzed. In the analysis the OT framework is assumed to demonstrate that both deletion and glottalization are motivated by a single motivation or conspiracy.

4.1 Phonology in Second Language Acquisition (SLA)

According to Eckman (2015), a phonologist's role in SLA is to formally describe learners' interlanguage grammar. Interlanguage is considered to be independent both of the target language and of the learners' first language, and according to Eckman, interlanguage grammar gradually becomes close to the grammar of the target language.

In order to lay out the phonological analysis of the data, Optimality Theory is used. According to Hancin-Bhatt and Bhatt (1997), in OT error rates and patterns in second language learning can be better captured and analyzed. In addition, in OT the motivation for a change, or in SLA the motivation for repair, can be clearly expressed by a high-ranked constraint in the analysis. Hence, in presenting a phonological analysis, the OT approach is used, so that i) error patterns can be captured, ii) the motivation for the repair can be expressed by the undominated constraint, and iii) the individual differences can be clearly explained by different constraint rankings.

4.2 OT Analysis

This section presents an OT analysis of the data. Section 4.2.1 presents the analysis of English. Section 4.2.2 presents a phonological analysis of deletion, and in Section 4.2.3, an analysis of glottalization is presented.

4.2.1 English

In English, G-V[ho] sequences surface faithfully. In other words, no deletion or insertion is observed in English. In OT terms, this can be expressed by the following faithfulness constraints ranked higher than those that motivate the change.

(5) **MAX** (McCarthy and Prince 1995)
Every segment of the input has a correspondent in the output (No Deletion).

(6) **DEP** (McCarthy and Prince 1995)
Every segment of the output has a correspondent in the input (No Epethesis).

One of the advantages of assuming the OT framework is that the motivation for a change, or repair, can be expressed by an undominated constraint. In English, the markedness constraint in (7) is low-ranked, but in the case of deletion or glottal stop epenthesis, the markedness constraint in (7) is undominated to enforce deletion or deletion along with epenthesis.

(7) **DISTINCT GLIDE (DIST-G)** (Rubach 2002:680; Kang 2014:164)
The onset glide cannot be a copy of the nucleus (No [j-i] / No [w-u]).

Finally, one of the differences between glottalization and deletion is the resulting syllable structure: the result of deletion without epenthesis is an onset-less syllable while epenthesis saves or keeps the CV syllable structure. Thus, when deletion occurs, whether glottal stop epenthesis is observed or not depends on the ranking of the constraint in (8).

(8) **ONSET** (Prince and Smolensky 1993)
Syllables must have onsets.

The English analysis with the constraints in (5) through (8) is presented in (9).

(9) MAX, DEP >> DIST-G Selects [ijld] with G-V[ho]: /jild/→[jild] 'yield'

$/j_1i_2l_3d_4/$	MAX	DEP	DIST-G	ONSET
☞a) $j_1i_2l_3d_4$			*	
b) $i_2l_3d_4$	*!			*
c) ʔ $i_2l_3d_4$	*(!)	*(!)		

In (9), subscript numbers indicate Input-Output correspondence. In (9a), every segment in the output form contains a subscript. This means that every output segment has a correspondent segment in the input (i.e. no DEP violation) and every input segment has a correspondent segment in the output (i.e. no MAX violation).

In (9b), since the input segment /j/ lacks its output correspondent (no output segment with the subscription number 1), this causes a MAX violation. (9c) is assumed to violate both MAX and DEP: the input /j/ lacks its output correspondent and the initial glottal stop in the output is not in a correspondent relationship with any input segment. In other words, the glottal stop in (9c) is assumed to be epethesized in place of the deleted glide.[2]

Tableau (9) shows that the ranking MAX, DEP >> DIST-G selects the actual form with G-V[ho], but no ranking argument for ONSET is provided by the analysis in (9). The ranking argument for ONSET is provided in (10), where there are no G-V[ho] sequences in the input.

(10) DEP >> ONSET Prohibits Unnecessary Epenthesis: /iər/ → [iər] 'ear'

$/i_1ə_2r_3/$	MAX	DEP	DIST-G	ONSET
☞a) $i_1ə_2r_3$				*
b) ʔ $i_1ə_2r_3$		*!		

In (10), both MAX and DIST-G are silent since neither one of the candidates contains a sequence of G-V[ho] and deletion is not observed in either one of the candidates. In (10), DEP serves as a tie-breaker and the ranking DEP >> ONSET blocks unnecessary epenthesis.

The two established rankings in (9) and (10), MAX >> DIST-G and DEP >> ONSET, account for the English case: MAX >> DIST-G guarantees that the input G-V[ho] sequence surfaces faithfully and DEP >> ONSET blocks unnecessary glottal stop epethesis.

4.2.2 Glide Deletion

The case of glide deletion is similar to the English case: glottal stop epenthesis is blocked and this can be achieved by the ranking DEP >> ONSET, as in English. The crucial difference between deletion and English grammar is that G-V[ho] sequence is avoided by deleting the preceding homorganic glide. The analysis of deletion is given in (11).

(11) Glide Deletion: DIST-G >> MAX, DEP >> ONSET Prefer Deletion: /jild/→ [ild]

/$j_1i_2$ld/	DIST-G	MAX	DEP	ONSET
☞ a) $i_2$ld		*		*
b) $j_1i_2$ld	*!			
c) $ʔi_2$ld		*	*!	

In (11), both (11a) and (11c) tie under MAX, and DEP prefers (11a), the deletion candidate, to (11c), in which glottal stop epenthesis is observed.

(11) shows the ranking DIST-G >> MAX, DEP >> ONSET accounts for deletion: the high-ranked DIST-G expresses the motivation for the repair, that is, this speaker fails to produce the [j-i] sequence because of the high-ranked DIST-G constraint. Then, the strategy for repair is determined by the ranking between DEP and ONSET. Since DEP outranks ONSET, this speaker choses to delete the glide but not to epenthesize a glottal stop in place of the glide.

In the next section, another case of repair, namely glottal stop epenthesis, is examined. In glottalization, the motivation for change is still to avoid a G-V[ho] sequence, but the different method of repair is expressed by the reversed ranking of DEP and ONSET.

4.2.3 Glottal Stop Epenthesis

The analysis of the third case, glottal stop epenthesis, is presented in (12).

(12) Epenthesis: DIST-G >> MAX, ONSET >> DEP Prefer Epenthesis: /jild/ → [ʔild]

/$j_1i_2$ld/	DIST-G	MAX	ONSET	DEP
☞a) $ʔi_2$ld		*		*
b) $j_1i_2$ld	*!			
c) $i_2$ld		*	*!	

In (12), (12a) and (12c) tie under MAX and the syllable well-formedness constraint ONSET prefers (12a) to (12c). Example (12) shows that the ranking DIST-G >> MAX, ONSET >> DEP selects the candidate in which a glottal stop is epenthesized.

Given the analysis presented in (11), one might ask why a glottal stop is preferred as an epenthesized segment. Following Kang (2014), I propose that the idea of harmonic alignment (Prince and Smolensky 1993:141) provides the solution. As stated in Hancin-Bhatt and Bhatt (1997) and Kang (2014), the idea behind harmonic alignment is that as a segment for syllable margin, including onset, the less sonorous a segment is the more harmonic a margin it is.

(13) Harmonic Alignment (Prince and Smolensky 1993)
    *M/V >> *M/r >> *M/l >> *M/nasal >> *M/obstruent >> *M/laryngeal

(13) states that vowels and glides are the least preferred segment as a syllable margin and laryngeal consonants are most preferred as a syllable margin consonant. I suggest that the ranking *M/l >> *M/obstruent >> *M/laryngeal excludes competing candidates, such as *[li₂ld] or *[ti₂ld], from /$j_1i_2$il/ and selects the candidate with the most harmonic syllable margin consonant, namely a glottal stop.

5. Summary and Discussion

Below, (14) presents the rankings obtained in Section 4.

(14) Ranking Summary
    14a) English: MAX, DEP >> DIST-G >> ONSET
    14b) Deletion: DIST-G >> MAX, DEP >> ONSET
    14c) Glottal Stop Epenthesis: DIST-G >> MAX, ONSET >> DEP

First, the difference between English and deletion is accounted for by the ranking of DIST-G: in English, DIST-G is low-ranked, which makes it possible for English speakers to produce G-V[ho] sequences. For deletion, the high-ranked DIST-G makes it impossible for such speakers to produce G-V[ho] sequences and the ranking DEP >> ONSET selects deletion for those speakers as a repair strategy. The high-ranked DIST-G also makes it impossible for epenthesis speakers to produce G-V[ho] sequences, but unlike in deletion the ranking ONSET >> DEP selects glottal stop epenthesis as a repair strategy for epenthesis speakers. To conclude, different interlanguage stages can be expressed by the different rankings of DEP and ONSET.

As stated, Eckman (2015) assumes that interlanguage grammar will gradually become closer to the grammar of a target language. Given this assumption, one might ask what motivates the ranking ONSET >> DEP in the grammar of glottal stop epenthesis speakers. As seen in (14), English requires the ranking DEP >> ONSET but (12) shows that ONSET must outrank DEP to guarantee epenthesis. As a result, a learner who epenthesizes a glottal stop is assumed to have acquired a grammar with a reversed constraint ranking.

To explore this question, it is necessary to consider the 'path' of phonological acquisition. Broselow (2004) reports that there are cases in which L2 learners first produce less marked structures before they start to produce more marked structures, but such production is not motivated by any L2 input. Broselow presents a case from Mandarin speakers learning English as a second/foreign language and reports that some Mandarin L2 English speakers produce a voiceless coda obstruent in place of a voiced one: that is, /bɛd/ is pronounced as *[bɛt] by such speakers before they accurately produce [bɛd]. In OT, coda devoicing can be explained by a TETU ranking IDENT (ONSET) [VOICE] >> *VOICE [OBSTRUENT] >> IDENT [VOICE], but Borselow argues that no input from English motivates this TETU ranking since English does not prohibit voiced obstruent codas. Still, as pointed out by Broselow, the fact is that there are cases in which some (but not all) of L2 learners first produce unmarked structures, which are not motivated by any L2 input, before they start to produce marked structures accurately.

It can be interpreted that learners with glottal stop epenthesis are exhibiting a similar phenomenon (even though (14c) is not a TETU ranking). No input from English will provide learners with the evidence for the ranking that enforces glottalization since English does not disallow onset-less syllables. However, as a result of glottalization, speakers achieve a less marked syllable structure, and this observation is consistent with Borselow's observation with Mandarin speakers learning English. Given these, I hypothesize that speakers with glottalization are in some phase of acquisition and that they are assumed to be in an interlanguage state in which they have learned to produce a less marked but unmotivated structure. Then, it is predicted that such speakers will learn to produce attested and more marked structures with a G-V[ho] sequence later in the course of acquisition.

6. Conclusion

In this article, it has been argued that it is not impossible for Japanese L2 English learners to produce English G-V[ho] sequences, but the majority of learners employ some repair strategies to avoid such sequences. As seen in the phonological analysis, the high-ranked DIST-G expresses the motivation for repair and the ranking between DEP and ONSET determines the choice of two of the common repair, deletion or glottalization.

There are still two questions that need to be investigated. The first question is whether it is possible to establish a correlation between the proficiency level of a speaker and the choice of repair. In the results presented in (1), it appears that glottalization is observed more among intermediate learners than among basic learners, and it also appears that basic learners employ deletion rather than glottalization as a repair strategy. The obvious problem with this generalization is, however, that there were so few participants from the basic level. One of the topics for the future research is to investigate whether it is possible to make generalizations between levels and repair. In order to do this, it is necessary to collect more data from speakers of different levels, especially from those in the basic level.[3]

Another question is related to the hypothesis that speakers with glottal stop epenthesis are in an interlanguage stage, in which they produce less marked but unmotivated structures. As Borselow points out, this 'unmarked' stage is just an intermediate stage and learners with an unmarked structure will eventually acquire the attested and more marked structures. To prove the validity of the hypothesis presented in this article it is presumably necessary to prove that speakers with epenthesis will eventually produce the more marked structure with G-V[ho] sequences. This may require a kind of longitudinal study and it is another possible direction to expand the study presented in this article.

Notes

[*]This paper was first presented at the Phonology Forum 2017. I would like to thank the participants of the forum for valuable comments and insightful discussions for this paper. My gratitude also goes to Professor Jill Beckman and Professor Elena Gavruseva of the University of Iowa and my research assistant for their help. Finally, I would like to express my special gratitude for two anonymous reviewers and for the editors of the journal for comments and patience. All mistakes are mine.

[1] To identify a glide in the spectrogram, visible formant structures, a sharp drop in F2, and continuous voicing are taken as indicators. These characteristics are suggested in Ladefoged (2006:196) as typical acoustic characteristics of a glide.

[2] Another possible interpretation of a surface glottal stop is to assume that it is in a correspondence with an input glide. However, candidates with such correspondence will incur faithfulness violations (because such a mapping involves so many changes in features) and will not be a winner.

[3] I would like to thank one of the anonymous reviewers for pointing out this issue.

References

Borselow, Ellen. 2004. Unmarked structures and emergent ranking in second language phonology. *International Journal of Bilingualism*. Volume 8. Number 1.51–65.

Dilley, Laura, Stefanie Shattuck-Hufnagel, Mari Ostendorf. 1996. Glottalization of word-initial vowels as a function of prosodic structure. *Journal of Phonetics* 24.423–444.

Eckman, Fred. 2015. Some aspects of second-language phonology: the characterization of interlanguage grammar. Handout. Paper presented at Phonology Forum 2015, Osaka, Japan.

Hacin-Bhatt, Barbara, Rakesh M Bhatt. 1997. Optimal L2 syllables interactions of transfer and developmental effects. *Studies in Second Language Acquisition* 19.331–378.

Kang, Sang-Kyun. 2014. *The acquisition of English glides by native speakers of Korean*. Ph.D. dissertation, University of Iowa.

Ladefoged, Peter. 2006. *A Course in phonetics*. Boston: Wadsworth Publishing.

McCarthy, John and Alan Prince. 1995. Faithfulness and reduplicative identity. *Papers in Optimality Theory* 249–384.

Prince Alan, and Paul Smolensky. 1993. Optimality Theory: constraint interaction in generative grammar. *Technical Report #2 of the Rutgers Center for Cognitive Science*.

Tsujimura, Natsuko. 1996. *An introduction to Japanese linguistics*. Malden, Oxford, Victoria: Blackwell Publishing.

Rubach, Jerzy. 2002. Against subsegmental glides. *Linguistic Inquiry* 32.672-687.

Vance, Timothy J. 2008. *The Sounds of Japanese*. Cambridge: Cambridge University Press.

後部要素が状態や動作をあらわす4字漢語のアクセントの
自然度評価

Naturalness Evaluation of Accent in Japanese Four-Kanji Compound Words with the Second Element Representing a State or Action

陳　曦

Chen Xi

大阪大学

Osaka University

ABSTRACT. This paper focuses on the accent in Japanese four-*kanji* compound words wherein the second element represents a state or action. Examining the accent pattern that is different from the predominant accent pattern of pronunciation, the naturalness evaluation of the accent was determined to be different between Group1 that was pronounced in Compound Accent Rule (CAR) and Group2 that was pronounced in Separated Compound Accent (SCA). We conducted a listening test to clarify this. Our results are as follows: when a subject listened to compound words with the accent pattern different from the predominant accent pattern of pronunciation, many words were evaluated as unnatural; however, when subjects listened to compound words that were pronounced in SCA predominantly with CAR, more words were felt to be natural than in the opposite case.

Keywords: accent, compound words, kanji (Sino-Japanese), Compound Accent Rule (CAR), Separated Compound Accent (SCA)

1. はじめに

　日本語の複合語には、[ジ「コボ ̄」ーエー][1]（自己防衛）のようにアクセントが中高型の1単位に融合する（以下「融合アクセント」）ものと、[「オ ̄」ーザボ「ーエー]（王座防衛）のように融合しない（以下「非融合アクセント」）ものがある。

　陳曦(2017)の発音調査では、後部要素が状態や動作[2]をあらわす4字漢語[3]のアクセントの融合・非融合を左右する要因として、（ア）要素間の統語的関係と（イ）要素の意味とがあることが明らかになった。そして、語によって大きく①融合傾向の強い語、②非融合傾向の強い語、③話者間のゆれと話者内のゆれが激しい語、といった3種類の4字漢語が観察された。

　しかし、窪薗晴夫(1995)の言うように、非融合アクセントで発音される複合語が少なからず観察される一方、融合アクセント（窪薗1995の「複合語アクセント規則」）はほとんどの複合語に生じている。つまり、複合語全体から見ると非融合アクセントは少数であると言えよう。こうした融合アクセントと非融合アクセントの複合語全体に占める割合の差を考えると、融合アクセントで発音される傾向が強い複合語について、それを非融合アクセントで発音した場合（以下「非融合化類」）の聴覚的自然度と、非融合アクセントで発音される傾向が強い複合語について、それを融合アクセントで発音した場

合(以下「融合化類」)の聴覚的自然度は異なる可能性がある。しかし、その実態は知られていないように思われる。

　また、非融合アクセントで発音しやすい構造を持つ語でも、慣用化、つまり使用頻度が上がるにつれ、融合アクセントで発音するようになることが多いとされている(窪薗1995、NHK放送文化研究所2016など)が、データは示されていない。したがって、実証的データで複合語に対する親密度とアクセントの融合・非融合との関係の有無を検証する必要があると思われる。

　そこで、非融合化類と融合化類とではアクセントの自然度評価への影響が異なるのか、もし異なるならば自然度に影響する要因はどこにあるのかを明らかにするために聴取調査を行った。さらに、複合語に対する親密度と、アクセントの融合・非融合の間に関係があるのかを明らかにするために親密度調査を実施した。

　本稿ではあらたに行った自然度評価の調査結果にもとづき、後部要素が状態や動作をあらわす4字漢語で非融合アクセントで発音されるものが、非融合アクセントから融合アクセントへと緩慢ながら移行しつつあり、また、その移行過程に前後要素のアクセント型の組み合せ及び、4字漢語に対する親密度が関与していることを示す。

2. 自然度評価のための聴取調査

　以下のような聴取調査を行った。テスト語は「後部要素が状態や動作をあらわす」4字漢語で、陳曦(2017)の発音調査でほぼ融合アクセントで発音された59語と、ほぼ非融合アクセントで発音された [4] 58語の、計117語である。

　テスト語を「××××がテーマです。」(「きょうの話は××××がテーマです。」のつもりで)に入れてテスト文を作成し、首都圏[5]で生まれ育った30歳台の東京方言話者1名に依頼して、その中のテスト語それぞれを融合アクセントと非融合アクセントの両方で発音してもらった。例えば、発音調査では融合アクセント([テ「ンポテ」ンカイ])で発音された「店舗展開」を[テ「ンポテ」ンカイ](融合)と[「テ」ンポテ「ンカイ](非融合)の両方で発音し、また発音調査では非融合アクセント([「オ」ーイケ「ーショー])で発音された「王位継承」を[「オ」ーイケ「ーショー](非融合)と[オ「ーイケ」ーショー](融合)の両方で発音したものを録音した。

　このようにして得た117×2=234の音声をランダムな順で首都圏で生まれ育った20〜36歳の日本語母語話者8名(女性2人、男性6人)に1音声につき繰り返し2回聞かせ(テスト文も文字で提示)、そのアクセントの自然度を5段階(1.非常に不自然　2.どちらかといえば不自然　3.どちらでもない　4.どちらかといえば自然　5.非常に自然)で評価してもらった。

　4字漢語に対する親密度とアクセントの融合・非融合の間に関係があるのかを明らかにするために、8名の評価者に対して聴取調査の終了後、117の調査語に対する親密度(どの程度見聞きするのか)を調査した。具体的には、「実際に見聞きする程度」によって5段階(1.全く見聞きしない　2.どちらかといえばよく見聞きしない　3.どちらでもない　4.どちらかといえばよく見聞きする　5.非常によく見聞きする)で判断してもらった。

3. 結果と考察

　第2章で述べたように、各語について、非融合アクセントと融合アクセントの2種類を聞かせたうえで、それぞれの発音に対し、その自然度が5段階で評価されている。これについて、ここでは評価

の結果が不自然か不自然でないかという観点から、1と2の評価をまとめて「不自然」、それ以外の3、4、5の評価をまとめて「不自然ではない」(おおまかに自然)とする。

そして、各語について、非融合アクセントまたは融合アクセントで聞く際、自然度が高か低かを、「不自然ではない」の回答数が回答者8名のうちの半数より小さい語、つまり0〜3名の語を「自然度低」、回答者8名のうちの半数より大きい語、つまり5〜8名の語を「自然度高」に分ける。自然度が低か高かのどちらかに該当するテスト語は102語である。以下、この102語を対象として分析する。

ここで、この102語は次の3つのタイプに分けられる。それは、①「非融合アクセントとして自然度が高く、融合アクセントとして自然度が低いもの」(つまり、非融合傾向が強い)、②「非融合アクセントとして自然度が高く、融合アクセントとしても自然度が高いもの」(つまり、融合アクセントと非融合アクセントが両方可能)、③「非融合アクセントとして自然度が低く、融合アクセントとして自然度が高いもの」(つまり、融合傾向が強い)である。そのそれぞれの語数を表1に示す。

表1 「不自然ではない」の割合から見たテスト語の融合・非融合の傾向

	語数	語例
非融合傾向が強い語	33 (32%)	名誉挽回
融合・非融合の両方可能な語	18 (18%)	辞表提出
融合傾向が強い語	51 (50%)	宇宙開発

3.1 発音調査結果と自然度に関する聴取調査結果の分析

3.1.1 非融合化と融合化の共通性

今回の自然度評価の聴取調査結果と陳曦(2017)の発音調査の結果との比較を表2に示す。

表2 陳曦(2017)の発音調査の結果と今回の聴取調査の結果の比較

発音調査の結果		聴取調査の結果		発音調査の結果と聴取調査の結果の関係	語例
ほぼ非融合	46語	非融合傾向が強い	33語	一致	名誉挽回
		融合・非融合の両方可能	13語	聴取調査では融合・非融合の両方可能	辞表提出
ほぼ融合	56語	融合傾向が強い	51語	一致	宇宙開発
		融合・非融合の両方可能	5語	聴取調査では融合・非融合の両方可能	意見表明

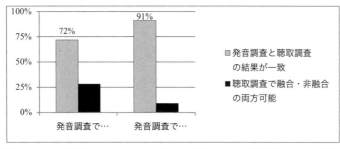

図1 発音調査でほぼ非融合の語と、ほぼ融合の語における聴取調査と発音調査の一致度

発音調査でほぼ非融合だったテスト語と、ほぼ融合だったテスト語について、聴取調査の傾向と一致している語数の割合を図1に示す。図1からは、発音調査でほぼ融合アクセントで発音されたもののうち91%が、ほぼ非融合アクセントで発音されたものでは72%が、聴取調査の結果と一致しており、いずれも高い割合であることが分かる。言い換えれば、融合か非融合かについて、発音調査で優勢なアクセントパターンとは違うアクセントパターンは不自然だと感じられる傾向が強いということである。これは、非融合化類と融合化類のどちらにおいても同様である。

このことから、今回調査した語の多くはおおよそ決まった融合か非融合のアクセントパターンを持っていることが分かる。つまり、後部要素が動作や状態をあらわす4字漢語の多くは、融合・非融合のどちらのアクセントも容認できるわけではないことが分かる。

3.1.2 融合化の非融合化に対する優位性

図1から言えるのは、発音調査でほぼ非融合アクセントで発音された語も、発音調査でほぼ融合アクセントで発音された語も、違うアクセントでの発音を聞いたとき自然度高（つまり、両方可能）と評価されたものは少ないことである。そして、ここで特に注目されるのは、「両方可能」の割合は、発音調査でほぼ融合アクセントで発音された語よりも、ほぼ非融合アクセントで発音された語の方が多いという点である。

発音調査と聴取調査の融合・非融合傾向が一致する語数と、それが一致しない(発音調査時は「ほぼ融合」「ほぼ非融合」のいずれかだが、聴取調査時には融合、非融合とも自然度が高い)語数の分布の均一性を正確確率検定(両側)を用いて検定した。その結果、発音調査でほぼ非融合の語であるか発音調査でほぼ融合の語であるかによって、聴取調査と発音調査のアクセントパターンとの一致の割合に有意差が認められた(p=0.017<0.05)。このことから、発音時の融合・非融合傾向が聴取時の自然度評価に影響を及ぼしていることが示唆される。

また、非融合化類より融合化類の方が自然度の高いものの割合が高いという傾向は、「所属語彙の少ない方の語は、所属語彙の多い安定型に代わりつつある」(NHK1985、NHK 放送文化研究所 1998)という考え方で説明できるのではないかと思われる。辞典類の見出しにあがっているような、安定的に一語だと言えるものの中では、融合アクセントの所属語彙が圧倒的に多く、非融合アクセントの所属語彙が少ない。したがって、後部要素が状態や動作をあらわす4字漢語で非融合アクセントで発音されるものが、複合語に「少なからず観察される」という非融合アクセントから「ほとんどの複合語に生じている」という融合アクセントへと緩慢ながら変わりつつあることが示唆されるのである。

3.1.3 非融合アクセントにおける頭高型+平板型

第3節冒頭において、聴取調査の結果にもとづいて、テスト語を①融合傾向が強い、②両方可能、③非融合傾向が強いに分けたが、ここでは、非融合傾向または融合傾向が特に強い語に何か特徴があるのかを知るために、非融合アクセントが「不自然ではない」という回答が8名中7または8名であると同時に、融合アクセントが「不自然ではない」が0または1名の語を「非融合傾向が非常に強い」、非融合アクセントが「不自然ではない」が0または1名であると同時に融合アクセントが「不自然ではない」が7または8名の語を「融合傾向が非常に強い」と呼ぶことにする。これらの語は発音調査時に得られたアクセントパターンしか許されない傾向が強い語だと考えられる。それらの語数を表3に示す。表3から、「非融合傾向が非常に強い」語より、「融合傾向が非常に強い」語の方が多いことが分かる。

表3　非融合傾向が非常に強い語と融合傾向が非常に強い語

	語数	語例
非融合傾向が非常に強い	11	王位継承
融合傾向が非常に強い	35	家庭訪問

表4　発音調査の結果がほぼ非融合だった語における、聴取調査の結果が非融合傾向が非常に強い語
（アクセント型の組み合せ別）

前後のアクセントの組み合せ	発音調査の結果	聴取調査の結果	
	ほぼ非融合の語数	非融合傾向が非常に強い語数	語例
平板型＋平板型	22	1	導入反対
頭高型＋平板型	21	9	王位継承
中高型＋平板型	2	1	一部改正
頭高型＋頭高型	1	0	（該当なし）

　さらに、「非融合傾向が非常に強い」11語を前後のアクセント型の組み合せ別に見ると、表4のようになるが、ここでは、今回用意した発音調査の結果がほぼ非融合だった語のうち、「中高型＋平板型」や「頭高型＋頭高型」の語数が極めて少ないため、「平板型＋平板型」と「頭高型＋平板型」だけに注目したい。その両者の聴取調査の際における「非融合傾向が非常に強い」語数とインプット語数（発音調査の結果がほぼ非融合だった語数）の分布の均一性を正確確率検定(両側)を用いて検定した。その結果、発音調査の結果がほぼ非融合だった語は前後のアクセント型の組み合せが「平板型＋平板型」か「頭高型＋平板型」かによって、聴取調査の際における「非融合傾向が非常に強い」語の割合に有意差が認められた(p=0.031 <0.05)。

　なぜ「平板型＋平板型」より、「頭高型+平板型」の方が発音調査時に得られた非融合アクセントしか許されない傾向が強いのか。その原因としてひとつ考えられるのが、融合しない「頭高型+平板型」の語を融合アクセントで聞く際、高低の配置の違いがより大きいため、不自然と感じてしまうのではないかということである。

　「頭高型+平板型」の「王位継承」と、「平板型+平板型」の「指針改定」は両方とも発音調査ではほぼ非融合アクセントで発音されている。一方、今回の聴取調査では、「頭高型+平板型」の「王位継承」は発音調査の傾向と一致し、非融合傾向が非常に強いが、「平板型+平板型」の「指針改定」は融合・非融合の両方が可能という結果になっている。

　「頭高型+平板型」（例：王位継承）も「平板型+平板型」（例：指針改定）も後部要素が平板型のため、融合アクセントになる時、両者とも後部要素の平板型が頭高型になるのである（「継承」：[ケ「ーショー → ケ˥ーショー]）（「改訂」：[カ「イテー → カ˥イテー]）。ここで、両者の違いである前部要素に注目したい。融合アクセントになる時、前部要素が頭高型のものは平板型になってから後部要素と接続する（「王位」：[「オ˥ーイ → オ「ーイ]）一方、前部要素が平板型のものはそのまま後部要素と接続するのである（「指針」：[シ「シン ＝ シ「シン]）。となると、「平板型+平板型」より、「頭高型+平板型」の方が非融合アクセントから融合アクセントへの（高低配置の）変化量が多いということになる。そのため、非融合アクセントの「頭高型+平板型」の方が融合アクセントになる際非融合アクセントとの区別をより感じやすく、それにより融合アクセントでの発音が許されず、発音時の非融合アクセントしか許されないのではないかという可能性がある。

複合語のアクセント規則を全体的に見た場合、前述の前部要素における変化量が見過ごされがちだが、今回の結果から、前部要素のアクセント型、ひいては前後要素のアクセント型の組み合せが、アクセントの融合・非融合に関与すると言えそうである。

3.2 親密度調査と聴取調査について

5段階の親密度調査の結果得られた各語の親密度評価点数について、8人の平均値をテスト語ごとに計算したものをヒストグラムの形で図2に示す。

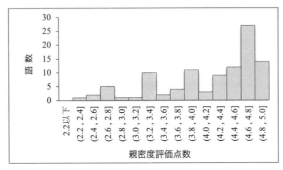

図2　親密度評価点数のヒストグラム

次に、親密度の高さが全102のテスト語の上位1/4にあたる25語(親密度上位)と下位1/4にあたる25語(親密度下位)について、聴取調査において非融合アクセントが「自然度低」と「自然度高」の語数を表5に示す。同様に、融合アクセントが「自然度低」と「自然度高」の語数を表6に示す。

表5　非融合アクセントの聴覚的自然度と親密度の関係

	親密度下位25語	親密度上位25語
非融合アクセントが自然度低	8	18
非融合アクセントが自然度高	17	7

表6　融合アクセントの聴覚的自然度と親密度の関係

	親密度下位25語	親密度上位25語
融合アクセントが自然度低	12	6
融合アクセントが自然度高	13	19

表5の親密度下位25語と親密度上位25語で非融合アクセントの聴覚的自然度が高と低の分布の均一性を正確確率検定(両側)で検定した結果、有意差が認められた($p=0.006 < 0.05$)。つまり、親密度の高低により、非融合アクセントを聞くとき自然度が変わるということになる。

一方、表6の親密度下位25語と親密度上位25語で融合アクセントの聴覚的自然度が高と低の分布の均一性を正確確率検定(両側)で検定した結果、有意差は認められなかった($p=0.140 > 0.05$)。

さらに、親密度下位25語と親密度上位25語における非融合アクセントが「自然度低」と「自然度高」の語の割合を図3に示す。そこから、親密度の低いものに非融合が「自然度高」のものが多いの

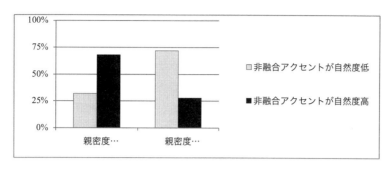

図3　親密度下位 25 語と親密度上位 25 語で非融合アクセントが自然度低の語と自然度高の語の割合

に対し、親密度の高いものに非融合が「自然度低」のものが多いことが読み取れる。

　複合語に対する慣用度とアクセントとして 1 つに融合するか否かとの関係について、窪薗(1995) は「慣用化の結果、言語使用者の側が複合語内部の意味構造を考えないまま、はじめから一語として処理し」、「一つのアクセント句にまとまる傾向が見られる」(p.75-76)としている。

　同じく後部要素が状態や動作をあらわす 4 字漢語でも、親密度の高いものの方が、使用者が 4 字漢語に対してその全体が結びつきの強い 1 単位であるという意識が強い結果、アクセント上も 1 単位に融合する発音になることが多いのではないかと思われる。

4. まとめ

　本研究では後部要素が状態や動作をあらわす 4 字漢語のアクセントの自然度を聴取調査で調べた。

　その結果、融合アクセントか非融合アクセントかという点で、発音時の優勢なアクセントとは違うアクセントを聞いた場合に不自然と評価される語が多かった。しかし、融合化類が非融合化類に比べて自然度が高いものの割合が高いこと、そして、「平板型+平板型」より、アクセント型の組み合せが「頭高型+平板型」のものは、非融合アクセント傾向が特に強い割合が高いことが分かった。

　さらに、複合語に対する親密度と聴取時の融合・非融合の自然度評価との関係について、親密度の低いものには非融合アクセントの自然度が高いものが多いのに対し、親密度の高いものには非融合アクセントの自然度が低いものが多いことが明らかになった。この結果は先行研究における記述の妥当性がある程度確認されたと言える。

　今回の結果を説明するのにひとつできる考え方として、後部要素が状態や動作をあらわす 4 字漢語で非融合アクセントで発音されるものが、多数派で安定型である融合アクセントへと緩慢ながら移行しつつあること，そしてその移行過程に前後要素のアクセント型の組み合せ及び、4 字漢語に対する親密度が関与するということがある [6]。

　しかし、今回の結果を、名詞句の音形を取る複合語が、親密度が上がるにつれ一語としての音形に移行するという傾向の反映ととらえる考え方もできる [7]。

　上記の結果の解釈についてはさらに検討を続ける予定であるが、今回は用意した発音調査の結果がほぼ非融合だった語のうち、「中高型＋平板型」や「頭高型＋頭高型」の語数が少ないため [8]、聴取時における非融合アクセントの傾向が強いか否かと前後のアクセントの組み合わせの関係などが十分検討できていない。今後は語数を増やし、さらに検証していきたいと考えている。また、本稿で扱っている融合アクセント・非融合アクセント間の非対称性と、陳曦(2017)によって明らかになったアク

セントの融合・非融合を左右する要因である、（ア）要素間の統語的関係、（イ）要素の意味、との関係に関する検討を、今後の課題としたい。

注

角括弧内の表音カナに付けられている記号「「」は上昇、「¬」は下降を表わす。上昇は句に属するものであり、句頭に起こる現象であるという考え方もあるが、本稿では郡(2004)に倣い、上昇は語頭に生じるものであり、アクセントの一部であるという立場をとる。

「後部要素が状態」は主に後部要素が『三省堂国語辞典 第七版』(2014)に「名」「形動ダ」「名・形動ダ」などと記載されている場合(例：原因不明)である。「後部要素が動作」は主に後部要素が辞典に「名・他サ」「名・自サ」「名・自他サ」と記載されている場合(例：王位継承)である。

本研究では日本語の複合語におけるアクセントの融合・非融合を研究する手始めとして、後部要素が状態や動作をあらわす4字漢語について検討する。また、「行方不明」のような前部要素が和語の語や「パワー全開」のような前部要素が外来語の語についても、今後は研究の視野に入れ、複合語のアクセントの融合・非融合と語種の関係について検討する予定である。

「ほぼ融合アクセント」と「ほぼ非融合アクセント」とは、陳曦(2017)の発音調査の結果、得られた非融合アクセントの発音回数(総発音回数は各語につき16)がそれぞれ0～3と13～16の語である。

ここで言う「首都圏」とは、おおむね東京都(島嶼部を除く)、埼玉県、千葉県、神奈川県を指す。

この解釈について、査読者から、融合アクセントが実態として多数派だとは言えないのではないかという旨の指摘をいただいているが、先にのべたように、筆者が考えているのは、辞典類の見出しにあがっているような安定的に一語だと言えるものについての多数派という意味である。

この考え方は同じ査読者の示唆にもとづく。

『NHK日本語発音アクセント新辞典』(NHK放送文化研究所2016)を見ても、非融合アクセントを記載する4字漢語の中で、「中高型＋平板型」と「頭高型＋頭高型」というアクセントの組み合せのものは少ないようである。

資料 分析対象語一覧

発音調査の結果		聴取調査の結果			語
ほぼ非融合 46語	非融合傾向が強い 33語	非融合傾向が非常に強い	11語	〈平板型＋平板型〉：導入反対、〈頭高型＋平板型〉：王位継承、名誉挽回、濃霧発生、意気消沈、大使任命、大臣就任、住所不定、効果抜群、理路整然、〈中高型＋平板型〉：一部改正
		上段以外	22語	〈平板型＋平板型〉：解任反対、交渉妥結、苦境脱出、交際順調、冷戦脱却、不振脱却、不況脱出、連敗脱出、性能向上、当選確実、前人未到、人気沸騰、決勝進出、原因不明、成績優秀、〈頭高型＋平板型〉：王位簒奪、勢力退潮、順次発売、再起不能、順次実施、経費節減
	融合・非融合の両方が可能 13語			〈平板型＋平板型〉：皇室稼入、指針改定、辞表提出、火災発生、顧客獲得、景気低迷、〈頭高型＋平板型〉：家事分担、領土拡大、名誉毀損、早期解決、新規参入、〈中高型＋平板型〉：一部緩和、〈頭高型＋頭高型〉：王位譲渡
ほぼ融合 56語	融合傾向が強い 51語	融合傾向が非常に強い	35語	〈平板型＋平板型〉：無線連絡、家電販売、街頭募金、政治不信、政権運営、財政不安、家庭訪問、国民投票、首脳会談、損害賠償、集団訴訟、正式発表、栄養補給、情報提供、殺人未遂、交通渋滞、完全燃焼、不正受給、〈頭高型＋平板型〉：社会進出、社会不安、水素爆発、宇宙開発、身体測定、自己啓発、軍事利用、事業展開、気分転換、自家発電、社会進出、自己紹介、〈頭高型＋頭高型〉：意識変化、現地調査、自己管理、自己嫌悪
		上段以外	16語	〈平板型＋平板型〉：過剰労働、首相発言、原発依存、災害対応、事前承認、環境保全、情報収集、気象観測、永久保存、有効活用、〈頭高型＋平板型〉：事故対応、都市経営、店頭展開、意思表明、心理分析、憲法違反
	融合・非融合の両方が可能 5語			〈平板型＋平板型〉：供給余剰、内政干渉、〈頭高型＋平板型〉：事業運営、意見表明、自己防衛

参照文献

秋永一枝(編) 2013『新明解日本語アクセント辞典 CD付き』東京：三省堂.

窪薗晴夫 1995『語形成と音韻構造』東京：くろしお出版.

見坊豪紀・市川孝・飛田良文・山崎誠・飯間浩明・塩田雄大(編) 2014『三省堂国語辞典 第七版』東京：三省堂.

郡史郎 2004「東京アクセントの特徴再考―語頭の上昇の扱いについて―」『国語学』55(2).16–31.日本語学会.

陳曦 2017「後部要素が状態や動作をあらわす四字漢語のアクセント融合」問題―統語的関係と意味の視点から―」『言語文化学』26.3–16. 大阪大学言語文化学会.

NHK(編) 1985『日本語発音アクセント辞典』東京：日本放送出版協会.

NHK放送文化研究所(編) 1998『NHK日本語発音アクセント辞典(新版)』東京：NHK出版.

NHK放送文化研究所(編) 2016『NHK日本語発音アクセント新辞典』東京：NHK出版.

Left-dominant Accent in Native Japanese: The Case of *Hito**

Chuyu Huang
The University of Tokyo / JSPS

ABSTRACT. This paper aims to provide more evidence to the hypothesis of left-dominant accentuation in word formation and compounds, claiming that the left-dominant accentuation exists not only in Sino-Japanese words but also native stratum. Moreover, the accent of the numeral *hitotsu* seems to be preserved in the data that was collected from a dictionary. This supports the hypothesis that the left member is the head in a complex word or a compound where the accent of the head should be preserved. The accentual change is also observed in words that are longer than four morae, which implies that the left-dominant accent might have changed in longer words.

Keywords: left-dominant accent, Tokyo Japanese, head projection, native stratum, numeral

1. Left or right
1.1 Right-dominant accent in Tokyo Japanese

Tokyo Japanese is known as language in which pitch accent is distinctive. In this language, an accented word can usually contain a so-called accent nucleus where a pitch fall is located[1]. What happens in a compound or a complex word composed of two accented words in most cases is that the accent of either the left member or the right member is reflected, rather than preserving them both. The compound accent rules in Tokyo Japanese are fundamentally right-dominant (McCawley 1968; Kubozono 1997; Kubozono *et al.* 1997; among others). The rules depend on the prosodic length of the second member. In regard to short second members which are less than three morae, three different types can be detected as shown in (1): deaccentuating morphemes that trigger deaccentuation in a compound, pre-accenting morphemes that cause an accent nucleus on the rightmost syllable of the left member, and initial-accenting morphemes that preserves the initial accent nucleus of the second member. This rule also seems to be applied in other lexical strata such as Sino-Japanese morphemes and foreign loanwords (' = the accent nucleus, while – at the word end = no accent. Morpheme boundaries are marked with #).

(1) McCawley (1968): words with short second members

    a. deaccenting morpheme:
      i. Native:
        [iro'] 'color' 色 → [aka#iro-] 'red(noun)' 赤色
                  [Murasaki#iro-] 'purple(noun)' 紫色
      ii. Sino-Japanese:
        [se'i] 'characteristics' 性 → [aku#sei-] 'malignant' 悪性,
                     [ryoo#sei-] 'benign' 良性
    b. preaccenting morpheme:
      i. Native:
        [mushi-] 'worm' 虫 → [imo'#mushi] 'green caterpillar' 芋虫
                 [aka'#mushi] 'bloodworm' 赤虫
      ii. Sino-Japanese:
        [ke'n] 'prefecture' 県
        → [akita'#ken] 'Akita Prefecture' 秋田県,
        [aomori'#ken] 'Aomori Prefecture' 青森県

c. initial-accenting morpheme:
    i. Native:
        [i'to] 'yarn' 糸 →   [tsumugi#i'to] 'silk yarn' 紬糸
                                [momon#i'to] 'cotton yarn' 木綿糸
    ii. Sino-Japanese:
        [su'u] 'number' 数 →   [kan#su'u] 'function' 関数,
                                [ten#su'u]'point' 点数

1.2 Left-dominant accent

As the name suggests, left-dominant accentuation indicates that the left member instead of the right member in a complex word dominates the accent of the word (Matsumori 2016; Kubozono 2017; Huang 2017a,b). Matsumori (2016) pointed out that some words in Tokyo Japanese are left-dominant. For example, *sake- > sakaya-* vs. *kutsu' > kutsu'ya*.[2] When the right member is *ya*, the left member decides whether the compound has an accent. In the other hand, Huang (2017a,b) claimed that left-dominant accent is observed in numerals and determiners and proposed that the linguistic motivation is due to head structure; phonological constraints prohibit candidates that do not preserve the accent nucleus of the first member.

Although the previous studies used the same term for non-right-dominant accent, it should be pointed out that what is called "left-dominant" might not be the same in each literature. In the examples that Matsumori and Kubozono mentioned, the accent of the left member does play a role in determining the accent. However, it is the right member rather than the left that triggers the accent. Returning to the *sakaya-* and *kutsu'ya* example, both words share the same second member. If we see accent determination as the competition between the first member and the second member, the *ya* example above should be taken to mean that *ya* yields the power of accent determining to the left-member. However, the left member does not "dominate" the accent accentuation in a strict sense. On the other hand, the following examples shown in Huang (2017a) show that the left member determines the accent type of the compound even if the second members are different:

(2) Sino-Japanese numerals preserve the accent of the first member (Huang 2017a)

    [ichi']+[go']   →[ichi'#go]
    'one word'   一語
    [ichi']+[o'ku]   → [ichi'#oku]
    'hundred million'   一億
    [ichi']+[gy'oo] → [ichi'#gyoo]
    'one row'   一行

When it comes to the linguistic motivation, Huang (2017b) suggests a determiner structure with a left-headed branch. Since the determiner, namely the left-member, is the morphological head in a complex word or a compound, its accent is preserved. Moreover, minimal pairs like [ho'nkoo] ('this school') and [honkoo-] ('the main school'), in which the first word preserves the accent of the determiner, also supports this analysis. These left-dominant accents may be the result of the accent preservation of the head element when the word is phonologically mapped. This mapping is realized phonologically in terms of an accent on the left member.

(3) Determiner structure

Some questions, however, are still left unanswered in this analysis. Some questions remain, for example, whether the left-dominant accent is observed in all the lexical strata or only in Sino-Japanese because only Sino-Japanese words were taken into account in Huang (2017a,b), and whether we really need a left-dominant analysis. As for the first question, if left-dominant accent only occurs in Sino-Japanese, the analysis should be questioned for its restricted validity. As for the second question, the left-dominant analysis, which assumes the accent of the left member is preserved, explains the left-dominant data, but we cannot know if the accent of the first member is really "preserved," or it is the result of the juncture accent in Kubozono (1995), Uwano (1997), and other studies. In the limited data of the numerals like *ichi'*, the accent always falls on *chi* which is also the juncture syllable. In order to answer the two questions above, this study first investigates the native numeral data and then shows the data which supports the left-dominant analysis but cannot be explained by other compound accent rules.

2. Left-dominance in native words

To tackle the issue of the lexical strata, words with a native numeral were examined. However, the data is restricted since not all native numerals are productive in modern Tokyo Japanese. Except for *hito* ('one') and *futa* ('two'), all other native numerals are no longer productive. Instead, Japanese speakers tend to use Sino-Japanese numerals for numbers larger than two. Among all the native numerals, *hito* might have the highest productivity. It can also co-occur with a loanword, e.g. *hitokappu* ('one cup' ひとカップ), which can be used as material to test the left-dominant hypothesis in the native stratum.

Hito is ultimately accented when being pronounced as a single word although it co-occurs with another word in most cases. The lone form of it is found in some social varieties, such as in the variety used in the Japanese Self-Defense Forces (Shintaro Kudo, p.c.).[3]

The data of accent type in each word was collected from *Sanseido Daijirin*. Native words beginning with *hito* were the target, and a total of 133 words were collected. As the table below shows, nearly all words containing *hito* preserve its accent in a complex word.

(4) The accent preservation of *hito* in compounds

	[hito']	[hito'] and other variations	other position	Total	Examples
3μ	10(100%)	0(0%)	0(0%)	10(100%)	[hito'e]
4μ	66(94.3%)	4(5.7%)	0(0%)	70(100%)	[hito'aji]
5μ	25(53.2%)	20(42.6%)	2(4.2%)	47(100%)	[hito'shizuku]
6μ	2(33.3%)	4(66.7%)	0(0%)	6(100%)	[hito'katamari]

These data show the high regularity with which the accent of the first member is preserved, as in the case of Sino-Japanese numerals. According to the dictionary data, words of six morae or less show the same tendency of accent preservation as shown below:

(5) Examples of complex words with [hito']

    a. Three-mora words:
       [hito'e] 一重, [hito'tsu] 一つ, [hito'me] 一目, [hito'ha] 一葉
    b. Four-mora words:
       [hito'ashi] 一足, [hito'aji] 一味, [hito'iki] 一息
    c. Five-mora words:
       [hito'kakera] ひと欠片, [hito'kamae] 一構え
    d. Six-mora words:
       [hito'anshin] 一安心

Words that are three-mora or four-mora long are relatively stable: there is almost no variation in the dictionary nor in the actual speech of Tokyo Japanese speakers. As for words longer than four morae, according to the dictionary data, five-mora words and six-mora words are pronounced with an accent nucleus falling on *to*. This might be the evidence that words in (5c, d) have a different structure compared to other compounds. Since the words in (5c, d) have a second member that is longer than two morae, the right-dominant compound accent rules would predict that the accent nucleus falls on the initial syllable of the second member or the syllable where the second member originally has an accent (e.g. Kubozono 2008). However, the accent as shown in (5c, d) seems to be changing. Many of them have more than one accent type in the dictionary, and some Tokyo Japanese speakers also pronounce these words different from the description in the dictionary. This accentual variation will be discussed later.

To summarize, native words show the same tendency of preserving the accent of the head just like Sino-Japanese words, which provides evidence for left-dominant accent outside the Sino-Japanese stratum.

3. Head projection of left-dominant words

Let us now turn to the question whether we really need the left-dominant accentuation. A possible criticism of the left-dominant accentuation is that most of the numerals used possess a penultimate accent and their accent can be accounted for by assuming the accent nucleus falls on the juncture syllable at the morpheme boundary.

Data with *hitotsu* might provide some evidence which supports the claim that left-dominance is necessary. Since the first element in a complex word is assumed as the head in Huang (2017b), in which the accent is preserved in a complex structure, it is expected that the accent of a complex word such as *hitotsu* (*hito* + *tsu*) is projected to the head position when another element follows (e.g. *hitotsu*). The head part of the determiner might keep its headness when being mapped onto a higher node in a larger recursive compound structure. Take a word like *hitotsu* which contains the assuming head *hito* for example, when a complex word is formed in a lower structure *hitotsu* is projected into the head position in a larger structure where *hitotsu* becomes the first element of the compound, e.g. in *hitotsukoto*, the accent of *hitotsu* which is the head, should also be preserved as *hito* in *hitotsu* is.

(6) Head projection

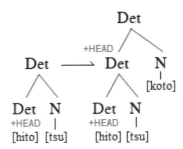

Not many words have the complex structure above, and most of them do not seem to follow the prediction of accent preservation. For example, *hitori'tabi*, which has an accent on *ri*, is composed of *hito'ri* and *tabi-*. If it has the structure above, the accent is predicted to fall on *to* like *hito'ri* does. However, we can still find some words where the accent of *hito'tsu* in the compound is preserved, such as those examples found in the data, suggesting that the head structure might be projected onto a higher node and cause the accent pattern as shown below:

(7) Examples of accent preservation

a. [hito'tsu]+[koto']   → [hito'tsu#koto]   '(one and) the same thing'   一つ事
b. [hito'tsu]+[kama-]   → [hito'tsu#kama]   'one kettle'   一つ釜
c. [hito'tsu]+[tokoro-] → [hito'tsu#tokoro-] 'one place'   一つ所

The data above provides evidence for the left-dominant analysis. The accents in the compounds in (7) explained with any of the compound accent rules proposed in the previous studies except the left-dominant hypothesis. Both the juncture accent rules proposed in Kubozono (1995) and Uwano (1997) that predict an accent appearing at the morpheme boundary (*i.e.* *tsu* or the first mora of the second member), as well as the antepenultimate rule that predict an accent nucleus on the antepenultimate mora *tsu* also fail to explain these cases. Contrary to these rules, the left-dominant rule predicts that the position of the accent nucleus of the head will be preserved in a complex structure, therefore the accent position of *hitotsu* is inherited in *hitotsukoto* and *hitotsukama*.

4. Accentual change and the correlation with *rendaku*

It should be mentioned that the pronunciation of some words in the data above seem to undergo a change for many Tokyo Japanese speakers. Also, the accentuation of the left-dominant structure seems to be correlated with *rendaku*. As a process broadly observed in Japanese, *rendaku* "replaces a morpheme-initial voiceless obstruent with a voiced obstruent." (Vance 2017)

4.1 Accentual change

Turning back to the examples in (5c, d), many Tokyo Japanese speakers do not pronounce these words with the accent described on the dictionary. Instead, the accent of these words mostly falls on the antepenultimate syllable as in (8c, d).

(8) Variations found in modern Tokyo Japanese

    a. Three-mora words: [hito'e] 一重, [hito'tsu] 一つ,
                        [hito'me] 一目, [hito'ha] 一葉
    b. Four-mora words: [hito'ashi] 一足, [hito'aji] 一味,
                        [hito'iki] 一息
    c. Five-mora words: [hito'kakera]~[hitoka'kera] ひと欠片,
                        [hito'kamae]~[hitoka'mae] 一構え
    d. Six-mora words: [hito'anshin]~[hitoa'nshin] 一安心

This shows that the data in the dictionary might be prescriptive data. The new variation is not totally unmentioned. In fact, both *NHK Accent Dictionary* and *Sanseido Daijirin* reflect the accentual change in progress to some extent by listing the variants with antepenultimate accent. On the other hand, the change does not seem to occur in three mora words and four mora words. A possible reason for this could be because four morae that form two feet are responsible for a number of phonological phenomena including deaccentuation which has been reported in previous studies (e.g. Itô and Mester 2016).

The accentual change can be accounted for by assuming that the antepenultimate accent is more unmarked than preserving the accent of the left member in a compound. The antepenultimate accent is also the most popular accent type in loanwords. This new accent variant shows that the left-dominant rule in longer words could be a remnant of older Japanese accent rules, which is also mentioned in Matsumori (2016). However, the left-dominant rule still works synchronically in words that are four morae or less. The accentual change can be generalized as below:

(9) Generalization of *hito* and *hitotsu* words

    If a word with *hito* or *hitotsu* is less than or equal to four morae: the accent of the left member is preserved. Otherwise, preserve the accent of the left member or put the accent on the antepenultimate syllable

4.2 A correlation with *rendaku*?

Another interesting fact is that the *hitotsu* data seems to show a correlation between the accent position and *rendaku*.

The correlation between accent and *rendaku* is still not clear. Sugito (1965) mentioned some cases where the *rendaku* form becomes unaccented, e.g. *shi'bata* 'Shibata (last name)' 柴田 vs. *imada-* 'Imada (last name)' 今田. Tanaka (2005) added some other examples such as *shima ~ jima* 'island' 島 (e.g. *tanega'shima* 'Tanega Island' 種子島 vs. *ishigakijima-* 'Ishigaki Island' 石垣島) to this hypothesis and further argues that both *rendaku* and accent serve as a boundary marker and therefore when one is applied, the other becomes redundant.

The *hitotsu* data shows a different relationship between *rendaku* and accent: words in which the second member undergoes *rendaku* have variants with antepenultimate accent, while words without *rendaku* application tend to preserve the accent of the first member. Due to the limitation of the lack of data, this issue awaits further study.

(10)　*Rendaku* in the *hitotsu* data[4]

    a.　*No rendaku and the accent of the left member is preserved:*
       [hito'tsu]+[koto'] → [hito'tsu#koto]
       '(one and) the same thing'　一つ事

    b.　*No rendaku and the accent of the left member is preserved:*
       [hito'tsu]+[kama-]→ [hito'tsu#kama]
       'one kettle'　一つ釜

    c.　*Rendaku and the antepenultimate syllable is accented:*
       [hito'tsu]+[hashi-]→ [hitotsu'#bashi]
       'bridge made of a piece of wood'　一つ橋

    d.　*Rendaku and the antepenultimate syllable is accented:*
       [hito'tsu]+[hanashi'] → [hitotsu#ba'nashi]
       'an repeated anecdote'　一つ話

5. Summary

This paper has four implications: (i) with the data of *hito* being provided, left-dominant accent is proved to exist in the Japanese native stratum, (ii) words with *hitotsu* support the determiner hypothesis, showing that the head is projected and its accent is inherited in some words, (iii) a thorough accentual change into the antepenultimate accent is observed in left-dominant words that are longer than four morae, and (iv) *rendaku* seems to be correlated with left-dominant accent, but the available data does not allow reliable conclusions to be drawn. It should be mentioned that the evidence in the present study cannot be generalized to all native numerals due to the limitation that most native numerals are not productive. However, the data of *hito* provides evidence for the left-dominant accent.

Although an accentual change is in progress, it does not deny the validity of left-dominant analysis, since the accentual change only occurs in words that are longer than four morae. As for the three and four mora words, the left-dominant accent rule, which assumes that the accent of the head on the left should be preserved, can still predict the accent of those words correctly.

Notes

[*] This study is supported by JSPS KAKENHI Grant Number 17J04129. An earlier version of this paper was presented at the Phonology Forum 2017 on August 24. I deeply appreciate all the comments from the audience. I would also like to thank two anonymous reviewers, Shin-ichi Tanaka, Takane Ito, Lynn Lethin, and Alina Kordesch, for giving me a lot of insightful suggestions. All errors are on my own.

[1] Tokyo Japanese also allows words without any accent, which will not be discussed in this paper.

[2] In the first example, [saka] is an allomorph of [sake]. The former form undergoes a vowel change and only appears in non-final position of words.

[3] Despite the lack of sufficient data that *hito* is used as a single word, native speakers seem to be aware of the morpheme boundaries of words with *hito* according to a pre-survey of this issue where ten Japanese native speakers were asked how many parts there are in a target word and where the morpheme boundaries of the target words with *hito* are located. All surveyed speakers answered with two and a boundary right after *hito*.

[4] One reviewer mentioned that words in (10) are mostly not frequently used words, which indicates the possibility that these words are lexical exceptions. For example, *hitotsukoto* is an outdated expression, and *hitotsukama* mostly appears in idioms like *hitotsukama-no meshi-o taberu* ('to eat the rice in the same pot', which means to have an intimate relationship with someone). This might also be a reason why the left-dominant accentuation in longer words is changing. Due to the low frequency of these words, speakers do not pronounce them in the left-dominant way, instead the default antepenultimate accent rule is applied.

References

Huang, Chuyu. 2017a. Left-dominant accentuation in Japanese. *Language and Information Sciences* 15.19–36.

Huang, Chuyu. 2017b. Accent of Sino-Japanese determiner compounds. *Phonological Studies* 20.47–54.

Ito, Junko, and Mester, Armin. 2016. Unaccentedness in Japanese. *Linguistic Inquiry* 47(3).471–526.

Kubozono, Haruo. 1995. Constraint interaction in Japanese phonology: Evidence from compound accent. *Phonology at Santa Cruz* 4.21–38.

Kubozono, Haruo. 1997. Lexical markedness and variation: A nonderivational account of Japanese compound accent. *WCCFL* 15.273–287.

Kubozono, Haruo, Itô, Junko, and Mester, Armin. 1997. On'inkōzō kara mita go to ku no kyōkai: fukugōmeishi akusento no bunseki. *Bunpō to onsei*, ed. by Spoken Language Research Group, 147–166. Tokyo: Kurosio Publications.

Kubozono, Haruo. 2008. Japanese accent. *Handbook of Japanese linguistics*, ed. by Shigeru Miyagawa and Mamoru Saito, 165–191. Oxford: Oxford University Press.

Kubozono, Haruo. To appear. Pitch accent. *The Cambridge handbook of Japanese linguistics*, ed. by Yoko Hasegawa. Cambridge: Cambridge University Press.

McCawley, James. 1968. *The phonological component of a grammar of Japanese*. The Hague: Mouton.

Matsumori, Akiko. 2016. Fukugōgoakusento ga nihongoshikenkyū ni teiki suru mono. *NINJAL Research Papers* 10.135–158. Tokyo: NINJAL.

Sugito, Miyoko. 1965. Shibata-san to Imada-san: Tango no chōkakuteki benbetsu ni tsuite no ichi kōsatsu. *Gengo Seikatsu.* 165.64–72. Tokyo: Chikuma Shobō.

Tanaka, Shin-ichi. 2005. *Akusento to Rizumu*. Tokyo: Kenkyūsha.

Vance, Timothy. 2017. Rendaku or sequential voicing in Japanese phonology. *Oxford research encyclopedia of linguistics.* http://linguistics.oxfordre.com/view/10.1093/acrefore/9780199384655.001.0001/acrefore-9780199384655-e-280 [accessed January 2018].

Two Sources of Optionality in Hebrew Imperatives[*]

Kazutaka Kurisu
Kobe College

ABSTRACT. In Modern Hebrew, colloquial imperatives are derived from future forms, and both faithful and subtracted forms are often available, exhibiting optionality. Bat-El (2002) analyzes subtracted imperative forms. Scrutiny reveals that her analysis encounters empirical and conceptual problems. The goal of this study is to present an alternative theoretical analysis that both accommodates optionality and overcomes problems with Bat-El's account. Part of Bat-El's failure resides in the unification of regular and irregular verbs. Teasing apart the two types of verbs, I claim that their different behavior is governed by different mechanisms. Optionality in regular verbs comes from two possible constraint rankings while optionality in irregular verbs results from two possible lexical representations.

Keywords: colloquial imperatives, Modern Hebrew, optionality, subtractive morphology

1. Introduction

Colloquial imperative forms are derived from future counterparts in Modern Hebrew. The faithful form identical to the future form is a possible imperative form, but a subtracted form is also permissible in many cases. As a result, optionality arises in the colloquial imperative formation. This word formation is described by Bolozky (1979) and Bat-El (2002) develops a detailed analysis of it in the framework of Optimality Theory (Prince and Smolensky 2004). It turns out that her analysis suffers from many serious problems.

This study has two goals. First, I review the core portion of Bat-El's (2002) analysis. Part of its failure comes from the unification of regular and irregular verbs. Second, I develop an analysis that separates the two types of verbs. This segregation largely simplifies the analysis and avoids the problems with Bat-El (2002). I argue that optionality in regular and irregular verbs is due to different principles. In regular verbs, on the one hand, optionality arises since one lexical representation is associated with two cophonological constraint rankings. On the other hand, irregular verbs are associated with a single constraint ranking, but there are two possible lexical representations for a colloquial imperative form. Thus, there are two sources of optionality if my proposal is on the right track.

This paper is mapped out as follows. Section 2 presents data of colloquial imperatives in Modern Hebrew. Section 3 reviews Bat-El (2002) and points out problems with the analysis. In section 4, I propose an alternative analysis. This paper is concluded in section 5.

2. Data

This section presents basic data to be discussed in this paper. Both regular and irregular verbs are considered in this study, so their distinction must be clarified. In regular verbs, all root consonants appear throughout the paradigm. In contrast, not all consonants of irregular verbs surface in the morphological paradigm. Their irregularity is not uniform. Initial, medial, and last consonants are potentially subject to phonologically unmotivated elision. Many other factors contribute to the classification of irregular verbs (see Schwarzwald 1984 and Zadok 2012). Imperative subtraction targets the left edge of a verb. For the purpose of this paper, the distinction of regular and irregular verbs is based on the behavior of the root-initial consonant. If it appears in the future, the verb is considered regular. Otherwise, the verb is irregular.

Representative examples of regular verbs are provided in (1). Colloquial imperative forms are derived from future forms. The future is expressed with different prefixes depending on the binyanim. A fully faithful imperative form identical to the future form is always possible, but a subtracted form is also available in many cases. Deleted phonological material is up to the first syllable of the input. Initial CV is elided when the first syllable is CVC, as in (1a). The prefix-internal vowel is deleted when the input begins with a CV syllable, as in (1b).

(1)

		Masculine		Feminine			Gloss
		Future	Imperative		Future	Imperative		
a.		ti-f.tax	tif.tax	ftax	ti-f.te.xi	tif.te.xi	fte.xi	open
		ti-v.rax	tiv.rax	vrax	ti-v.re.xi	tiv.re.xi	vre.xi	run away
		tit.-pa.ʃet	tit.pa.ʃet	tpa.ʃet	tit.-paʃ.ti	tit.paʃ.ti	tpaʃ.ti	undress
		tit.-la.beʃ	tit.la.beʃ	tla.beʃ	tit.-lab.ʃi	tit.lab.ʃi	tlab.ʃi	dress
b.		ti.-ka.nes	ti.ka.nes	tka.nes	ti.-kan.si	ti.kan.si	tkan.si	enter
		te.-na.ʃek	te.na.ʃek	tna.ʃek	te.-naʃ.ki	te.naʃ.ki	tnaʃ.ki	kiss
		te.-xa.bes	te.xa.bes	txa.bes	te.-xab.si	te.xab.si	txab.si	launder

Bat-El (2002) gives convincing evidence for the derivation of colloquial imperatives from their future counterparts. First, initial fricatives as in [ftax] and [vrax] are due to an identity effect with future forms. Examples like [patax] 'opened' and [barax] 'ran away' suggest that the initial fricatives are due to post-vocalic spirantization. Second, Modern Hebrew has no prefix that produces a complex onset with the initial consonant of a verbal stem. Therefore, imperative-initial [t] that appears in many examples in (1) cannot be an imperative prefix.

Irregular verbs are exemplified in (2). Both faithful and subtracted forms are permitted. When subtraction applies, initial CV segments undergo deletion.

(2)

		Masculine		Feminine			Gloss
		Future	Imperative		Future	Imperative		
a.		ti.-kax	ti.kax	kax	ti-k.xi	tik.xi	kxi	take
		ti.-ten	ti.ten	ten	ti-t.ni	tit.ni	tni	give
b.		ta.-kum	ta.kum	kum	ta.-ku.mi	ta.ku.mi	ku.mi	get up
		ta.-sim	ta.sim	sim	ta.-si.mi	ta.si.mi	si.mi	put

Bolozky (2009) claims that deletion of prefixal /i, e/ is phonetic elision general in casual speech (see Bolozky and Schwarzwald 1990 for casual speech). He also claims that /a/ resists elision due to its high sonority and stability and that the subtracted forms in (2b) come from the normative register. These claims are not valid. First, faithful and subtracted forms are not synonymous. Subtracted forms convey more direct and forceful commands (Bolozky 1979). Second, /i/ is more stubborn than /a/ (Bat-El 2002). Imperative subtraction is morphological.

3. Reviewing Bat-El (2002)

This section reviews Bat-El's (2002) analysis. Her analysis of regular verbs is illustrated in (3) and (4). TRUNC is a descriptive constraint that requires segmental deletion. It may be replaced by ¬MAX (Alderete 1999) or REALIZE MORPHEME (Kurisu 2001). When the input begins with a CVC syllable, vowel deletion creates a tri-consonantal cluster penalized by $*_\sigma$[CCC, so initial CV segments are elided, as in (3). As shown in (4), only a vowel is deleted when the first syllable of the input is CV because $*_\sigma$[CCC is not offended.

(3)

	/ti-f.tax/	TRUNC	ONSET	$*_\sigma$[CCC	MAX
a.	tif.tax	*!			
b.	if.tax		*!		*
c.	tftax			*!	*
d. ☞	ftax				**

(4)

	/ti.-ka.nes/	TRUNC	ONSET	$*_\sigma$[CCC	MAX
a.	ti.ka.nes	*!			
b.	i.ka.nes		*!		*
c. ☞	tka.nes				*
d.	ka.nes				**!

Turning to irregular verbs, the analysis above erroneously predicts vowel deletion in (2b) and the masculine forms in (2a). Stress falls on the penultimate syllable in the feminine forms in (2b), and the final syllable attracts stress in all the other examples in (2). Bat-El (2002) observes that stressed syllables remain unaffected in (2b) and the masculine forms in (2a). Building upon this observation, she proposes the faithfulness constraint in (5).

(5) FAITHσ́: Corresponding stressed syllables are segmentally identical.

Bat-El's analysis of the masculine forms in (2a) is presented in (6). Given the constraint in (5), CV deletion is compelled in order to have stressed syllables match between the input and the output. The examples in (2b) are analyzed in the same way.

(6)

	/ti.-káx/	TRUNC	ONSET	FAITHσ́	MAX
a.	ti.káx	*!			
b.	i.káx		*!		*
c.	tkáx			*!	*
d. ☞	káx				**

FAITHσ́ is not always satisfied (e.g., /ti-f.táx/→[ftáx] 'open-MASCULINE'), but violation of FAITHσ́ is limited to cases where a stem segment would be required to disappear in order to respect FAITHσ́. This suggests that MAX$_{STEM}$ dominates FAITHσ́. As demonstrated in (7), this ranking blocks deletion of stem segments even if FAITHσ́ is sacrificed.

(7)

	/ti-f.táx/	MAX$_{STEM}$	FAITHσ́	MAX
a. ☞	ftáx		*	**
b.	táx	*!		***

This analysis implies that deleting affixal segments costs less than deleting stem segments. This prediction is falsified by the verbal morphology of Modern Hebrew. Probably, the most convincing case is the denominal verb formation exemplified in (8). It is word-based rather than root-based (Bat-El 1994; Ussishkin 1999). The input-output mapping looks as follows: /cad-i e/→[cided]. The melodic overwriting here implies that MAX$_{AFFIX}$ outranks MAX$_{STEM}$.

(8)

Nouns	Gloss	Denominal verbs	Gloss
cad	side	cided	side
dam	blood	dimem	bleed
mana	portion	minen	apportion

Let us continue to look at irregular verbs. All the examples in (9) are similar in that their root-initial sonorants disappear in the future. In colloquial imperatives, initial CV deletion may take place in (9a, b), but subtracted forms are unacceptable in (9c). The examples in (9c) are not expected by Bat-El's analysis so far.

(9)

		Past	Future	Imperative		Gloss
	a.	ja.rad	te.réd	te.réd	réd	descend
		ja.ʃav	te.ʃév	te.ʃév	ʃév	sit
		ja.tsa	te.tsé	te.tsé	tsé	go out
	b.	na.tan	ti.tén	ti.tén	tén	give
		na.sa	ti.sá	ti.sá	sá	travel
		la.kax	ti.káx	ti.káx	káx	take
	c.	ja.raʃ	ti.ráʃ	ti.ráʃ	*ráʃ	inherit
		ja.nak	ti.nák	ti.nák	*nák	suck
		ja.rak	ti.rák	ti.rák	*rák	spit
		ja.ʃan	ti.ʃán	ti.ʃán	*ʃán	sleep

Bat-El argues that the past tense plays a crucial role. The future form is compared with its past counterpart. She claims that the vowel immediately after future-initial [t] is prefixal if the initial consonant of the past form appears in the future form, as illustrated in (10a). If the first consonant in the past does not appear in the future, the first future vowel corresponds to the past-initial consonant, as shown in (10b). The morphological affiliation of the first future vowel is determined by comparison with its past counterpart.

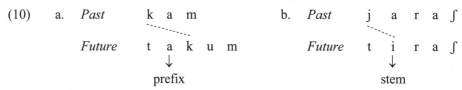

(10) a. *Past*   k a m   b. *Past*   j a r a ʃ

      Future t a k u m   *Future* t i r a ʃ
                      ↓   ↓
                   prefix   stem

With the background stated above, Bat-El assumes the multiple correspondence constraint in (11). This constraint is dormant in (10a) because the two relevant correspondents are both consonants. The constraint is active only when the first vowel in the future is regarded as part of a stem.

(11) IDENT[high]CV:
      The first past consonant and the first future vowel must agree in [±high] in the colloquial imperative formation if they correspond to each other.

Incorporating this multiple correspondence constraint, Bat-El's analysis is demonstrated below. In (12), the initial glide of the past form is absent from the future counterpart (i.e., the input to the colloquial imperative). Since the first vowel is a mid vowel in (12a), it disagrees with past-initial [j] in height. As a result, the candidate incurs a violation of IDENT[high]CV. The three constraints ranked over MAX are crucially unranked with respect to one another in Bat-El's analysis, so violation of TRUNC is fatal in (12a). To avoid a violation of the multiple correspondence constraint, the mid vowel right after the future prefix [t-] is eliminated. In (13), IDENT[high]CV is satisfied by the fully faithful candidate because past-initial [j] and the first vowel in the candidate are both [+high] segments. Fully faithful (13a) is more harmonic than (13b) since the latter incurs gratuitous violations of MAX.

(12)		/t-e.réd/ [ja.rad]$_{Past}$	IDENT[high]CV	TRUNC	MAX$_{STEM}$	MAX
	a.	te.réd	*	*!		
	b. ☞	réd			*	**

(13)		/t-i.ráʃ/ [ja.raʃ]$_{Past}$	IDENT[high]CV	TRUNC	MAX$_{STEM}$	MAX
	a. ☞	ti.ráʃ		*		
	b.	ráʃ			*	*!*

The analysis demonstrated above is problematic for several reasons. First, it is puzzling why the height (dis)agreement of a past-initial consonant and a vowel in the imperative form directly affects the grammaticality of subtractive morphology. Given that a consonant is often taken out in irregular verbs, Hebrew speakers need to pay attention to a broad morphological paradigm to identify verbal roots. However, this paradigmatic reference does not entail that interrelated forms exercise influence over the colloquial imperative formation.

Second, the fact that the first consonant of a past form is absent from its future form does not imply that the consonant corresponds to the first future vowel. This correspondence is not a logical consequence since we cannot exclude the possibility that the first vowel of a future form belongs to a future prefix. [ti-] and [te-] are widely accepted as future prefixes.

Finally, the mechanism that determines the morphological affiliation of the vowel right after the future prefix [t-] is attenuated by exceptional binyan-I verbs. Binyan-III future forms take [ta-], but it is attached to binyan-I verbs in (14). Bat-El argues that these two examples are misconceived as binyan-III verbs by Hebrew speakers because their rightmost stem vowel is [i], a segmental property characteristic to binyan-III future forms.

(14)

Past	Future	Imperative			Gloss
rav	ta.rív	ta.rív	*trív	*rív	quarrel
ʃar	ta.ʃir	ta.ʃir	*tʃir	*ʃir	sing

Representative examples of binyan-III verbs are given in (15). They show that binyan-III resists imperative subtraction (Bolozky 1979; Dekel 2014). Therefore, only the forms faithful to their future counterparts are available to binyan-III.

(15)

Masculine			Feminine			
Future	Imperative		Future	Imperative		Gloss
taz.kír	taz.kír	*zkír	taz.kí.ri	taz.kí.ri	*zkí.ri	remind
taf.sík	taf.sík	*fsík	taf.sí.ki	taf.sí.ki	*fsí.ki	stop
ta.kím	ta.kím	*kím	ta.kí.mi	ta.kí.mi	*kí.mi	raise
ta.píl	ta.píl	*píl	ta.pí.li	ta.pí.li	*pí.li	drop
ta.ví	ta.ví	*ví	ta.ví.(ʔ)i	ta.ví.(ʔ)i	*ví.(ʔ)i	bring

Bat-El attempts to analyze the examples in (14) and (15) in a parallel way. She assumes with no justification that the first vowel of a past form in binyan-III is part of a stem rather than part of the past prefix (e.g., [h-iz.kir]/*[hi-z.kir] 'reminded'). This vowel corresponds to the first vowel of the future form, so it follows that the latter is also a stem vowel, as shown in (16).

(16)

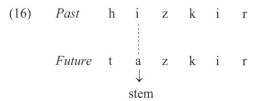

Building upon the assumption above, Bat-El's analysis of the data in (15) is presented in (17). The four undominated constraints are assumed to be crucially unranked. (17c) is ruled out due to its cumulative violations of *σ[CCC and MAX_STEM. Among the other forms, only the fully faithful candidate in (17a) satisfies the two lower ranked constraints. (17b) and (17d) are eliminated by MAX and FAITHσ, respectively. It is crucial here that the first vowel of a future form is a stem vowel. If the vowel were instead assumed to be part of the future prefix, (17d) would satisfy MAX_STEM and win the competition erroneously.

(17)

		/t-az.kír/	TRUNC	ONSET	*σ[CCC	MAX_STEM	FAITHσ	MAX
a.	☞	taz.kír	*					
b.		az.kír		*				*!
c.		tzkír			*	*!	*	*
d.		zkír				*	*!	**

Besides the problem that the assumption depicted in (16) is not justified, the analysis in (17) cannot be applied to the data in (14). The morphological status of the vowel immediately after future-initial [t] is crucial. Binyan-I past forms take no past prefix. The initial consonant of a past form is present in its future counterpart. Thus, the vowel right after future-initial [t] cannot be part of the verbal stem. As illustrated in (18), it follows that the vowel is part of the future prefix, according to Bat-El's (2002) logic.

(18) *Past*   r   a   v

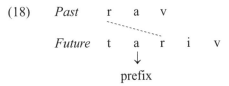

     Future   t   a   r   i   v
                  ↓
              prefix

The tableau in (19) shows that the output with CV deletion is undesirably generated by Bat-El's (2002) analysis. Unlike in (17), where her analysis of binyan-III verbs is presented, deletion of the vowel right after future-initial [t] does not lead to a violation of MAX$_{STEM}$. The faithful candidate in (19a) (i.e., the intended winner) is eliminated, so the examples provided in (14) and (15) cannot be explained in a parallel fashion.

(19)

/ta-.rív/		TRUNC	ONSET	FAITH$\acute{O}$	MAX
a. ☹	ta.rív	*!			
b.	a.rív		*!		*
c.	trív			*!	*
d. ☞	rív				**

Bat-El (2002:674) suggests the possibility that Hebrew speakers draw the generalization that future forms with [i] in the stem-final syllable do not tolerate subtraction in the colloquial imperative formation. This suggestion is tantamount to giving up a phonological analysis of the data in (14) and (15). This suggestion contradicts Bat-El's analysis in which blocking of subtraction in (14) and (15) is accounted for in phonological terms. Furthermore, this move is empirically falsified. [i] is the rightmost stem vowel in [sim] and [si.mi] provided in (2b), but subtraction is permitted. They must be treated as lexical exceptions, a situation preferably to be avoided.

Summarizing this section, Bat-El (2002) analyzes the colloquial imperative formation in regular and irregular verbs. Her analysis tries to unify the two kinds of verbs in phonological terms, but it encounters many problems. The problems are both internal and external to the colloquial imperative formation in Modern Hebrew.

4. Separating regular and irregular verbs

The goal of this section is to develop an analysis toward our better understanding of the colloquial imperative formation in Modern Hebrew. Part of the problems with Bat-El (2002) has to do with the unification of regular and irregular verbs. Furthermore, optionality is not taken into consideration in her account. My analysis below segregates the two types of verbs. It is designed not only to overcome the problems with Bat-El's theoretical account but also to explain optionality.

The core part of my analysis is summarized in (20). In colloquial imperatives of regular verbs, there is a single lexical representation, and this unique representation is associated with two constraint rankings. In irregular verbs, MAX » TRUNC is the only constraint ranking, but there are two conceivable lexical representations. This analysis has two notable features. First, regular and irregular verbs are analyzed individually. It is well known that they exhibit quite different phonological behavior, so separating them is a natural move. Second, optionality in the two kinds of verbs is governed by different principles. The source of optionality is two constraint hierarchies in regular verbs, but it is two lexical representations in irregular verbs.

(20)

	Regular verbs	Irregular verbs
Lexical representations	/[prefix+stem]$_{Future}$/	/[prefix+stem]$_{Future}$/ /[stem]$_{Future}$/
Constraint rankings	MAX » TRUNC TRUNC » MAX	MAX » TRUNC

The two constraint rankings in (20) (i.e., MAX » TRUNC and TRUNC » MAX) are described in more detail in (21). They are partially ordered (Anttila 1997, 2002; Anttila and Cho 1998; Anttila and Fong 2004).

(21)   a.   MAX » TRUNC: ONSET, *$_\sigma$[CCC, MAX » TRUNC
        b.   TRUNC » MAX: ONSET, *$_\sigma$[CCC, TRUNC » MAX

In regular verbs, a colloquial imperative form is identical to its future form when MAX » TRUNC is chosen. By contrast, subtracted forms are obtained when TRUNC » MAX is chosen. In this case, the analysis looks exactly as in (3) and (4). ONSET and *$_\sigma$[CCC determine the well-formedness of subtracted forms. In irregular verbs, on the other hand, the future form surfaces faithfully when /[prefix+stem]$_{Future}$/ is selected while no future prefix appears in the colloquial imperative when /[stem]$_{Future}$/ serves as the input. Given MAX » TRUNC, the picked lexical representation surfaces as it is in the output representation. This analysis explains the data in (1), (2), and (9a, b).

The two different mechanisms of optionality are required. Regular verbs are not explained with the mechanism of irregular verbs because cases where part of a future prefix surfaces are not accounted for. Also, the behavior of irregular verbs does not follow from the analysis of regular verbs. When subtraction takes place, a whole prefix would not undergo deletion when the input begins with a CV syllable.

Our next task is to analyze the examples in (9c) and (14). They are irregular verbs and subtraction is not an available option. I simply suggest that the examples in (9c) and (14) are associated only with /[prefix+stem]$_{Future}$/. This analysis is not explanatory. However, this lack of explanatory adequacy is a virtue rather than a weakness. First, there are only a handful of data as in (9c) and (14). The small population of data indicates that they are presumably real exceptions. Second, there are fluctuating data. Bat-El (2002) finds that the subtracted forms in (22) are grammatical for some Hebrew speakers but ungrammatical for others. In (22), the past-initial sonorant disappears in futures and imperatives, just as in (9). She classifies [te.da] 'know' into (9a) and [ti.pol] 'fall' into (9b), respectively. The small number of relevant data and the existence of fluctuating data indicate that the grammaticality and ungrammaticality of subtracted forms is unsystematic in (9) and (14). Such examples should not be analyzed in phonological terms since no phonological descriptive generalization is likely to be robust.

(22)
	Past	Future	Imperative		Gloss
	ja.da	te.da	te.da	(*)da	know
	na.fal	ti.pol	ti.pol	(*)pol	fall

Finally, the behavior of binyan-III is explained in the same way as (9c) and (14). In (15), subtracted forms are not tolerated. This fact follows from the assumption that binyan-III is categorically associated with /[prefix+stem]$_{Future}$/ and MAX » TRUNC. The parallel behavior of binyan-I verbs in (14) and binyan-III verbs in (15) is nothing surprising because they take the same prefix. In Bat-El's (2002) analysis, by contrast, it is inexplicable why Modern Hebrew speakers misunderstand the binyan-I verbs as binyan-III. She attributes this misidentification to the quality of the rightmost stem vowel in (14). Given her assumption that the binyan-III future prefix is /t-/, however, it is a puzzle why /t-/ is not prefixed in the future forms in (14).

My analysis dispenses with some of the central constraints in Bat-El (2002). First, my analysis obviates FAITHσ́ since it does not make reference to prosodic information. FAITHσ́ is required in her account to unify regular and irregular verbs. In my account that separates the two kinds of verbs, their different phonological behavior requires no phonological analysis. Second, my analysis does away with MAX$_{STEM}$. My analysis does not predict that stem vowels are more resistant than affixal vowels. Consequently, my account is not incompatible with the denominal verb formation in (8) in which affixal vowels are given priority over stem vowels.

Finally, IDENT[high]CV is not necessary in my analysis since past forms play no role. This is a significant advantage of my account. IDENT[high]CV is assumed in Bat-El (2002) in order to explain the set of the examples in (9). As discussed in section 3, reference to past forms is not motivated, and the mechanism of how the constraint works is not logical. I also discussed in this section that the examples in (9) should not be explained in phonological terms because the available data are not reliably systematic.

The discussion above reveals that the problems with Bat-El's (2002) analysis largely have to do with the constraints unrequired in my analysis. Obliterating such constraints not merely makes us possible to develop a better and coherent theoretical account but also simplifies the analysis. In colloquial imperatives in Modern Hebrew, the importance of phonology is much less than discussed by Bat-El (2002).

5. Conclusion

The goal of this study was two-fold: reviewing Bat-El's (2002) analysis of the colloquial imperative formation in Modern Hebrew and developing a theoretical analysis that not only avoids problems with Bat-El (2002) but also accommodates optionality. Her account faces a variety of empirical and conceptual problems. I proposed an analysis that teases apart regular and irregular verbs. Optionality arises in regular verbs since a single lexical representation is associated with two cophonological constraint hierarchies. By contrast, optionality is ascribed to two possible lexical representations in irregular verbs. There are two sources of optionality in the colloquial imperative formation in Modern Hebrew.

Note
* I am most grateful to Outi Bat-El for sharing with me her wisdom of Hebrew phonology. I also thank the audience of Phonology Forum 2017 for discussion, especially Elan Dresher and Yu Tanaka. Finally, my thanks go to two anonymous reviewers for valuable comments on earlier drafts. All errors are mine.

References
Alderete, John. 1999. *Morphologically governed accent in Optimality Theory*. Doctoral dissertation. University of Massachusetts, Amherst.
Anttila, Arto. 1997. Deriving variation from grammar. In *Variation, change and phonological theory*, ed. by Frans Hinskens, Roeland van Hout and Leo Wetzels, 35–68. Amsterdam: John Benjamins.
Anttila, Arto. 2002. Morphologically conditioned phonological alternations. *Natural Language and Linguistic Theory* 20. 1–42.
Anttila, Arto and Young-mee Yu Cho. 1998. Variation and change in Optimality Theory. *Lingua* 104. 31–56.
Anttila, Arto and Vivienne Fong. 2004. Variation, ambiguity and noun classes in English. *Lingua* 114. 1253–1290.
Bat-El, Outi. 1994. Stem modification and cluster transfer in Modern Hebrew. *Natural Language and Linguistic Theory* 12. 571–596.
Bat-El, Outi. 2002. True truncation in colloquial Hebrew imperatives. *Language* 78. 651–683.
Bolozky, Shmuel. 1979. On the new imperatives in colloquial Hebrew. *Hebrew Annual Review* 3. 17–24.
Bolozky, Shmuel. 2009. Colloquial Hebrew imperatives revisited. *Language Sciences* 31. 136–143.
Bolozky, Shmuel and Ora Rodrigue Schwarzwald. 1990. On vowel assimilation and deletion in casual Modern Hebrew. *Hebrew Annual Review* 12. 23–48.
Dekel, Nurit. 2014. *Colloquial Israeli Hebrew*. Berlin and Boston: Water de Gruyter.
Kurisu, Kazutaka. 2001. *The phonology of morpheme realization*. Doctoral dissertation. University of California, Santa Cruz.
Prince, Alan and Paul Smolensky. 2004. *Optimality Theory: constraint interaction in generative grammar*. Malden, Massachusetts: Blackwell Publishing.
Schwarzwald, Rodrigue Ora. 1984. Analogy and regularization in morphophonemic changes: the case of the weak verbs in post-biblical and colloquial Modern Hebrew. *Afroasiatic Linguistics* 9. 87–100.
Ussishkin, Adam. 1999. The inadequacy of the consonantal root: Modern Hebrew denominal verbs and output-output correspondence. *Phonology* 16. 401–442.
Zadok, Gila. 2012. *Similarity, variation, and change: instability in Hebrew weak verbs*. Doctoral dissertation. Tel Aviv University.

日本語複合名詞の非標準的アクセント型について＊

On "Nonstandard" Accent Patterns of Japanese Compound Nouns

太田　聡

Satoshi Ohta

山口大学

Yamaguchi University

Abstract. This paper claims that in order to explain the nonstandard accent pattern of such compound nouns as *kenpookaisei* "amendment of the Constitution", we should invoke the argument structure of the head element. I propose that when the head is derived from a verb which requires an internal argument "theme", for example, and the theme is incorporated into the compound as its first element, the accent of the first element has to be assigned independently from that of the second.

Keywords: compound accent rule, lexicon, argument structure

1. はじめに

　日本語複合名詞の標準的なアクセント型の規則としては、以下の 3 種がよく知られている（窪薗（1995）を参照）。下向きの矢印は、直前のモーラにアクセント核があり、ピッチがそこで落ちることを表している（矢印がついていない場合には、その語のアクセントは平板式／無アクセントとする）。

(1)　a. 後半要素が 1〜2 モーラのときは、前半要素の最後に複合語アクセントを置く。

　　　例）じんじ↓ぶ（人事部）、すみだ↓がわ（隅田川）

　　b. 後半要素が 3 モーラ以上のときは、後半要素の最初に複合語アクセントを置く。

　　　例）おんなご↓ころ（女心）、きたア↓メリカ（北アメリカ）

　　c. 後半要素がいわゆる中高型のアクセントを持つときは、それが複合語全体のアクセントとして継承される。

　　　例）げんじ＋ものが↓たり → げんじものが↓たり（源氏物語）

(1a)と(1b)の規則は、「2 つの要素の切れ目に近いところにアクセントが与えられる」という具合にまとめることもできよう。

　ところが、例えば「憲法改正」という複合語は、後半要素が 4 モーラなので、(1b)に従えば「けんぽうか↓いせい」と予測されるのだが、実際には、「け↓んぽうかいせい」というアクセント配置になる。本論では、こうした一見不規則と思われるアクセントを持つ例がなぜ生じるのか、その理由を探り、アクセント付与に関する文法の仕組みについて論じることにする。

2. 窪薗(1995)の分析とその問題点

　窪薗(1995: 70-71)は、(1)に示した原則が当てはまらない例の一種として、「消息不明」、「自信喪失」、「首位攻防」、「選手宣誓」、「門戸開放」などを挙げ、これらに「格関係」という分類名称を与えている。この格関係について、窪薗は「複合語を構成する 2 要素が基底において［主語+動詞］、［主語+形容（動）詞］、［目的語+動詞］といった意味構造を成すものであり、特に漢語を含む場合に複合語アクセント規

則の適用を受けにくくなってしまう」と述べている。「憲法改正」も、その意味は「憲法を改正すること」なので、窪薗流に言えば、［目的語＋動詞］という結びつきであり、通常の規則を受けないとなろう。この意味に基づいた観察・指摘（前半要素が主語や目的語と解釈できる例のアクセント型は一般的なものとは異なりやすいということ）は、抽象的なことを言っているわけではないので、とても理解しやすい。しかし、なぜ主語や目的語に当たるものが前半要素として取り込まれると、複合語アクセント規則が適用されにくくなるのであろうか。事実の指摘はされていても、理由が説明されているわけではない。さらに、文法全体の仕組みを考慮した場合、窪薗の言説には、大きな問題点がある。

主語や目的語を定義することは難しいが、一般的には、「文」もしくは「節」という単位に基づいて述べられる。例えば、Crystal (2008)は、主語と目的語を共に“A term used in the analysis of grammatical functions to refer to a major constituent of sentence or clause structure, ...”としている。また、生成文法の標準理論(Chomsky 1965)の有名な定義では、「主語はSに直接支配された(immediately dominated) NPであり、目的語はVPに直接支配されたNPである」となる。よって、主語や目的語とは、統語論的な（あるいは、文や句を構成した際の）単位・概念ということができる。そして、統語論（統語部門）の働きは、ごく単純化して言えば、レキシコン（語彙部門）から提供される語に、併合(merge)や移動(move)などの統語操作を加えて、句や文を作ることである。文法全体の流れがわかるように、現在のミニマリスト・プログラムの枠組み（の例）で示せば、以下のようになる（田中(2013: 2)より）。

(2)

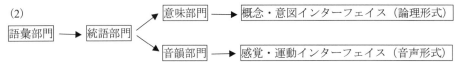

つまり、文法体系内の順序としては、語が収められているレキシコンよりも、統語部門は後に位置づけられているはずである。ところが、窪薗のように、語のアクセントの不規則性を説明するために統語的に作られる単位（そしてその意味解釈）を頼りにしなくてはならないとなると、統語的な構造を先に作った上で、その情報をレキシコンに後戻りさせるようなシステムを（一部の例の説明のためだけに）提案することになり、納得がいかない。

統語部門（あるいはそれ以降にある部門）の単位や概念に頼らずに、レキシコンの段階で利用できる情報のみに基づいて、複合語の一見例外に見えるアクセント型も予測・説明ができないであろうか。次節では、まずは事実確認のために、複合語（的なもの）ではあるが、後半要素ではなく、前半要素にアクセントが置かれ、(1)の規則が当てはまらないものをアクセント辞典から抽出し、その特徴を調べることにする。

3. アクセント上の切れ目がある複合語類

例えば、「はつかね↓ずみ（二十日鼠）」、「こくさいく↑うこう（国際空港）」、「ガールフレ↓ンド」のように、前半要素が修飾部(modifier)で、後半要素が主要部(head)という関係で結びついた複合語の多くは、語種が和語であっても、漢語であっても、外来語であっても、そのアクセントパターンは通常の複合語アクセント規則（すなわち(1)）に従う。そして、こうした例は1語として一息に発音されるので、途中に幾分かの切れ目（小さな間）を置くことはない。

一方、「憲法改正」などでは、前半要素と後半要素の間にアクセント上の切れ目が生じうる。そして、前半要素に（あるいは、より正確には、前半要素と後半要素のそれぞれに独立した）アクセントを与えることになる。『新明解日本語アクセント辞典』(以下では『新明ア』と略す)では、こうした切れ目を、例えば、「アキノ・ナナクサ（秋の七草）」、「ジガ（・）ジサン（自画自賛）」のように中点を用いて表

している[1]。そこで、この辞典にある中点つきの例をもれなく抽出していくことにした。ただし、本稿の議論では、窪薗が取り上げたように、漢語複合名詞を特に対象として論じることにするので、漢語名詞ではないものや、漢語ではあっても、別の要因が働いていると思われるものを、考察対象から外していくことにした。考察対象外としたのは、以下のような例である（なお、『新明ア』では、2つ以上のアクセント型を併記するときには、標準語アクセントとして望ましいと思われる方を先に示している。よって、第2候補として切れ目の中点がつけられた例は、抽出対象とはしなかった）。

(3) a. 品詞が名詞以外のものや、主要部が漢語ではないもの

　　　　例）興味津津、媚び諂う、虎視眈眈、切羽詰る、丁々発止、どうのこうの、とつおいつ、多摩モノレール、引きも切らず、滅多矢鱈、等々

　　b. 人名や題名など

　　　　例）芥川龍之介、鴨長明、西郷隆盛、魏志倭人伝、義経千本桜、等々

　　c. 3つ以上の要素が含まれているもの

　　　　例）海軍兵学校、国家公安委員会、日本電信電話公社、日本放送協会、内閣総理大臣、等々

　　d. 並列(apposition)関係になっているものや、畳語の類

　　　　例）一朝一夕、虚虚実々、質疑応答、神社仏閣、大義名分、明明白白、真行草、等々

　　e. 数詞と名詞や助数詞を組み合わせたもの

　　　　例）一姫二太郎、一世一代、三十一日、十人十色、七転八倒、二十四時間、等々

　　f. 句の形（「AのB」）をしているものや、慣用句、諺、四字熟語など[2]

　　　　例）後の祭り、以心伝心、言わぬが花、鬼に金棒、温故知新、呉越同舟、言語道断、森羅万象、大器晩成、体育の日、美辞麗句、付和雷同、油断大敵、臨機応変、寄らば大樹の陰、等々

　　g. 部分関係になっているもの

　　　　例）皇居外苑、有史以前、有史以来、等々

　　h. 前部がアクセントを取りやすい接頭語（辞）であるもの

　　　　例）環太平洋、現時点、全日本、第一線、第六感、半永久、等々

(3)に挙げたもののいくつかについて、少し補足説明をしておく。(3c)に関しては、例えば、x, y, z という3つの項目から成る複合語で、[x[yz]]というまとまりを持つもの——右枝分かれの構造になっている場合——は、x と y の間に構造上の切れ目があるので、x が独立したアクセントを持ちやすいと分析できる。(3d)で触れた並列や畳語の例というのは、2つの要素が対等の関係で並んでいるため、それぞれがアクセントを取ることは不思議ではなかろう。(3f)で挙げた句の形をしたものは、（例えば、「なまざ↓かな（生魚）」と「な↓まのさかな（生の魚）」を対比させてみればわかるように、）前半要素がアクセントを取ることこそが、普通である。また、慣用句や諺や四字熟語とは、短い語句の中に、人類の長年の英知を伝えたり、文で表現するような深い意味合いを込めたりしているわけであるから、それぞれの要素にアクセントがつけられるのはうべなるかなである。つまり、前半と後半のどちらの要素も同じくらい重要であるので、両方にアクセントが配置されるべきである。(3g)の部分関係で言わんとすることは、例えば「関東北部」や「明治以降」のように、空間的にも時間的にも、あるところを基点・基準にして、そこからさらに絞り込みを行う場合には、前後の両要素にアクセントが与えられやすく、「皇居外苑」などもそうした類と見なせるということである。なお、(3)では一応8つのグループに分けて列挙したが、これらは完全に別の特徴を持つというわけではなく、ある例が2つ以上のグループにまたがっている面がある。例えば、(3a)や(3d)に挙げた例には、四字熟語でもある（すなわち(3f)に入れてもよい）ものがある。また、人名は「〜家の〇〇」という部分関係になっているので、(3g)と

まとめることもできよう。

　さて、『新明ア』に中点つきで示された例で、(3)に該当しなかった複合語は、案外少なくて、以下の25例であった。

　　(4) 意気投合、意識不明、医薬分業、機会均等、議事妨害、憲法改正、憲法発布、公私混同、産学協同、住所不定、初志貫徹、心機一転、審議未了、人事不省、神経過敏、前後不覚、男女共学、男女同権、天下太平、八宗兼学、眉目秀麗、分相応、本末転倒、免許皆伝、門戸開放

なお、窪薗の挙げた「消息不明」という例には、『新明ア』ではなぜか中点が付されていなかった。また、窪薗が挙げた「身元不明」、「自信喪失」、「首位攻防」、「選手宣誓」、「音声多重」、「新旧交代」、「内閣改造」などの複合語は、『新明ア』に見出し語としては載っていなかった。それゆえ、こうした例は（(4)の例と同類ではあるが、）(4)には加えていない。

　窪薗が指摘したように、漢語の場合には通常の複合語アクセント規則が適用されにくくなるが、それはなぜかをここで考えてみよう。（後半要素が）和語である複合語の場合には、次の(5a)の例のように、前半要素の最後もしくは後半要素の最初の拍にアクセントをつけるか、(5b)のように後半要素のはじめを連濁させるか、(5c)に示したように、その両方を用いるか、といったことが多い（連濁した箇所には下線を付した）。もっとも、(5d)のようにどちらの方法も示さない例もないわけではない。

　　(5) a. そら↓まめ（空豆）、いしあ↓たま（石頭）
　　　　b. うみ<u>が</u>め（海亀）、ひと<u>ざ</u>と（人里）
　　　　c. やま↓<u>で</u>ら（山寺）、うし<u>が</u>↓える（牛蛙）
　　　　d. したさき（舌先）、くろふね（黒船）

(5a)‐(5c)のパターンは、結局、2つの要素の境界がどこにあるかを伝え、意味解釈が容易になるようにする手段だと思われる。例えば、「ヨザ↓クラ（夜桜）を見に行く」という例を、連濁もアクセントもなしで、「ヨサクラ」と発音すると、2つの要素の切れ目・つながりがあいまいになり、わかりにくくなる（聞いた者は、「与作たちに会いに行くのだろうか？」、「ヨサという種類の蔵／倉でも見に行くのだろうか？」など混乱するであろう）。このように、和語の複合語では、構成要素の境界を知らせる手段が2重になっているわけであるが、漢語の場合には、基本的に、連濁が生じない。よって、要素間にどのようなまとまりと切れ目があるのかを知らせるために、アクセントの働きがより重要となる。そのため、漢語複合語の場合には、後半要素以外にもアクセントを付与するパターンを発達させたのではないかと推察できる。なお、外来語複合語の場合には、連濁は起こらないし、アクセントも、前半要素に置かれることはまずない。では、なぜ漢語の方が外来語よりもアクセントパターンを多様にしたのかというと、それは、やはり語数の多さのためであろう。外来語複合語の数は、漢語に比べれば少ないので、様々な区別は不要であったのであろう。

　それでは、次節で、「憲法改正」などが、統語的な情報に頼らずとも、レキシコンにおいて得られる情報だけから、修飾・被修飾という関係で結びつく複合語とは異なるアクセント型を取ることを、いかにして決められるのか、というメカニズムを考えてみることにする。

4. 複合語形成と項構造

　まず、語彙記載項——すなわち、語がレキシコンの中で備えている情報——の例を示すことからはじめよう。次の例は、英語の cut という動詞の記載内容である（中村・金子・菊池(2001: 28)より）。

　　(6) cut　(i)　[kʌt]
　　　　　　(ii)　a. V

b. [＿＿ NP]

(iii) a. [Agent, Theme[−Abstract]]

b. x divides y by separating with a sharp edge or instrument.

(i)が音韻情報、(iia)が統語範疇、(iib)は厳密下位範疇化(strict subcategorization)の情報を示す。そして、(iiia)は項構造(argument structure)、すなわち、どのような意味役割(semantic role)を持つ要素を要求するかを表しており、(iiib)がこの語の意味内容を記述している。この中で特に項構造について補足しよう。例えば、英語の put という動詞は、「置く」という行為をする動作主(Agent)と、その対象物である主題(Theme)と、その場所(Location)が要ることが語彙的に決まっているので、例えば、She put the vase on the table.というような文ができる。これは、文を作ってみてはじめて put がどのような種類の意味を持った要素をいくつ取るかがわかる、というものではない。日本語の場合にも、同様に、動詞や（動詞と同じく用言と分類される）形容詞・形容動詞などの述語になりうる語には、句や文を形成していく際に、どのような意味役割を持った要素を必要とするかという情報が、レキシコンの段階から付与されていると考えられる。よって、「改正（する）」といった動詞も、文を作ってみずとも、『改正』するからには、それをする人――動作主――と、その対象――主題――が必要である」といったことはわかる・決まっているはずである。また、「同権（である）」という語も、「平等」という形容動詞と同じように、「○○が『同権』だ」という具合に、同権である主体（もしくは経験者(Experiencer)）を表現するように決まっているはずである。つまり、述語になりうる語には、どのような意味役割あるいは主題役割(thematic role)を持つ要素と組み合わされるかという情報が、はじめから備わっていると考えてよい。ゆえに、「憲法改正」の「改正」や「男女同権」の「同権」は、以下のような項構造を備えているといえよう（＜ ＞はいわゆる内項(internal argument)を表すために用いた。＜ ＞のついていないものはいわゆる外項(external argument)となる）。

(7) カイセイ： Agent〈Theme〉

ドウケン： Experiencer

　一方、例えば、修飾・被修飾の関係で結びつき、通常の複合語アクセントを持つ「赤とんぼ」、「国語辞典」、「地域社会」などでは、その主要部の語が動作主や主題などを要求するといったことはない。となれば、「主語」や「目的語」といった概念・単位に依らずとも、(4)に挙げた語群（およびその同類語）に対しては、「（結果として主語になる）外項や（結果として目的語になる）内項といった項構造を持った語が主要部になる複合語は、アクセント付与において、項構造を持たない語が主要部となる複合語とは異なるふるまいを示す」という一般化が可能であろう。例えば、英語の複合語の場合にも、伝統的に、windmill のように主要部が動詞から派生されていないものは語根複合語(root compound)、hand washing のように主要部が動詞から派生されたもので、非主要部はその項であるという関係になっているものは総合複合語(synthetic compound)と呼ばれ、区別されてきた（Lieber (2016)などを参照）。よって、主要部の品詞・項構造の違いに基づいて複合語を分類して論じることは妥当である。

　では、なにゆえ、外項や内項を取る語が、その外項や内項の語と結びついて複合語を形成するときには、途中にわずかながら間を置き、前半と後半が独立したアクセントを持つようになるのであろうか。前部（の名詞や形容詞）が後部（の名詞）を修飾する関係で結びついて複合語となる場合には、構造を括弧で示せば、(8a)のようになる。それぞれの要素（＝語）に括弧をつけたので、前半要素と後半要素の境界は"]["という表示になっている。この程度の切れ目は、アクセント付与の妨げになるものではなく、全体を一塊と捉えてアクセントの計算を行うことができる。

(8) a. [[N/A][N]]ɴ （⇐ 全体を 1 語としてアクセント付与）

b. $[[[N]]_{N+}[V/A]]$
       ↓（⇐前半要素と後半要素のアクセントを別々に付与）
   $[[N]\cdot[N]]_N$

これに対して、主要部が動詞や形容（動）詞由来の名詞であり、それらが取る項を前部要素として取り込む場合には、(8b)の構造と派生が仮定できよう。例えば、put が Agent と Theme と Location という主題役割を取るということは、既述のように、She put the vase on the table.などの文を生み出すことであり、*She put vase table.といった文は現れない。つまり、項構造の項は、文の中では名詞句（あるいは決定詞句(DP)）や前置詞句(PP)といった「句」の形で具現される。ならば、「改正（する）」が「憲法」を取る場合にも、「憲法」に名詞句的な資格を与えることは穏当であろう。レキシコンの段階では、基本的に句はまだ仮定できないが、句になる資格を備えた語よりは大きな塊という意味で、範疇記号の横にプラス(+)を加えて N+と記した。こうすれば、語としての括弧の外側に句的なものとしての括弧も持つことになる。その結果、2 つの要素の間の境界は、"]][" となり、(8a)の場合に比べて、切れ目がより大きなものとなる（Chomsky and Halle (1968)の用いた形式素境界(＋)と語境界(#)のような違いが、(8a)と(8b)にはあるとたとえることもできよう。また、壁／境界が 1 つでなく 2 つになると要素間の結びつけができなくなるというのは、統語論の下接の条件(subjacency condition)を連想させるものがある）。よって、前半要素は後半要素から独立してアクセントが与えられ、それに伴い、後半要素も独立してアクセントの計算をせざるを得ないわけである。結果として、前半要素にアクセントがある例（「憲法改正」、「男女同権」）や、全体が平板式という例（「消息不明」、「自信喪失」など）、すなわち通常の複合語とは異なるアクセント型を持つものが生じる。そして、最終的には、前半要素の資格は句的なものから語に改められ、また、主要部の動詞や形容動詞の「する／だ」などの語尾が削除されて、名詞へと変換され、途中にアクセントの切れ目がある複合名詞が現れることになる。

5. 語彙的複合語と統語的複合語について

　影山・柴谷(1989)や Kageyama (2016)は、例えば、「新婚旅行」、「山歩き」、「国立大学」などは通常の（語彙的）複合語であるが、「受験生：増加」、「韓国：訪問」、「格差：解消」などは、統語的複合語──より正確には、統語部門より後(postsyntactic)の音韻部門で形成される複合語──とする（彼らは、コロンを、構成要素が各々のアクセントを伴い、途中に若干の切れ目を置いて発音することを表すために用いている）。では、影山・柴谷が唱える統語的複合語は、通常の複合語とは、2 要素間にある若干の切れ目という音声的なこと以外に、何が違うのかを確認してみよう。

　複合語を特徴づける用語の 1 つとして、語彙的統合性(lexical integrity)というものがある。よく知られているように、複合語は 1 語にまとまっているので、途中に他の要素を挿入したり、一部分だけを修飾したり、一部分だけを削除・代用したりするといった、統語的な句には許される操作が許されない。影山・柴谷は、例えば、「二人はきのう〔新婚旅行〕に出かけた」を「*二人は〔新婚きのう旅行〕に出かけた」とはできないように、「急激な〔受験生：増加〕を見込む」を「*〔受験生：急激な増加〕を見込む」とはできないことなどから、統語的複合語も、語彙的統合性は備えているとしている。つまり、「統語的」複合語とはいえ、あくまで語であって、句ではないというわけである。しかしながら、次のような点で、統語的複合語は、通常の複合語とはふるまいが異なると影山・柴谷は指摘する。(9)に示したように、語彙的複合の内部には生起しない尊敬語接辞を、統語的複合語には含ませることができ、それは、句の場合と並行的である（影山・柴谷 1989: 151）。

(9) a. *先生は〔新婚ご旅行〕／〔山お登り〕に出かけられた。
    b. 皇太子の〔韓国：ご訪問〕に伴い……

c. 皇太子の韓国のご訪問に伴い……

また、(10)に例示したように、語彙的複合語では許容されない削除や代用が、統語的複合語では可能となる（影山・柴谷 1989: 158-159）。

(10) a. *職場が国立ᵢ大学からφᵢ病院に移った。

　　b. このぶんでは格差ᵢ：解消もφᵢ／そのᵢ是正も期待できない。

つまり、統語的複合語と名づけられた例では、句の場合と同じような操作が許されるわけであるから、それが形成される場所は、統語部門、もしくは、それより後の音韻部門であるという議論は、なるほど興味深い。

　では、前節までで問題にした「憲法改正」という語は、どちらのタイプなのであろうか。影山・柴谷流のテストに当てはめると、以下のようになる。

(11) 憲法ᵢ改正は、むしろそのᵢ／φᵢ改悪だという意見もある。

また、(現実には反するが、仮の話であれば、)「天皇の憲法ご改正」という言い方ができる。これらの結果からすれば、「憲法改正」は統語的複合語ということになりそうでる。しかしながら、省略などの操作や「ご」の付加が、ある複合語に対してできたとしても、そのことから直ちに、その複合語が統語部門（以降）で作られると断定できるのであろうか。もう少し慎重な観察と考察が必要であろう。

　上で挙げた「韓国訪問」のような例は、新聞の見出しなどで、「Xの／が韓国の／をご訪問」という表現から助詞等を省略した形で、よく使われるものである。また、「韓国」の部分を他の国名・都市名などに入れ替えれば、ほぼ無限と言ってよいほど多くの例を作り出すことが可能である。よって、非常に高い生産性を示すそうした例をわざわざ辞書に載せることはまずない（ゆえに、「韓国訪問」のような例を統語的複合語と見なすことには特に異論はない）。一方、「憲法改正」などは国語辞典にも載っているものであるので、ヒト（＝日本語話者）の心的辞書に収められているとすべきであり、統語的複合語とする必要はまったくあるまい。「憲法改正」や「意識不明」のような例が、もし(4)のところで挙げたように20〜30例しかなければ、よく耳にする語でもあるので、そのアクセント型を例外的なものとして暗記しているのだという考え方も成り立つであろう。しかし、そのアクセント型は、例えば、「刑法改正」、「民法改正」、「商法改正」、「原因不明」、「安否不明」など、他の例にも当てはめていくことができる。つまり、ある程度の生産性が見られるのである。では、なぜ暗記しているわけではなさそうな例に対しても同じ計算ができるのかと言えば、それはやはり、レキシコンの中にある項構造の情報を頼りに、同じ法則を適用していると考えられるのである。

　さらに、次の(12)に示したような相違点にも注目されたい。

(12) a. 先生が生徒の家を〔家庭訪問〕する。

　　b. *外務大臣が〔韓国：訪問〕する。

　　c. ?首相が〔憲法・改正〕する必要を説く。

「家庭訪問」のように完全に語彙化されている例は、通常の複合語アクセントをとり、「する」の付加が可能である。しかし、「韓国訪問」の場合には、アクセントを前半要素に置いたまま「する」を付加することはできない。ところが、「憲法改正」の場合には、アクセントを変えなくても、「する」の付加がそれほどおかしくはない。したがって、やはり「憲法改正」のような例は、「韓国訪問」のような例とは違って、レキシコンの中で作られるタイプのものであると推察できる。

6. 残された課題

　本稿は、窪薗が特に漢語複合語のアクセントに関して行った説明を批判する形で展開したので、漢

語の複合語を中心に論じてきた。しかし、例えば「バイク買い取り」、「図書貸し出し」、「資料持ち出し」のような主要部が和語の例にも、「憲法改正」と同じアクセント型が観察される（和田学氏からの個人談話によるご指摘）。ところが、「バイク<u>買い取り</u>」のように後半が複合動詞由来の 4 モーラ語の場合には、たしかに「憲法改正」と同じように前半にアクセントがくるが、例えば、「バイク探し」、「資料<u>作り</u>」、「図書<u>集め</u>」のように後半が単純動詞の連用形由来の 3 モーラ語になると、後半にアクセントが置かれる。今後は、このように主要部が和語である例にも注目して、アクセント付与の仕方が何の違いによって変化するのかを考察していく必要がある。

7. まとめ

　「憲法改正」のような複合語のアクセント型は、一般的な複合語が示すものとは異なる。しかし、だからと言って、そのような複合語が統語部門（以降）で作られると仮定したり、そのアクセントを例外的なものとして指定したりする必要はない、ということを本論は明らかにした。レキシコンの段階で利用できる項構造に着目すれば、複合名詞の主要部を、基底において、主題役割を持つ語を外項や内項として要求するものとしないものに分けることができる。そして、この違いによって、アクセント付与の仕方も異なるという議論を行った。つまり、（統語的複合語という類はあるにせよ、）本論の主張は、複合語形成は基本的にレキシコンの中で完了し、統語的な情報に頼る必要はないというものであった。

注

* 本論は、JSPS 科研費（課題番号 16K02772）の助成を受けている。原稿の段階で 2 名の査読委員の方から大変貴重な批評をいただき、改稿に役立てることができた。ここに記して感謝申し上げたい。

1 「ジガ（・）ジサン」のように、中点に括弧がついているものは、切れ目がなくなることもあることを表す。切れ目があれば「サン」の部分は高く発音されるが、なければ、「サン」の部分は低くなる。

2 四字熟語の辞典に収録されている語であっても、本論での議論の対象としている「憲法改正」や「消息不明」と同じタイプのもの、すなわち、主要部が動詞／形容動詞由来の名詞で、前半要素を A、後半の主要部を B とした場合、その意味が「A を／に B する」もしくは「A が B である」と解釈できる例は、ここには含めず、次の(4)に含めることにした。

参照文献

Chomsky, Noam. 1965. *Aspects of the theory of syntax*. Cambridge MA: MIT Press.

Chomsky, Noam and Morris Halle. 1968. *The sound pattern of English*. Harper and Row, New York.

Crystal, David. 2008. *A dictionary of linguistics and phonetics*. 6th edition. Malden MA: Blackwell.

影山太郎・柴谷方良 1989「モジュール文法の語形成―『の』名詞句からの複合語」久野暲・柴谷方良（編）『日本語学の新展開』くろしお出版，139–166.

Kageyama, Taro 2016 Noun-compounding and noun-incorporation. *Handbook of Japanese Lexicon and Word Formation* ed. By Taro Kageyama and Hideki Kishimoto, 237–272. Boston: Walter de Gruyter.

窪薗晴夫 1995『語形成と音韻構造』東京：くろしお出版.

金田一春彦監修 2014『新明解日本語アクセント辞典　第 2 版　CD 付き』東京：三省堂.

Lieber, Rochelle. 2016. *Introducing Morphology*. 2nd edition. Cambridge: Cambridge University Press.

中村捷・金子義明・菊地朗 2001『生成文法の新展開―ミニマリスト・プログラム―』東京：研究社.

田中智之 2013『統語論』東京：朝倉書店.

講演 / LECTURES

Contrastive Feature Hierarchies in Synchronic and Diachronic Phonology[*]

B. Elan Dresher
University of Toronto

ABSTRACT. This paper presents the main tenets of contrastive hierarchy theory, aka Modified Contrastive Specification or "Toronto School" phonology. I propose that the language learner's task is to arrive at a set of ordered contrastive features that account for the phonological patterning of the input language. I then show how contrastive features supplemented by post-phonological enhancement features contribute to synchronic (Tokyo Japanese) and diachronic (West Germanic) accounts of phonological patterns.

Keywords: phonological contrast, feature hierarchies, enhancement, Tokyo Japanese, West Germanic

1. Introduction

Contrastive hierarchy theory[1] (Dresher 2009) posits that contrastive features are computed hierarchically, and that only contrastive features are manipulated by the phonology. Additional features become available in the post-lexical component or later; an important class of such features are those that enhance the effects of contrastive features. I will briefly set out the main tenets of this theory in §2, and then illustrate how it applies to the synchronic phonology of Tokyo Japanese in §3. In §4, I show how an enhancement feature in West Germanic can become contrastive, and how "deep allophones" can exist in the lexical phonology.

2. Contrastive hierarchy theory

I have argued (Dresher 2009) that contrasts are computed hierarchically by ordered features that can be expressed as a branching tree. Branching trees are generated by what I call the Successive Division Algorithm (Dresher 2009:16–17), given informally in (1).

(1) The Successive Division Algorithm
     Assign contrastive features by successively dividing the inventory until every phoneme has been distinguished.

I assume that the ordering of features is language particular. Therefore, it is necessary to have criteria for selecting and ordering the features. Phonetics is important in that the selected features must be consistent with the phonetic properties of the phonemes. However, the contrastive specification of a phoneme can deviate from its surface phonetics. In some dialects of Inuktitut, for example, an underlying contrast between /i/ and /i/ is neutralized at the surface, with both /i/ and /i/ being realized as phonetic [i] (Compton and Dresher 2011). In this case, /i/ and /i/, which behave differently and have different effects on neighboring sounds, would be distinguished by a contrastive feature, even though their surface phonetics are identical.

As the above example shows, the way a sound *patterns* can override its phonetics (Sapir 1925). Thus, we consider as most fundamental that features should be selected and ordered so as to reflect the *phonological activity* in a language, where activity is defined as in (2) (adapted from Clements 2001:77).

(2) Phonological activity
     A feature can be said to be *active* if it plays a role in the phonological computation; that is, if it is required for the expression of phonological regularities in a language, including both static phonotactic patterns and patterns of alternation.

A second major tenet has been formulated by Hall (2007) as the Contrastivist Hypothesis:

(3) The Contrastivist Hypothesis
The phonological component of a language L operates only on those features which are necessary to distinguish the phonemes of L from one another.

That is, *only* contrastive features can be phonologically active. If this hypothesis is correct, then (4) follows as a corollary:

(4) Corollary to the Contrastivist Hypothesis
If a feature is phonologically active, then it must be contrastive.

Another assumption is that features are binary, and that every feature has a marked and unmarked value. I assume that markedness is language particular (Rice 2003; 2007) and accounts for asymmetries between the two values of a feature, where these exist. I will designate the marked value of a feature F as [F], and the unmarked value as [non-F]. I will refer to the two values together as [±F].

Unless a vowel is further specified by other contrastive features (originating in another vowel or in the consonants), it is made more specific only in a post-phonological component. Stevens et al. (1986) propose that feature contrasts can be *enhanced* by other features with similar acoustic effects (see also Keyser and Stevens 2006). Thus, the feature [back] on a non-low vowel can be enhanced by adding {round}, and [non-low] can be enhanced by {high}.[2] Enhancements are not universally necessary, however (Dyck 1995; Hall 2011).

Finally, the assumption that the contrastive feature hierarchy is innate makes it unnecessary to posit that individual features are innate. I assume that features must inevitably "emerge" in the course of language acquisition because it is the learner's task to arrive at a set of hierarchically ordered contrastive features. The contrastive hierarchy and Contrastivist Hypothesis together account for why phonological systems resemble each other in terms of representations, without requiring individual features to be innate (Dresher to appear a, b). On this view, the concept of a contrastive hierarchy is the glue that binds phonological representations and makes them appear similar from language to language.

3. Tokyo Japanese vowel features (Hirayama 2003)

Hirayama's (2003) analysis of Tokyo Japanese vowels illustrates a number of the principles set out in the previous section. Hirayama bases her analysis on patterns of activity, including epenthesis into loan words from English, vowel coalescence, affrication of consonants, and vowel devoicing.

3.1 Epenthesis into loan words from English

A vowel is inserted into a loan word from English that contains a consonant cluster or word-final consonant (Kubozono 2001). After most English consonants /u/ is inserted, as shown in (5). If /u/ is the default epenthetic vowel, we will assume, with Hirayama (2003), that it has no marked features, other things being equal.[3]

(5) Epenthetic /u/ after most English consonants

	English	Gloss	Japanese
a.	/paɪp/	'pipe'	/paipu̲/
b.	/bif/	'beef'	/biihu̲/
c.	/krɪsməs/	'Christmas'	/ku̲risumasu̲/
d.	/θrɪl/	'thrill'	/su̲riru̲/

The vowel /i/ is inserted after English /ʃ, tʃ, dʒ/ (6a–c) and, in older loans, after front /k/ (6d). Hirayama observes that /i/ is chosen so as to maintain the palatality of the preceding consonants, which presumably share a front feature with /i/. Hirayama (2003) calls this feature [coronal]; I will call it [front], but it amounts to the same thing.

(6) Epenthetic /i/ after English /ʃ, tʃ, dʒ/ and front /k/

	English	Gloss	Japanese	Phonetic
a.	/brʌʃ/	'brush'	/burasi/	[buraɕi]
b.	/bitʃ/	'beach'	/biiti/	[biːt͡ɕi]
c.	/dʒʌdʒ/	'judge'	/djaddi/	[d͡ʑaɟːʑi]
d.	/keɪk/	'cake'	/keikki/	[keeki]

An /o/ is inserted after English /t, d, h/ (7). Hirayama (2003) suggests that /u/ is not chosen because it would create allophones of the preceding consonants that would make them too far from the English sounds.

(7) Epenthetic /o/ after English /t, d, h/

	English	Gloss	Japanese	*Result before /u/
a.	/tɛnt/	'tent'	/teNto/	*[…t͡ɕu]
b.	/dræmə/	'drama'	/dorama/	*[d͡zu…]
c.	/hwaɪt/	'white'	/howaito/	*[ɸu…t͡ɕu]

Based on epenthesis, we conclude that [front] is marked in Japanese. We assume that /u/ is also not marked for height: Hirayama proposes that the height feature is [low], comprising /e, o, a/. I will call this feature [open], since the only vowels that are [non-open] are the high vowels. It remains to distinguish /o/ and /a/. I depart from Hirayama's analysis in this regard: I suppose that /a/ is more marked than /o/, because /o/ is epenthetic after /t, d, h/, not /a/. I will call this third feature [low].

We have seen no evidence that would decide the ordering of [±front] and [±open] in the hierarchy; either ordering would work. For concreteness, I will put [±front] first.[4] Then [±open] is ordered second and [±low] is ordered after [±open]. This gives the feature ordering [±front] > [±open] > [±low], where "[±F] > [±G]" indicates that feature [±F] is ordered before [±G]. A tree diagram of the vowel features of Tokyo Japanese is given in (8).

(8) Tokyo Japanese vowel feature hierarchy: [±front] > [±open] > [±low]

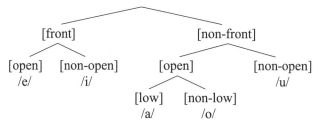

The terminal contrastive features for each vowel in (8) are given in (9). They give the desired markedness values with respect to the choice of epenthetic vowel: /u/ has no marked features, and is the default epenthetic vowel; /i/ is the least marked [front] vowel, when [front] is required; and /o/ is the next-least marked [non-front] vowel.

(9) Contrastive features for each Tokyo Japanese vowel

/i/	/e/	/a/	/o/	/u/
[front]	[front]	[non-front]	[non-front]	[non-front]
[non-open]	[open]	[open]	[open]	[non-open]
		[low]	[non-low]	

3.2 Vowel coalescence

Another process involving vowels is vowel coalescence, whereby two adjacent vowels combine to form one long vowel (Kubozono 1999, 2001; McCawley 1968); some examples are given in (10).

(10) Examples of vowel coalescence

	Underlying	Gloss	Surface	Coalescence pattern
a.	/osie+te/	'tell me'	*oseete*	/ie/ > [ee]
b.	/sugo+i/	'amazing'	*sugee*	/oi/ > [ee]
c.	/mazu+i/	'bad in taste'	*mazii*	/ui/ > [ii]
d.	/atarasi+ku/	'new'	*atarasjuu*	/iu/ > [uu]
e.	/uma+i/	'good'	*umee*	/ai/ > [ee]
f.	/omae/	'you'	*omee*	/ae/ > [ee]
g.	/taka+ku/	'tall, high'	*takoo*	/au/ > [oo]

Hirayama (2003) follows Causley (1999) in proposing that the resolution of vowel hiatus should reflect the feature specifications of the vowels involved. Specifically, all things being equal, it is the *marked* features that decide the quality of the resultant vowel, while unmarked features are inert in coalescence (see also St-Amand 2012 for a similar analysis of vowel coalescence in Québec French). In Japanese, markedness decides the *height* of the resulting vowel; the *place* is determined by the place of the rightmost vowel.

When /i/ coalesces with /e/ (10a), the result is [ee]. The place is taken from the second vowel, /e/; this yields [front] (11b). Height comes from marked features: in this case, the only marked height feature also comes from /e/, which contributes [open] (11c). The result is a vowel that is [front, open], which yields [ee].

(11) Coalescence of /ie/ > [ee]

a.	Underlying segments	V1 = /i/	V2 = /e/
	Features	[front, non-open]	[front, open]
b.	Place from V2	[front]	
c.	Height: marked features	[front, open]	= [ee]

When /o/ coalesces with /i/ (10b), the result is again [ee]. The place is taken from /i/, yielding [front]. The only other marked feature is [open], from both /o/ and /e/; the result is [front, open] = [ee].

When /u/ coalesces with /i/ (10c), the result is [ii]. The only marked feature is [front], on /i/. Since /i/ is the second vowel, its place feature is transferred to the resultant vowel (12b). There are no marked height features in either /u/ or /i/; but there is no Japanese vowel that is just [front]. Therefore, to achieve an interpretable representation, we must add the default height (12c), which is [non-open], resulting in [ii].

(12) Coalescence of /ui/ > [ii]

a.	Underlying segments	V1 = /u/	V2 = /i/
	Features	[non-front, non-open]	[front, non-open]
b.	Place from V2	[front]	
c.	Add default height	[front, non-open]	= [ii]

When /i/ coalesces with /u/ (10d), the result is [uu]. The place is taken from /u/, yielding [non-front]. As there are no more marked features, the default height [non-open] is added as in (12), now yielding [uu].

When /a/ coalesces with /i/ (10e), the result is [ee]. The place is taken from V2, /i/, giving [front] (13b). /a/ has two marked height features, [open] and [low]. However, the combination [front, open, low] does not exist in Japanese, and cannot be created by coalescence.

Therefore, one of [open] or [low] must be deleted. Since [low] depends on [open], it is deleted (13d); the result is [front, open] = [ee]. The coalescence of /a/ with /e/ (10f) is similar.

(13) Coalescence of /ai/ > [ee]

		V1 = /a/	V2 = /i/	
a.	Underlying segments			
	Features	[non-front, open, low]	[front, non-open]	
b.	Place from V2	[front]		
c.	Height: marked features	[front, open, low]		*(ill-formed)*
d.	Delete [low]	[front, open]		= [ee]

When /a/ coalesces with /u/ (10g), the result is [oo]. As Hirayama (2003) points out, there is a problem here. The place feature, [non-front], comes from /u/, which is correct. However, /a/ contributes the marked features [open] and [low]. The result is a vowel specified [non-front, open, low], that is, *[aa], which is incorrect.

In order to obtain [oo], we need to add a feature to /u/ that /a/ does not have; Hirayama (2003) suggests [peripheral], defined by Rice (2002) as dorsality or labiality or both. However, the only way we can add more vowel features is by enhancement or by other post-lexical processes. Hirayama (2003) argues that vowel coalescence does in fact occur in the post-lexical component (Pulleyblank 1983; P. Kiparsky 1985). The reason is that vowel coalescence in Japanese is variable and depends on style differences. According to Lombardi (1996), an optional process that depends on style and speed is post-lexical (or later).

Following Hirayama's (2003) account, I will suppose that vowels that are not [low] enhance their [non-front] feature with another place feature. Rather than {peripheral}, I will call it {back}. This enhancement does not apply to [low] vowels, hence it does not apply to /a/. I assume also that high vowels enhance [non-open] with {high}. Adding these enhancement features to the representations in (9) gives us the post-lexical representations in (14).

(14) Post-lexical features for each Tokyo Japanese vowel

/i/	/e/	/a/	/o/	/u/
[front]	[front]	[non-front]	[non-front]	[non-front]
			{back}	{back}
[non-open]	[open]	[open]	[open]	[non-open]
		[low]	[non-low]	
{high}				{high}

Returning to the coalescence of /a/ + /u/ to /oo/, once we add the enhancement features (15a), we transfer [non-front] and {back}, the place features of /u/ (15b).[5] There are three marked height features (counting enhancement features as marked): [open] and [low] from /a/, and {high} from /u/ (15c). The features [low] and {high} cancel each other out (or alternatively, are not compatible with the features {back} and [open]); we are left with [non-front], {back} and [open], which is ill-formed, but can be remedied by adding the unmarked [non-low] (15e), yielding [oo].

(15) Post-lexical coalescence of /au/ > [oo]

		V1 = /a/	V2 = /u/	
a.	Underlying segments			
	Contrastive features	[non-front, open, low]	[non-front, non-open]	
	Enhancement features		{back, high}	
b.	Place from V2	[non-front], {back}		
c.	Add marked height features	[non-front], {back}, [open], [low], {high}		
d.	Delete [low] and {high}	[non-front], {back}, [open]		*(ill-formed)*
e.	Add default height	[non-front], {back}, [open], [non-low]		= [oo]

3.3 Affrication and high vowel devoicing

Two processes that involve the high vowels /i/ and /u/ are affrication of coronal consonants and high vowel devoicing. Coronal plosives /t, d/ are affricated before high vowels /i, u/ (16), and the high vowels /i, u/ devoice between voiceless obstruents (17) (Hirayama 2003, citing Kubozono 1999; Sugito 1997; Vance 1987; see also Hirayama 2009).

(16) Affrication of /t, d/ before the high vowels /i, u/

  a.   /t, d/ ⟶ palatal affricate   [c͡ɕ, ɟ͡ʑ] / ____ *i, j*
  b.   /t, d/ ⟶ alveolar affricate [t͡s, d͡z] / ____ *u*
  c.   /t, d/ ⟶ dental plosive   [t̪, d̪] / ____ elsewhere (*e, a, o*)

(17) Devoicing of high vowels /i, u/ between voiceless obstruents

/i, u/ ⟶ [–voice] [i̥, u̥] /   C   ____   C   [ku̥tsu̥ɕi̥ta] 'sock(s)'
           [vl, obst]   [vl, obst]

Hirayama (2003) proposes that these processes are also postlexical, because they create allophones rather than change one phoneme into another. Hirayama (2009) points out that high vowel devoicing shows other characteristics of post-lexical rules: it applies across a word boundary, it has no exceptions, its outputs are gradient, and it is not categorical. Therefore, as these rules are post-lexical, they are able to refer to the enhancement feature {high}, which picks out /i/ and /u/.[6]

Without disputing that these rules apply post-lexically in Japanese, I observe that it is possible to have rules that create allophones in the lexical (contrastive) phonology. The West Germanic pre-history of Old English and Old High German gives an example of this, as well as illustrating how an enhancement feature can become contrastive.

4. Contrastive hierarchies in diachronic phonology: West Germanic *i*-umlaut[7]

At a certain time, the West Germanic vowel system had five short and five long vowels (Antonsen 1965; Ringe and Taylor 2014:106). I have argued (Dresher 2017) that at this stage West Germanic had the vowel feature hierarchy [±low] > [±front] > [±high], as shown in (18).[8] The feature [round] is *not* contrastive at this point.

(18) West Germanic vowel feature hierarchy 1: [±low] > [±front] > [±high]

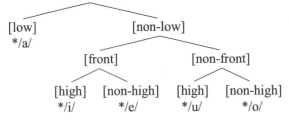

The rule of *i*-umlaut began in early Germanic as a phonetic process that created fronted allophones of the back vowels when */i(ː)/ or */j/ followed. Given our analysis of the West Germanic vowel system, the result of fronting */u, o/ in the contrastive phonology would be to simply make them identical to */i, e/. But *i*-umlaut crucially preserves the rounded nature of the fronted vowels: */u, o/ become *[y, ø], respectively. Therefore, the enhancement feature {round} must be in play at the point that */u, o/ are fronted. This conclusion is consistent with the assumption of many commentators, beginning with V. Kiparsky (1932) and Twaddell (1938), that *i*-umlaut began as a late phonetic (or post-lexical) rule.

There is evidence, however, that over time *i*-umlaut became a lexical rule, even while it was still creating fronted allophones of the vowels */u/ and */o/ (Janda 2003; P. Kiparsky

2015). I posit that at a certain stage learners began to conclude that [round] was a contrastive vowel feature, along with [front] and [high]. A new feature hierarchy can be constructed in which [round] is contrastive over the non-front vowels; [low] is now demoted (19).

(19) West Germanic vowel feature hierarchy 2: [±front] > [±round] > [±high]

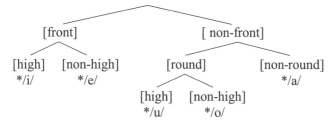

Now, changing the [non-front, round] vowels to [front] results in new front rounded vowels which begin as allophones of */u, o/. Although they are allophones, they can arise in the contrastive phonology because they consist only of contrastive features. They are thus what Moulton (2003) calls "deep allophones," referring to the Old English voiced fricatives which also arise early in the lexical phonology. Deep allophones are possible because contrastive features are not all necessarily unpredictable in a hierarchical approach.

Notes

* This paper is based on portions of a talk presented at the Phonological Society of Japan Phonology Forum, held at the Tokyo Metropolitan University, Minami-Osawa Campus, August 2017. I would like to thank the organizers for inviting me, and Forum participants for their comments and questions. Special thanks to Manami Hirayama for her analysis of the Tokyo Japanese vowel system and for her help with arrangements. Parts of the talk that could not be included here for reasons of space will appear in Dresher (to appear a; b). See also the publications and talks listed at http://homes.chass.utoronto.ca/~dresher/publications.html.

[1] The theory has gone under various names: Modified Contrastive Specification (Avery and Rice 1989; Dresher et al. 1994), Contrast and Enhancement Theory (Hall 2011), or "Toronto School" phonology. See Dresher (2015) for a more complete summary of the theory.

[2] I follow Purnell and Raimy (2015) in indicating enhancement features in curly brackets.

[3] One can imagine that epenthetic vowels in some languages must have certain marked features; however, I assume that we require positive evidence that this is the case.

[4] I follow Trubetzkoy (1939:92) in positing the front/back contrast as the main one in Japanese vowels.

[5] It is not clear whether markedness continues to play a role once enhancement features are added, and how enhancement features fit in. I will assume here that it does, and that enhancement features are considered to be marked.

[6] Note that [non-open] also applies only to high vowels. I assume that phonology can refer to unmarked features.

[7] See Dresher (2017) for more detailed discussion and references of the material in this section.

[8] I will henceforth disregard vowel length, as the short and long vowel systems were symmetrical at this time.

References

Antonsen, Elmer H. 1965. On defining stages in prehistoric Germanic. *Language* 41.19–36.

Avery, Peter and Keren Rice. 1989. Segment structure and coronal underspecification. *Phonology* 6.179–200.

Causley, Trisha Kathleen. 1999. *Complexity and markedness in Optimality Theory*. Ph.D. dissertation, University of Toronto.

Clements, G. N. 2001. Representational economy in constraint-based phonology. *Distinctive feature theory*, ed. by T. Alan Hall, 71–146. Berlin: Mouton de Gruyter.

Compton, Richard and B. Elan Dresher. 2011. Palatalization and "strong *i*" across Inuit dialects. *Canadian Journal of Linguistics/ Revue canadienne de linguistique* 56.203–228.

Dresher, B. Elan. 2009. *The contrastive hierarchy in phonology*. Cambridge: Cambridge University Press.

Dresher, B. Elan. 2015. Contrastive hierarchy theory: An overview. The combined slides (in two parts) presented at UConn and UMass, Amherst. http://homes.chass.utoronto.ca/~dresher/talks/Combined_UConn-UMass_slides-PART1.pdf and -PART2.pdf. Last accessed Sept. 16, 2017.

Dresher, B. Elan. 2017. Contrastive feature hierarchies in Old English diachronic phonology. *Transactions of the Philological Society*, doi:10.1111/1467-968X.12105.

Dresher, B. Elan. To appear a. Contrastive feature hierarchies in phonology: Variation and universality. *Variable properties: Their nature and acquisition* (*Proceedings of GURT 2017*), ed. by David W. Lightfoot. Washington, DC: Georgetown University Press.

Dresher, B. Elan. To appear b. Contrastive hierarchy theory and the nature of features. *WCCFL 35: Proceedings of the 35th West Coast Conference on Formal Linguistics, April 2017*, ed. by Dennis Storoshenko. Somerville, MA: Cascadilla Proceedings Project.

Dresher, B. Elan, Glyne L. Piggott and Keren Rice. 1994. Contrast in phonology: Overview. *Toronto Working Papers in Linguistics* 13(1).iii–xvii.

Dyck, Carrie. 1995. *Constraining the phonology-phonetics interface, with exemplification from Spanish and Italian dialects*. Ph.D. dissertation, University of Toronto.

Hall, Daniel Currie. 2007. *The role and representation of contrast in phonological theory*. Ph.D. dissertation, University of Toronto.

Hall, Daniel Currie. 2011. Phonological contrast and its phonetic enhancement: Dispersedness without dispersion. *Phonology* 28.1–54.

Hirayama, Manami. 2003. Contrast in Japanese vowels. *Toronto Working Papers in Linguistics* 20.115–132.

Hirayama, Manami. 2009. *Postlexical prosodic structure and vowel devoicing in Japanese*. Ph.D. dissertation, University of Toronto.

Janda, Richard D. 2003. "Phonologization" as the start of dephoneticization – or, on sound change and its aftermath: Of extension, generalization, lexicalization, and morphologization. *The handbook of historical linguistics*, ed. by Brian D. Joseph and Richard D. Janda, 401–422. Oxford: Blackwell.

Keyser, Samuel Jay and Kenneth N. Stevens. 2006. Enhancement and overlap in the speech chain. *Language* 82.33–63.

Kiparsky, Paul. 1985. Some consequences of lexical phonology. *Phonology Yearbook* 2.85–138.

Kiparsky, Paul. 2015. Phonologization. *The handbook of historical phonology*, ed. by Patrick Honeybone and Joseph Salmons, 563–579. Oxford: Oxford University Press.

Kiparsky, Valentin. 1932. Johdatusta fonologiaan. *Virittäjä* 36.230–250.

Kubozono, Haruo. 1999. *Nihon-go no onsei [The sounds of Japanese]*. Tokyo: Iwanami Shoten.

Kubozono, Haruo. 2001. Epenthetic vowels and accent in Japanese: Facts and paradoxes. *Issues in Japanese phonology and morphology*, ed. by Jeroen van de Weijer and Tetsuo Nishihara, 111–140. Berlin: Mouton de Gruyter.

Lombardi, Linda. 1996. Postlexical rules and the status of privative features. *Phonology* 13.1–38.

McCawley, James D. 1968. *The phonological component of a grammar of Japanese*. The Hague: Mouton.

Moulton, Keir. 2003. Deep allophones in the Old English laryngeal system. *Toronto Working Papers in Linguistics* 20.157–173.

Pulleyblank, Douglas. 1983. *Tone in Lexical Phonology*. Dordrecht: D. Reidel.

Purnell, Thomas and Eric Raimy. 2015. Distinctive features, levels of representation and historical phonology. *The handbook of historical phonology*, ed. by Patrick Honeybone and Joseph Salmons, 522–544. Oxford: Oxford University Press.

Rice, Keren. 2002. Vowel place contrasts. *Language universals and variation*, ed. by Mengistu Amberber and Peter Collins, 239–269. Westport, CT & London: Praeger.

Rice, Keren. 2003. Featural markedness in phonology: Variation. *The second Glot International state-of-the-article book: The latest in linguistics*, ed. by Lisa Cheng and Rint Sybesma, 387–427. Berlin: Mouton de Gruyter.

Rice, Keren. 2007. Markedness in phonology. *The Cambridge handbook of phonology*, ed. by Paul de Lacy, 79–97. Cambridge: Cambridge University Press.

Ringe, Donald and Ann Taylor. 2014. *A linguistic history of English. Volume 2: The development of Old English*. Oxford: Oxford University Press.

Sapir, Edward. 1925. Sound patterns in language. *Language* 1.37–51.

St-Amand, Anne. 2012. *Hiatus and hiatus resolution in Québécois French*. Ph.D. dissertation, University of Toronto.

Stevens, Kenneth N., Samuel Jay Keyser and Haruko Kawasaki. 1986. Toward a phonetic and phonological theory of redundant features. *Symposium on invariance and variability of speech processes*, ed. by Joseph S. Perkell and Dennis H. Klatt, 432–469. Hillsdale, NJ: Lawrence Erlbaum.

Sugito, Miyoko. 1997. *Onsei hakee wa kataru [Sound waves speak]*, Volume 4 of *Nihongo onsei no kenkyu [Study of Japanese Sounds]*. Osaka: Izumi Syoin.

Trubetzkoy, N. S. 1939. *Grundzüge der Phonologie*. Göttingen: Vandenhoek & Ruprecht.

Twaddell, W. Freeman. 1938. A note on Old High German umlaut. *Monatshefte für deutschen Unterricht* 30. 177–181.

Vance, Timothy J. 1987. *An introduction to Japanese phonology*. Albany: State University of New York Press.

Effect of L1 Influence and L2 Proficiency
on the Perception and Production of Foreign Sounds

Hinako Masuda
Seikei University

ABSTRACT. This paper provides an overview of one production and four perception experiments on non-native speech processing by Japanese learners of English, and explores the effect of non-native language proficiency as well as traces of first language influence. Experiment 1 investigates the degree of vowel epenthesis in the production of consonant clusters, Experiment 2 investigates the perception of English consonants in background noise, Experiment 3 investigates the perception of English consonants in reverberation and noise+reverberation, Experiment 4 investigates the effectiveness of perceptual training of English consonants in background noise, and Experiment 5 investigates the role of predictability in word identification in background noise. All in all, listeners' proficiency in the non-native language affected both perception and production; however, traces of first language influence were observed in the consonant voicing patterns in production and the confusion patterns in perception.

Keywords: L2 production, L2 perception, non-native, background noise, reverberation, proficiency

1. Introduction

Unlike first language (L1) acquisition, learning a new language as second language (L2) learners can be challenging, because it usually begins after one has been exposed to their L1. Because L2 learners have varying linguistic backgrounds, factors such as age of learning the second language, experience of residing abroad, and overall L2 proficiency play important roles. This paper provides an overview of the author's research concerning the effect of L2 proficiency and L1 influence on L2 perception and production by introducing five experiments: 1) production of consonant clusters (Masuda and Arai 2010), 2) perception of English consonants in background noise (Masuda *et al.* 2015), 3) perception of English consonants in reverberation and noise+reverberation (Masuda 2016), 4) perceptual training of English consonants in background noise (Masuda 2016), and 5) role of predictability in word identification in background noise (Masuda, to appear).

L2 processing difficulties are observed in both perceptual and production domains, and at both segmental and suprasegmental levels. For example, a typical production error caused by suprasegmental differences in Japanese and English is the native Japanese speakers' insertion of epenthetic vowels. Since Japanese syllables almost always end with a vowel with exceptions of nasals and geminates, consonant clusters are illegal in Japanese phonotactics. Therefore, Japanese are likely to insert [u] after a consonant except after [t, d] and [ʧ, ʤ], in which case [o] and [i] are inserted, respectively, to avoid open syllables (e.g. "book" [bukku̲], "street" [su̲tori̲to̲]) (Kubozono 1999).

Difficulties are also observed at the segmental level. L2 learning theories (e.g. Best 1995) suggest that we listen to sounds of a new language based on the knowledge of our L1. L2 perception requires the listener's close attention to the similarity and dissimilarity of the target sound to the closest sound in their L1 phonology (Best 1995). One of the well-known example of perceptual difficulty is the discrimination of English phonemes /r/ and /l/ (e.g. Miyawaki *et al.* 1975; Logan *et al.* 1991), which is caused by the differences in the inventories of Japanese and English phonemes. The two English liquid phonemes are thus often, though not symmetrically, perceptually assimilated into a single Japanese /r/ (e.g. Sheldon and Strange 1982; Aoyama *et al.* 2004; Masuda *et al.* 2015).

Although perceiving non-native sounds seems like a great obstacle, numerous studies have also shown that non-native listeners perform surprisingly well in tasks that involve low-level (e.g. singleton consonants and vowels) (e.g. Nabelek and Donahue 1984; Takata and Nabelek 1990; Cutler *et al.* 2008) and high-level processing (e.g. words) (e.g. Rogers *et al.* 2006; Jin and Liu 2012), if the sounds are presented to the listeners in a quiet environment. However, when learners are presented with non-native sounds in background noise and/or reverberation, accurate perception becomes challenging for most, if not all, non-native listeners regardless of their proficiency (e.g. Nabelek and Donahue 1984; Florentine 1985; Takata and Nabelek 1990; Mayo *et al.* 1997; Lecumberri and Cooke 2006; Rogers *et al.* 2006; Cutler *et al.* 2008; Jin and Liu 2012; Masuda 2016). A question arises then, whether learners can finely adjust their categories within their phonological space to acquire non-native sounds. Perceptual training on non-native listeners to identify non-native sounds have been attempted for several decades (e.g. Logan *et al.* 1991; Lively *et al.* 1993; Bradlow *et al.* 1997), and its effectiveness has been reported, at least for Japanese listeners' identification of English /r/ and /l/. However, these perceptual trainings were conducted in quiet listening environments, and the effectiveness of perceptual training in a noisy listening environment has not fully been investigated. An interesting question is, therefore, does perceptual training in adverse listening environments aid in increased identification accuracy?

Another important factor to consider in perceptual experiments is the nature of the stimuli. Observing perceptual patterns of singleton consonants in a non-word context is beneficial in detecting how listeners use acoustical information. However, this method does not fully comprehend how listeners are perceiving speech in real life – in real life communication we use not only acoustical information but contextual information. The final question addressed in this paper is the non-native listeners' use of predictability in word identification; are non-native listeners able to use contextual information to accurately identify words in sentences, even if the sounds are distorted by background noise?

2. Experiments
2.1 Experiment 1: Production of consonant clusters [Masuda and Arai, 2010]
Vowel epenthesis is a common, well-known error made by Japanese learners of English. However, how L2 proficiency influences epenthesis has not been fully investigated. The purpose of Experiment 1 is to investigate the impact of L2 proficiency and phonetic context (consonant voicing) on the production of non-native consonant clusters.

A total of 39 Japanese learners of English participated, of which 17 were advanced-level learners of English, and 22 were intermediate level learners. Ten native American English speakers also participated as the control group. Participants were asked to produce 9 pseudo-words that contained non-native consonant clusters (abge, egdo, ibdo, akmo, ashmi, okna, ekshi, ishto, oshat) (Dupoux *et al.* 1999). Acoustical analysis was performed on 441 utterances (49 participants x 9 words) using Praat (2008). Utterances were categorized into one of the three categories according to the degree of epenthesis: full epenthesis, partial epenthesis, and no epenthesis (see Masuda and Arai (2010) for detailed criteria).

Chi-square tests showed significant differences in the degree of vowel epenthesis produced by advanced and intermediate level learners ($p<0.001$) as well as advanced level learners and English speakers ($p<0.01$). When averaged out among all nine words, the highest percentage of the degree of epenthesis was full epenthesis for intermediate level learners, partial epenthesis for advanced level learners, and no epenthesis for English speakers. This result shows that learners with higher proficiency were able to pronounce consonant clusters with less degree of epenthesis, i.e. more native-like, compared to those with lower proficiency.

The consonant voicing combinations also had an effect. In C[+voice]-C[+voice] and C[-voice]-C[+voice], intermediate level learners inserted full vowels, whereas a high proportion of utterances by advanced level learners and English speakers had no vowels in C[+voice]-C[+voice]. In C[-voice]-C[+voice], approximately 66% of English speakers did not insert vowels and 96% of advanced level learners inserted partial vowels. In C[-voice]-C[-voice], both intermediate and advanced level learners inserted partial vowel the most, whereas English speakers still did not insert any vowels. These results indicate that voiced consonants are more likely to prompt epenthesis in intermediate level learners compared to advanced level learners, but the presence of voiceless consonants reduces the degree of epenthesis in Japanese speakers, both intermediate and advanced. The latter was also observed in English speakers, though not as robust.

The effect of consonant voicing on the degree of epenthesis may be the result of the devoicing phenomenon in Japanese. Vowel devoicing in Japanese is common in /i/ and /u/, especially between voiceless consonants, or after a voiceless consonant followed by a pause (Vance 2008). In addition, Arai *et al.* (2007) found that vowel devoicing is also common in spontaneous Japanese speech in a more non-typical devoicing context, such as high vowels preceded by a voiceless consonant and followed by a voiced consonant. These two studies show that the presence of voiceless consonants in consonant clusters can reduce the degree of epenthesis – a result we see in both advanced and intermediate level leaners in Experiment 1.

Another interesting point worth mentioning is the variations observed in the articulation of the first consonant in the C[+voice]-C[+voice] cluster. In English, stop consonants such as /b/ and /g/ are sometimes reduced and devoiced to /b̥/ and /g̊/ (Jones 1989), whereas they are sometimes reduced and spirantized to, for example, /β/ and /ɣ̊/, in Japanese (Kawakami 1977; Arai *et al.* 2007). The acoustical analyses of the first consonant in the C[+voice]-C[+voice] clusters showed that 45% of intermediate level learners spirantized them, whereas 33% of advanced level learners devoiced them, supposedly triggered by Japanese and English consonant reduction tendencies.

2.2 Experiment 2: Perception of English consonants in noise [Masuda *et al.* 2015]

Perception of non-native speech in background noise has been extensively studied (see Lecumberri *et al.* (2010) for review), and it is clear that the presence of background noise hinders accurate perception in all listeners, both native and non-native. It is obviously more challenging for non-native listeners, however, as they have less exposure and experience perceiving non-native speech in noise compared to native listeners. The purpose of Experiment 2 is to investigate how learners' proficiency affects identification of non-native consonants in background noise.

A total of 23 Japanese learners of English and 12 American English listeners participated in a consonant identification task. The 23 American English consonants [p b t d k g tʃ dʒ m n f v θ ð s z ʃ ʒ h ɹ j w l] were embedded in [aCa] context to form non-words (e.g. [ata]). The sounds were presented to the listeners in 1) noisy listening environments at Signal-to-Noise Ratios (SNR) of 10 dB, 5 dB, and 0 dB (in randomized order), and 2) quiet listening environment. Multispeaker babble noise (Varga and Steeneken 1993) was selected as background noise, because a similar experiment in a previous study by Lecumberri and Cooke (2006) showed that multispeaker babble noise showed the most salient differences between non-native and native listeners among other types of noise. The computer program Praat was used to run the experiment and to collect responses. All participants were given 23 practice trials before proceeding to the main set which consisted of 460 trials (23 consonants x 4 listening conditions x 5 repetitions). Each stimulus was presented only once, and the participants were asked to identify the consonant they heard from a list of 23 consonants on the experimental interface (e.g. B as in Be, D as in Do, G as in Go, etc.).

The results showed that there was no significant difference between the two groups of listeners in this particular set of participants. However, there was a significant effect of learners' proficiency on the identification rates. The learners' TOEIC® scores were used as an objective measure to look at learners' English proficiency. The correlation (identification and proficiency) coefficient values and p-values in quiet, SNR = 10 dB, 5 dB, and 0 dB were $r=0.87$ ($p<0.001$), $r=0.56$ ($p<0.05$), $r=0.66$ ($p<0.01$), and $r=0.38$ (*n.s.*), respectively. All values showed positive correlations with the learners' TOEIC® scores, with the one in the quiet environment being the strongest and SNR = 0 dB being the weakest. These results indicate that learners with higher TOEIC® scores were able to accurately identify English consonants significantly higher in a quiet environment than those with lower TOEIC® scores, but having higher TOEIC® scores was not beneficial in the most noisy environment.

Further analyses were performed to look closer into the listeners' confusion patterns. The learners were separated into two groups according to their TOEIC® scores: those with scores over 800 (N=15) were grouped as advanced level learners, and those with scores below 800 (N=8) were grouped as intermediate level learners. One of the consonants that exhibited prominent effect of proficiency was the English lateral approximant /l/. The Japanese listeners' difficulty in accurately identifying English /l/ has been documented in previous research (e.g. Sheldon and Strange 1982; Aoyama *et al.* 2004), and the identification rates and confusion patterns obtained from the present experiment was no exception. Specifically, the accurate identification rates of /l/ in the quiet environment by English and advanced level listeners were over 90% and 75%, respectively, whereas intermediate level listeners achieved 48%. As the listening environment became more adverse, the differences between the groups also became larger; in SNR = 0 dB, accuracy rates were 60% (Eng), 30.8% (adv), and 16% (inter). We clearly see a decrease in accuracy rates, in both quiet and noisy environments, as proficiency level becomes lower. Regarding confusion patterns of /l/, a strong influence of the learners' first language (Japanese) was observed. While the most common confusion pattern by English listeners in SNR = 0 dB was /l/ to /m/, both advanced and intermediate level listeners shared the same pattern of confusing /l/ as /ɹ/ and /w/ where we can clearly see the influence from the first language.

2.3 Experiment 3: Perception of English consonants in reverberation [Masuda, 2016a]

Listeners are often exposed to not just background noise but also reverberation and the two combined together in daily life, for example in classroom settings, train stations, airports, etc. However, the impact of reverberation on non-native speech perception has not been as extensively researched as background noise. We do know, from limited literature, that reverberation is known to also hinder speech perception, and that the difficulty is larger for non-native listeners (e.g. Nabelek and Donahue 1984; Takata and Nabelek 1990). The purpose of Experiment 3 is to investigate how learners' proficiency affects identification of non-native consonants in reverberation as well as background noise+reverberation.

A total of 22 Japanese learners of English and 23 American English listeners participated in a consonant identification task. The 23 American English consonants (same as Experiment 2) were embedded in "You are about to hear [aCa]" context. The sounds were presented to the listeners in 1) reverberation at Reverberation Times (RT) at 0.78 seconds, 1.12 seconds, and 1.43 seconds (in randomized order), 2) multispeaker babble noise (SNR = 10 dB) + reverberation (RT = 0.78s), and 3) quiet environment, in that order. The computer program Praat was used to run the experiment and to collect responses. All participants were given 23 practice trials before proceeding to the main set which consisted of 575 trials (23 consonants x 5 listening conditions x 5 repetitions). Each stimulus was presented only once, and the participants were asked to identify the consonant they heard from a list of 23 consonants on the same experimental interface used in Experiment 2.

The results showed that although English listeners always outperformed the Japanese listeners, there was no significant difference between the two groups. Further analysis was performed on a subset of 11 consonants [f dʒ ʒ l ɹ s ʃ θ ð v z] that are often difficult for Japanese listeners to identify. In this subset, there was a significant difference between the two language groups. However, there was no significant interaction between language groups and listening environments, suggesting that non-native disadvantage was not accentuated by the degrading listening environment. Table 1 shows the correlation coefficient r and p-values between accurate identification rates and 1) Japanese listeners' TOEIC® scores and 2) length of residence in English-speaking countries. Both Japanese listeners' TOEIC® scores and length of residence in English-speaking countries had positive correlations with the accurate identification of the 11 subset consonants in all environments, suggesting that higher TOEIC® scores and longer length of residence led to higher identification rates not only in quiet but also reverberant and noisy+reverberant environments.

	Quiet	RT=0.78s	RT=1.12s	RT=1.43s	Noise+Rev
TOEIC	r=0.58, p=0.004	r=0.45, p=0.03	r=0.64, p=0.001	r=0.62, p=0.001	r=0.58, p=0.004
LOR	r=0.39, p=0.06	r=0.43, p=0.04	r=0.52, p=0.01	r=0.41, p=0.05	r=0.44, p=0.03

Table 1 *Correlation coefficient r and p-values between accuracy and (1) Japanese listeners'*
TOEIC® scores and (2) length of residence (LOR) in English-speaking countries

Japanese listeners were further divided into two groups according to their TOEIC® scores: listeners with TOEIC® scores higher than 700 were labeled as advanced, and those below 620 were labeled as intermediate level listeners. Regarding the confusion patterns, intermediate level listeners achieved 70% in the identification of /l/ and misperceived it as /r/ by 28.3% even in the quiet environment, whereas both English and advanced level listeners achieved 98.3% and 96%, respectively. In the noisy+reverberant environment, intermediate level listeners' accurate identification of /l/ decreased to 33.3%, misperceiving it as /r/ by 28.3%, as /w/ by 15% and as /m/ by 10%, advanced level listeners achieved 48%, misperceiving it as /r/ by 24%, as /w/ by 16%, and 0% as /m/, and English listeners achieved 64.2%, misperceiving it as /m/ by 16.7%, as /w/ by 8.3%, and as /r/ by 5.8%. Although the three groups show similar confusion patterns, the proportion of misperceiving /l/ as /r/ and /w/ demonstrated robustness particular to Japanese listeners.

2.4 Experiment 4: Perceptual training of English consonants in noise (Preliminary) (Masuda 2016b)

The negative impact that adverse listening environments have on speech perception is decisive. This brings us to the next question: can listeners be trained to accurately identify consonants in such environments? The purpose of Experiment 4 is to investigate whether perceptual training in noisy environment increases consonant identification accuracy in noise.

A total of 13 Japanese learners of English participated in the training task. The target sounds were 13 American English fricatives and approximants / f h ʒ l ɹ s ʃ θ ð v w j z/ embedded in the carrier phrase "You are about to hear [aCa] on the tape again." where one of the 13 consonants were inserted in C (e.g. /afa/). The stimuli were presented to the listeners in two listening environments: in multispeaker babble noise at SNR 10dB and quiet environments. The participants were instructed to listen to the stimuli, and to choose the consonant that they heard from a choice of 23 American English consonants /b ʧ d f g h ʤ ʒ k l m n p ɹ s ʃ t θ ð v w j z/. The computer program TP (Rauber *et al.* 2012) was used to run the experiment and to collect responses.

The experiment consisted of three parts: pre-test, training sessions, and post-test. The pre- and post- tests were identical. All participants completed 20 practice trials (10 in multispeaker babble noise at SNR 0dB and 10 in quiet environment), before proceeding with the main trials of the pre-test. The pre-test consisted of 260 trials; 130 trials in multispeaker babble noise at SNR 0dB and 130 trials in quiet environment, in that order. After the pre-test, participants were instructed to participate in five training sessions. Each training session consisted of 130 trials in multispeaker babble noise at SNR 0dB. Similarly to the pre-test, participants were presented with the sentence "You are about to hear [aCa] on the tape again." and were asked to choose the consonant they heard from the list of 23 choices. All participants participated in the post-test within one to two weeks after completing the training sessions.

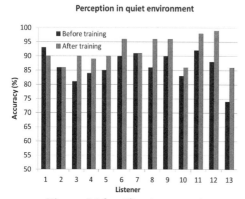

***Figure 1** Identification rates in quiet environment*

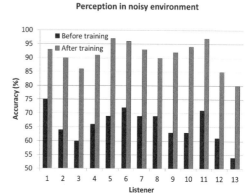

***Figure 2** Identification rates in noise*

The participants' correct identification rates of pre- and post-tests were compared to examine whether the training sessions in noise improved consonant identification in noise and quiet environments. Figures 1 and 2 show the improvement of identification rates in quiet and background noise, respectively. All participants' identification rates improved after the training sessions in both quiet and noise, except for Participant 1 in quiet environment. Average identification rates increased from approximately 86% to 91% in the quiet environment and from approximately 65% to 91% in background noise after participating in the training sessions. Repeated measures Analysis of Variance found significant differences between identification rates and listening condition ($F[1,37]=175.2$, $p<0.0001$) and identification rates and training ($F[1,37]=273.5$, $p<0.0001$), i.e. listeners performed significantly worse in noise compared to quiet environment, and identification rates were significantly higher after participating in the training sessions in both quiet and noise.

2.5 Experiment 5: Role of predictability in word identification in noise (to appear, Masuda 2017)

Although focusing on singleton consonants in non-words is an effective and efficient way to observe the listeners' perceptual characteristics, testing perception in real-word context is also important, as that is the way we perceive sounds when we communicate. The purpose of Experiment 5 is to investigate whether non-native listeners can make use of predictability in word identification in noise.

A total of 17 Japanese learners of English participated in the perception experiment. The stimuli consisted of 140 sentences (70 words * 2 predictability types) which were formed based on the Speech in Noise Test (SPIN) (Kalilow and Stevens 1977). One hundred sentences were presented in multispeaker babble noise at SNR 5 dB and 0 dB, and 40 sentences were presented in a quiet listening environment. The target word was always the last word of the sentence, and was always monosyllabic. Half of the sentences in each listening environment (50 in noise and 20 in quiet) were contextually predictable, and the remaining half were contextually unpredictable. The target words in noise and quiet listening environments were different. The experiment was run on the computer software Praat. A word identification task was designed, in which participants listened to the stimulus through headphones and wrote down the target word on the answer sheet provided by the experimenter.

Figure 3 shows the average accuracy rates in each listening condition (quiet/noisy) and predictability type (high/low). Predictable words in quiet condition had the highest accuracy rate at 80.9%, and unpredictable words in noisy condition had the lowest accuracy rate at 40.1%. Analysis of variance (ANOVA) was performed to investigate the effect of listening conditions and predictability types on accuracy. There were significant main effects in listening condition ($F(2, 48)=32.72$, $p<0.01$) and predictability type ($F(1, 32)=22.7$, $p<0.01$), and a significant interaction between the two factors ($F(3, 67)=29.44$, $p<0.01$).

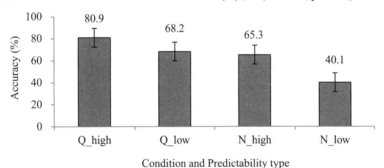

Figure 3 *Average accuracy rates (%) in each listening condition and predictability type*

Post-hoc comparisons by the Tukey-Kramer test showed significant differences in Q_high/N_high, Q_high/N_low, Q_low/N_low, and N_high/N_low ($p<0.01$), and Q_high/Q_low ($p<0.05$), but not in Q_low/N_high. These results illustrate that 1) learners have difficulty with accurate perception in noise even with predictable words, 2) learners have most difficulty with perceiving unpredictable words in noise, 3) accurate perception is difficult either in quiet or noise unless the target word is predictable, and 4) difficulty level is similar in unpredictable words presented in quiet environment and predictable words presented in noise.

Correlation coefficient among environment (Quiet/high, Quiet/low, Noisy/high, Noisy/low) and the listeners' TOEIC® scores were $r=0.41$ ($p=0.01$), $r=0.24$ ($p=0.03$), $r=0.68$

($p=0.0001$) and $r=0.33$ ($p=0.9$), respectively. Strongest correlation was observed when predictable words were presented in noisy environment, and weakest correlation was observed when unpredictable words were presented in quiet environment. In other words, all listeners regardless of their TOEIC® scores performed similarly in quiet environment when words were unpredictable, but listeners with higher TOEIC® scores made better usage of word predictability in noisy environment.

Further analysis was performed to investigate how experience of residing abroad influences perception, under the assumption that such experience increases exposure to listening to non-native sounds in noise. Figure 4 shows the accuracy rates of participants with (N=5) and without (N=12) experience of residing in English-speaking countries. Participants with experience always outperformed those without experience, and the difference was largest at Q_high, with Q_low and N_high close second behind, and lowest at N_low. This result suggests that having the experience of residing abroad, i.e. having more experience being exposed to perceiving English words in noise, generally has an advantage in accurate perception, but the advantage diminishes as conditions become more difficult.

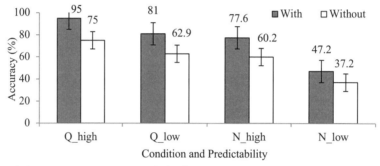

Figure 4 *Average accuracy rates (%) of participants with or without experience of residing in English-speaking countries*

3. General Discussion and Conclusion

The series of five experiments introduced in the present paper aimed to observe how one's L2 proficiency and native language impact non-native speech processing. TOEIC® scores were mainly used as an objective means for measuring the English learners' proficiency. The results demonstrated clear advantage of higher proficiency in both production and perception. However, detailed analyses also revealed that native language influence is not completely eliminated. For example, Japanese learners of English with high proficiency in English performed native-like in the production of voiced consonant clusters, i.e. inserted lesser degree of epenthetic vowels, although the degree of epenthesis increased, as did those with lower English proficiency, when voiceless consonants were introduced. Regarding perception of English consonants in VCV non-word context in adverse listening environments, i.e. in background noise and/or reverberation, advantage of higher proficiency was observed through positive correlations between accuracy and proficiency. However, while higher proficiency resulted in higher accuracy rates, both ends of proficiencies shared common confusion patterns that were not present in English listeners. The advantage of higher proficiency continued to show in the perception of real words; those with higher proficiency performed significantly higher than those with lower proficiency when predictable words were presented in noisy listening environment. In other words, the ability of detect contextual cues seem to improve with increased level of proficiency. This tendency was corroborated also by the result that Japanese learners of English that had the experience of residing in English-speaking countries, i.e. having more experience in being exposed to English in adverse listening environments, generally performed higher compared to those that have no experience of residing abroad. Finally, the results of Experiment 4 showed that training English consonants in VCV non-word context in noisy listening environment significantly improved accuracy in perception, although proficiency was not a part of the post hoc analysis due to the small number of participants.

What we have come to understand through looking at the data is that although having higher proficiency is advantageous in both speech production and perception, it still leaves them room for improvement. This is especially important in the perceptual domain, as we see in the results of Experiment 2 (identification of consonants in noise), 3 (identification of consonants in reverberation and noise+reverberation), and 5 (identification of words in noise), as we see confusions of English /r/ and /l/ among other consonants that are some of the notorious confusion patterns observed in Japanese, and the difficulty of perceiving unpredictable words in both quiet and noisy listening environments. Although a much larger set of stimuli as well as participants are necessary to substantiate this claim, the preliminary results of Experiment 4 (training to identify consonants in noise) indicate that training can be effective in improving perceptual accuracy in background noise.

Acknowledgments

The author thanks Takayuki Arai, Shigeto Kawahara, Shigeko Shinohara, and Kensaku Yoshida for working together on some of the experiments introduced in the paper. The experiments introduced in this paper were supported by Sophia University Open Research Center from MEXT, JSPS Kakenhi (Grant numbers 24820043, 2658011 and 17K13509), Waseda University Grants for Special Research Projects (Grant number 2014S-100), and Seikei University Grant-in-Aid for Scientific Research.

References

Aoyama, Katsura, James Emil Flege, Susan G. Guion, Reiko Akahane-Yamada and Tsuneo Yamada. 2004. Perceived phonetic dissimilarity and L2 speech learning: the case of Japanese /r/ and English /l/ and /r/. *Journal of Phonetics* 32.233-250.

Arai, Takayuki, Natasha Warner and Steven Greenberg. 2007. Analysis of spontaneous Japanese in a multi-language telephone-speech corpus. *Acoustical Science & Technology* 28.46-48.

Best, Catherine T. 1995. A direct realist view of cross-language speech perception. *Speech perception and linguistic experience: Issues in cross-language research*, ed. by Winifred Strange, 171-204. Timonium, MD: York Press.

Boersma, Paul and David Weenink. 2008. *Praat: doing phonetics by computer* (Version 5.0.09) [Computer program]. Retrieved April 3 2008 from http://www.praat.org/.

Bradlow, Ann R., David Pisoni, Reiko Akahane-Yamada and Yoh'ichi Tohkura. 1997. Training Japanese listeners to identify English /r/ and /l/: IV. Some effects of perceptual learning on speech production. *Journal of the Acoustical Society of America* 101.4.2299-2310.

Cutler, Anne, M.L. Garcia Lecumberri and Martin Cooke. 2008. Consonant identification in noise by native and non-native listeners: Effect of local context. *Journal of the Acoustical Society of America* 124.2:1264-1268.

Dupoux, Emmanuel, Kazuhiko Kakehi, Yuki Hirose, Christophe Pallier and Jacques Mehler. 1999. Epenthetic vowels in Japanese: A perceptual illusion? *Journal of Experimental Psychology: Human Perception and Performance* 35.6.1568-1578.

Florentine, Mary. 1985. Non-native listeners' perception of American-English in noise. *Proceedings of Inter-noise* 85.1021-1024.

Fujimoto, Masako and Seiya Funatsu. 2008. Vowel epenthesis in consonant clusters by Japanese speakers. *IEICE Technical Report* SP2007-204.105-109.

Jin, Su-Hyun and Chang Liu. 2012. English sentence recognition in speech-shaped noise and multi-talker babble for English-, Chinese-, and Korean-native listeners. *Journal of the Acoustical Society of America* 132. EL391.

Jones, Daniel. 1989. *An outline of English phonetics* (9th edition). Cambridge: Cambridge University Press.

Kalikow, D.N. and K.N. Stevens. 1977. Development of a test of speech intelligibility in noise using sentence materials with controlled word predictability. *Journal of the Acoustical Society of America* 61.5.1337-1351.

Kawakami, Shin. 1977. *Nihongo onsei gaisetsu*. Tokyo: Ōfusha.

Kubozono, Haruo. *Nihongo no onsei*. Tokyo: Iwanami Shoten.

Lecumberri, M.L. Garcia, Martin Cooke and Anne Cutler. 2010. Non-native speech perception in adverse conditions: A review. *Speech Communication* 52.864-886.

Lecumberri, M.L. Garcia and Martin Cooke. 2006. Effect of masker type on native and non-native consonant perception in noise. *Journal of the Acoustical Society of America* 119.4.2445-2454.

Logan, John, Scott Lively and David Pisoni. 1991. Training Japanese listeners to identify English /r/ and /l/: A first report. *Journal of the Acoustical Society of America* 89.2.874-886.

Masuda, Hinako. 2016. Misperception patterns of American English consonants by Japanese listeners in reverberant and noisy environments. *Speech Communication* 79.74-87.

Masuda, Hinako. 2016. Preliminary analysis of training non-native sounds in noise (abstract). *Journal of the Acoustical Society of America* 140.3342.

Masuda, Hinako. To appear. Word identification in adverse listening conditions by Japanese learners of English – role of predictability. IEICE Technical Report.

Masuda, Hinako and Arai, Takayuki. 2010. Processing of consonant clusters by Japanese native speakers: Influence of English learning backgrounds. *Acoustical Science & Technology* 31.5.320-327.

Masuda, Hinako, Takayuki Arai and Shigeto Kawahara. 2015. Identification of English consonants in intervocalic contexts in multispeakers babble noise by Japanese listeners: Correlation between English proficiency and consonant identification ability. *Acoustical Science & Technology* 36.1.31-34.

Mayo, Lynn Hansberry, Mary Florentine and Søren Buus. 1997. Age of second-language acquisition and perception of speech in noise. *Journal of Speech, Language, and Hearing Research* 40.3.686–693.

Miyawaki, Kuniko, Winifred Strange, Robert Vergrugge, Alvin Liberman, James Jenkins and Osamu Fujimura. 1975. An effect of linguistic experiment. The discrimination of [r] and [l] by native speakers of Japanese and English. *Perception & Psychophysics* 18.5.331-340.

Nabelek, Anna K. and Amy M. Donahue. 1984 Perception of consonants in reverberation by native and non-native listeners. *Journal of the Acoustical Society of America* 75.2.632-634.

Rauber, Andreia Schurt, Anabela Rato, Denise Cristina Kluge, Giane Rodrigues dos Santos and Marcos Figueiredo. 2013. TP 3.1 Software: A tool for designing audio, visual, and audiovisual perceptual training tasks and perception tests. *Proceedings of Interspeech*. 2095-2098.

Rogers, Catherine L., Jennifer J. Lister, Dashielle M. Febo, Joan M. Besing and Harvey B. Abrahams. 2006. Effects of bilingualism, noise, and reverberation on speech perception by listeners with normal hearing. *Applied Psycholinguistics* 27.465–485.

Sheldon, Amy and Winifred Strange. 1982. The acquisition of /r/ and /l/ by Japanese learners of English: Evidence that speech production can precede speech perception. *Applied Psycholinguistics* 3.243-261.

Tajima, Keiichi, Donna Erickson and Kyoko Nagao. 2000. Phonetic analysis of vowel epenthesis in native Japanese speakers' production of English words. *Proceedings of the 14th General Meeting of the Phonetic Society of Japan* 195-200.

Takata, Yoji and Anna K. Nabelek. 1990. English consonant recognition in noise and in reverberation by Japanese and American listeners. *Journal of the Acoustical Society of America* 88.2.663-666.

Vance, Timothy J. 2008. *The Sounds of Japanese*. Cambridge: Cambridge University Press.

Varga, Andrew and Herman J.M. Steeneken. 1993. Assessment for automatic recognition II: NOISEX-92: a database and an experiment to study the effect of additive noise on speech recognition systems. *Speech Communication* 12.3.247-251.

Perception of English Word-final Stops in Clearly Articulated Connected Speech by Japanese L2 Learners of English*

Kikuyo Ito

National Institute of Technology, Kagawa College

ABSTRACT. This study investigated the perception of place-of-articulation contrasts of English word-final stops /p-t-k/, /b-d-g/, and /m-n-ŋ/ in running speech by adult Japanese second language (L2) learners of English, using real words. Minimal triplets differing in place of articulation of the word-final stop (e.g., *sip*, *sit*, and *sick*), followed by adverbs starting with /p/, /t/, or /k/ in sentences were presented in clearly articulated speech. Participants chose one of three written options of the target words after listening to a sentence, such as *He said the word sit positively* (or *tauntingly* or *cautiously*).

Results showed that Japanese listeners had difficulty identifying word-final unreleased oral stops, indicating their heavy reliance on the release. Japanese listeners also showed marked difficulty in correctly perceiving word-final nasal stops, in contrast to American listeners' ceiling-level performance.

Keywords: L2 phonetic perception, word-final consonants, connected speech

1. Introduction

English word-final consonants are realized differently in connected speech from the same word-final consonants produced in isolation because of coarticulation with the following segment. Their realization also varies with speaking rate and style (e.g., Gay 1981; Manuel *et al.* 1992). Although some variations are reported to be less intelligible than their base forms (e.g., Householder 1956; Nolan 1992; Gaskell and Marslen-Wilson 2001), first language (L1) listeners generally seem to be capable of recovering the underlying forms of phonetic segments from coarticulated speech when they are presented in context (e.g., Sumner and Samuel 2005; Gow 2002, 2003; Manuel 1995). In the case of non-native perception, however, how well second language (L2) listeners can perceive the underlying representations of phonetic segments in connected speech has not been well explored yet. The goal of the present study was to investigate L1 and L2 perception of English word-final oral and nasal stops with different places of articulation in connected speech.

The study examined the identification of English words ending with an oral or nasal stop followed by a word beginning with an oral stop /p/, /t/, or /k/ in clearly articulated connected speech. Native speakers of Japanese (JP) and American English (AE) participated in the experiment.

Since the present study adopted real words for the target stimuli, the lexical influence on word identification was analyzed by examining the correlation of percent accuracy of the experiment with word familiarity and with word frequency of the target words. The correlations between perceptual performance of JP listeners and their length of residence (LOR) and age of arrival (AOA) in English-speaking countries, and their English proficiency were also examined.

2. Methods
2.1. Participants

Twenty-four adult native speakers of JP living in the U.S. and a control group of twelve adult native speakers of AE participated in the experiment. The information of JP and AE participants is presented in Table 1.

Language Group	Gender Distribution	Mean Age (Range)	Mean LOR (Range)	Mean AOA (Range)
JP (N = 24)	3 males 21 females	32.3 (22 – 44)	5y 8m (1m – 17y 8m)	25.5 (17 – 34)
AE (N = 12)	4 males 8 females	30 (23 – 44)		

Table 1 Biographical information on Japanese and AE participants

2.2. Stimulus Materials

A total of 54 target words, constituting 18 monosyllabic CVC minimal triplets, each of which differed in only the place of articulation of the word-final stops, such as *sip-sit-sick*, *lab-lad-lag*, and *sum-sun-sung*, were constructed. (The places of articulation of the target words, Labial, Alveolar, and Velar, are called *target place*, hereafter.) These triplets were subdivided into three groups, according to the types of contrast of the final stops (*contrast type*, hereafter): Voiceless contrasts (/p/-/t/-/k/), Voiced contrasts (/b/-/d/-/g/), and Nasal contrasts (/m/-/n/-/ŋ/).

The target words were followed by one of the following three adverbs: *positively*, *tauntingly*, or *cautiously*, creating a total of 162 two-word sequences. The two-word sequences, therefore, contained 27 types of consonantal sequences at the word boundary: 9 final stops of the target words (/p/, /t/, /k/, /b/, /d/, /g/, /m/, /n/, and /ŋ/) × 3 initial stops of the following adverbs (/p/, /t/, and /k/). In addition, a total of 72 filler sequences using word-initial minimal triplets, such as *pick-tick-kick* were included. All two-word combinations including the fillers are presented in the appendix.

All two-word sequences were preceded by "He said the word ..." in the recording, such as, "He said the word *sit* cautiously," making syntactically and semantically viable English sentences. The stimulus sentences were produced by a 29-year-old phonetically trained male native speaker of AE from the New York area. The speaker was instructed to read the sentences "as if speaking to a non-native English listener or speaking in a noisy environment." All sentences were digitally recorded using a microphone (SHURE SM 48) in a sound-attenuated room at a sampling rate of 22,050 Hz, monaural, with 16-bit resolution, supported by SOUND FORGE 4.5 software.

A total of 468 stimulus sentences, which included two physically different tokens of 162 target and 72 filler sentences, were presented in the experiment.

The presence or absence of the oral stop release and the magnitude of the release, measured by multiplying the amplitude of each release by its duration, were examined and summarized in Figure 1. The following context (*following place*, hereafter) was categorized into *Different* or *Same* context for each contrast type, depending on whether the following place coincides with the target place.

A clear pattern seen in the data is that the word-final stops of the target words (*target stops*, hereafter) were not released in most cases in Same contexts whereas they were almost always released in Different contexts. This pattern was seen in both Voiceless and Voiced contrasts, and was most clearly seen in Labial in which the stops were never released in Same contexts and were always released in Different contexts.

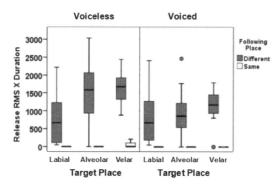

Figure 1 *Magnitude of Oral Stop Release Compared by Following Context*

2.3. Procedures

Participants were tested individually in a sound-attenuated room in the Speech-Language-Hearing Sciences department at the Graduate Center of the City University of New York, using the computer software, Paradigm. The experiment consisted of the main experiment and a word familiarity rating task, both of which were self-paced, followed by a standardized English proficiency test called the Versant™ English Test (for JP participants only). The entire session was completed within two hours for JP participants and within one and a half hours for AE participants.

2.3.1. Main experiment

The stimuli were presented binaurally through headphones (Telephonics TDH 39) in random order. For each trial, a stimulus sentence with one member of a triplet as the target word (e.g., "He said the word *sit* positively") was presented, and participants were asked to identify the target word by clicking on one of the three written alternatives appearing on the computer screen (e.g., *sip, sit* and *sick*).

The experiment consisted of 12 blocks, each of which contained 39 trials. One repetition of each sentence was presented in the first 6 blocks and the other repetition in the remaining 6 blocks. In order to avoid fatigue effects, 5-minute breaks were inserted after the third, the sixth, and ninth blocks.

2.3.2. Word familiarity rating task

The main experiment was followed by a word familiarity rating task that asked participants to rate their familiarity with the written target words by clicking on one of seven boxes corresponding to the seven levels of familiarity (1 = I don't know the word at all, 7 = I know the word very well).

2.3.3. Versant English test

The Versant™ English Test, a 20-minute computerized telephone test, was administered only to JP participants. It assesses English spoken language skills of non-native speakers by the overall score with four diagnostic subscores (Pronunciation, Fluency, Sentence Mastery, and Vocabulary). It has been reported that extended one-on-one interviews by two experts correlate scores greater than 90% (Bernstein 2009).

3. Results
3.1. Language effect (AE vs. JP)

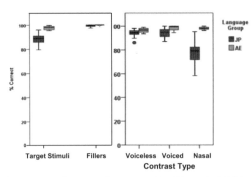

Figure 2 *Percent Correct Accuracy by JP and AE Listeners*

The left panel in Figure 2 illustrates the overall response accuracy by AE and JP listeners. The performance on the filler items by both JP and AE listeners was at ceiling level whereas their performance on the target stimuli exhibited the language effect showing better performance by AE listeners than JP listeners (median response accuracy 88.9% by JP *vs.* 98.5 % by AE). The overall response accuracy by AE listeners was significantly higher than that of JP listeners [Mann Whitney U, $U = 3$, $z = -4.74$, $p < 0.001$], with a very large effect size [$r = 0.79$].

The JP and AE performance on each contrast type (Voiceless, Voiced, Nasal) is presented in the right panel of Figure 2. The JP performance was significantly lower than the AE performance on all contrast types [Mann Whitney U with Bonferroni adjustments, $U = 63$, $z = -2.74$, $p < 0.01$ for Voiceless, $U = 48$, $z = -3.25$, $p < 0.001$ for Voiced, $U = 0$, $z = -4.84$, $p < 0.001$ for Nasal]. The language effect was larger for Nasal [$r = 0.81$] than for Voiceless [$r = 0.45$] and Voiced [$r = 0.53$] contrasts.

Figure 3 shows the performance on each target place (Labial, Alveolar, Velar) of each contrast type. While the JP performance on Voiceless Alveolar /t/ and Voiced Alveolar /d/ was significantly poorer than the AE performance [Mann Whitney U with Bonferroni adjustments, $p < 0.001$ for /t/, $p < 0.0056$ for /d/] with large effect sizes [$r = 0.53$ for /t/, $r = 0.77$ for /d/], their performance on Labial /p/, /b/ and Velar /k/, /g/ did not differ significantly from that of AE listeners. The results indicate that the language effects observed for Voiceless and Voiced contrasts are attributable to the JP group's significantly worse performance only on Alveolar stops. On the other hand, the JP performance on Nasal contrasts of all target places were significantly worse than the corresponding AE performance, with very large to medium effects [$r = 0.77$ for /n/, $r = 0.81$ for /ŋ/, $r = 0.49$ for /m/].

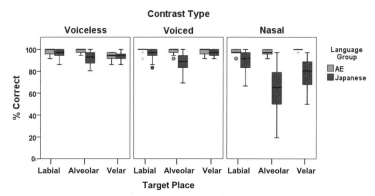

Figure 3 *Percent Correct Accuracy on Target Place by AE and JP Listeners*

3.2. Contrast type comparisons (Voiceless *vs.* Voiced *vs.* Nasal)

The performance differences between contrast types and those between target places within each contrast type were examined within each language group and are briefly summarized below. For the AE group, a non-parametric Friedman's test and three separate Wilcoxon Signed-Rank tests with Bonferroni adjustments were carried out because of the heterogeneity of variance and ceiling effects. A one-way repeated measures ANOVA and three separate repeated measures ANOVAs with Bonferroni adjustments were adopted for the JP group.

The AE performance on Voiceless contrasts was significantly worse than that on Voiced contrasts and Nasal contrasts. The difference in performance between Voiced and Nasal contrasts was not significant, showing the following relationship in terms of the goodness of the performance: Voiceless < Voiced ≈ Nasal. The results indicate that word-final voiceless stops are relatively harder to perceive than voiced and nasal counterparts even for native listeners.

The JP performance on Nasal contrasts was significantly poorer than that on both Voiced and Voiceless contrasts with very large effect sizes ($\eta_p^2 > 0.8$ for both contrasts). The difference in their performance between Voiced contrasts and Voiceless contrasts did not differ significantly, showing the following relationship regarding the goodness of the performance: Nasal < Voiceless ≈ Voiced. The results indicate marked difficulty in correctly perceiving the place of articulation of word-final nasal stops in a sentence, showing a very different perceptual pattern from that seen in the AE results.

3.3. Following place comparisons (Different *vs.* Same)

Wilcoxon Signed Rank Tests with Bonferroni adjustments revealed no significant difference between Different and Same contexts in the AE performance except for Voiceless Velar /k/ that showed better performance on Different than on Same context.

The JP performance seemed to be more affected by following place. JP listeners' mean response accuracies on Same and Different contexts with standard errors are presented in Figure 4.

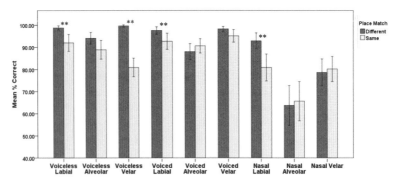

Figure 4 *Mean Percent Correct Accuracy by JP on Following Place*

Repeated measures ANOVAs revealed that four out of nine target stimulus types showed better performance on Different than on Same context and that Same context was never perceived better than Different context in any of the contrast types in the JP performance. Since the release of a word-final oral stop in Same context was either deleted or critically reduced, the JP listeners' pattern showing better performance on Different context than on Same context for oral stops suggests that JP listeners were utilizing stop release cues for place identification of word-final oral stops. The next part examines the listeners' reliance on the release cues for the perception of word-final oral stops more directly by examining the correlations between the magnitude of the stop releases and the corresponding performance.

3.4. Correlations between magnitude of stop release and performance

The correlations between the magnitude of the oral stop releases of the target words with the corresponding performance by JP and AE listeners were examined, by multiplying the RMS amplitude of the release by duration as the indicator of the magnitude of the release. Spearman rank order correlations revealed positive correlations of the JP performance on both Voiceless [rho=0.55, p < 0.01] and Voiced [rho=0.34, p < 0.01] tokens, indicating JP listeners' heavy reliance, especially for Voiceless stops, on the place information in the stop release. As for AE listeners, significant correlations were seen in performance on Voiceless tokens only [rho=0.300, p < 0.01], showing similar but much weaker patterns of correlations than those of the JP performance.

3.5. Lexical effects on performance: word frequency and word familiarity

The lexical effects were analyzed by examining the correlation of performance on the main experiment with scores on the word familiarity task and with word frequency of the target words based on the SUBTLEXUS corpus. The SUBTLEXUS norms are reported to predict lexical decision times quite consistently (Brysbaert and New 2009). Spearman rank-order correlations showed no correlations between the percent correct accuracy on target words and the corresponding word familiarity scores by either of the language groups. None of the correlations between the response accuracy and word frequency scores were significant either, indicating that there were no lexical effects on the performance.

3.6. Correlations with LOR, AOA, and language proficiency.

The correlations of the JP listeners' performance with their LOR, AOA, and English proficiency measured by the Versant™ English Test (*Versant Test*, hereafter) were examined by adopting Spearman rank order correlations. The scatter plots showing the correlations of the overall accuracy of JP listeners with their LOR, AOA, and Versant Test scores are presented in Figure 5. Strong positive correlations of LOR were seen not only with the overall performance but also with the performance on all three contrast groups.

The correlations of the JP listeners' performance with their AOA were much weaker than those with LOR. A significant negative correlation was only seen with the performance on Voiceless contrasts.

The correlations of the JP performance with the overall scores of the Versant Test were almost as strong as those of LOR. Among the subscores of the Versant Test, Pronunciation and Fluency scores showed higher correlations with performance than the other subscores.

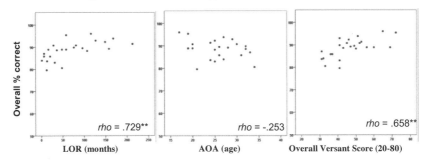

Figure 5 *Correlations of JP Performance with LOR, AOA, and Language Proficiency*

4. Discussion

Results of the present study indicated that the language effect predicting less accurate perception by JP than AE listeners was evident in the performance of the main experiment on all contrast types. No correlations between performance and word familiarity or word frequency were found in either of the language groups, indicating no lexical effects on their place perception of word-final stops in connected speech. Perceptual patterns by JP and AE listeners observed in this study are discussed below.

4.1. JP listeners' perceptual difficulty in identifying word-final nasal stop

The JP listeners' difficulty in identifying word-final nasal stops was clearly indicated in the result showing the JP group's much lower performance on Nasal contrasts than the corresponding AE performance, as well as in the result showing the JP group's much poorer performance on Nasal contrasts than their performance on Voiceless and on Voiced contrasts.

The observed difficulty by JP listeners is explicable by attributing it to the negative L1 influence caused by the place assimilatory nature of the Japanese moraic nasal. The place of articulation of the moraic nasal /N/ is underspecified because of its obligatory place assimilation to the following segment, resulting in several allophonic variations including [m], [n] and [ŋ] (Amanuma *et al*. 1983; Vance 1987; Nakajo 1990). This archiphonemic nature of Japanese moraic /N/ create L1-based perceptual patterns of syllable-final nasals by JP listeners (e.g., Otake *et al*. 1993, 1996), which are likely to be applied to non-native inputs (e.g., Cutler and Otake 1994, 1998). Aoyama (2003) reported that these L1-based perceptual patterns cause confusion in identifying the place of articulation of English word-final nasals produced in isolation. The results of the present study support the Aoyama study, extending the argument to the perception of English word-final nasals followed by other consonants in connected speech.

4.2. Influence of oral stop releases on performance

Results comparing the performance on Same and Different contexts of Voiceless and Voiced contrasts revealed that the JP performance in Same contexts was less accurate than that in Different contexts for the target places /p/, /k/, and /b/. No significant trend in the opposite direction was found. The AE performance showed no difference between Different and Same contexts except for /k/, which showed better performance on Different than on Same context.

The JP listeners' less accurate perception of oral stop contrasts in Same context than in Different context suggests their heavy reliance on acoustic information in stop releases because the release of a word-final oral stop in Same context was either deleted or critically reduced. The positive correlations between the magnitudes of the oral stop releases and the JP performance on the corresponding tokens strongly supported this assumption. The AE performance on Voiceless contrasts showed a weaker positive correlation, but their performance on Voiced contrasts did not show a correlation, indicating that AE listeners were much less dependent on the acoustic cues in stop releases. The results are consistent with past findings that listeners whose L1 has no or limited word-final stops rely on L2 stop releases (e.g., Flege 1989; Flege and Wang 1989) and that AE listeners are able to tap into anticipatory acoustic information available in the preceding vowel and transitional segments of English word-final stops (Warren and Marslen-Wilson 1987, 1988).

4.3. Correlations of JP Performance with language experience and proficiency

The JP listeners' overall performance as well as their performance on all contrast types was more strongly correlated with their LOR than AOA, indicating that LOR is a better predictor of performance. In the scatter plots, however, the improvement of the performance as a function of LOR is not clearly seen after four to five years of LOR, which may indicate a possible cut-off point of the effects of L2 immersion on perceptual accuracy. This observation is in line with the notion that a long LOR alone may not guarantee the acquisition of difficult L2 contrasts, as has often been pointed out by Flege and colleagues (e.g. Flege and Liu 2001).

The JP performance on all contrast types was also positively correlated with their language proficiency as measured by the Versant Test. Among the subscores, the pronunciation score and fluency score were better correlated with the performance than the sentence mastery score and the vocabulary score, suggesting a close relationship between L2 phonetic perception in connected speech and L2 production skills.

4.4. Future direction

The present study is based on the author's dissertation study, which investigated the JP listeners' place perception of English word-final stops followed by word-initial stops in clearly articulated speech (*clear speech*, hereafter), as well as in casually produced fast speech (*fast speech*, hereafter). The current study only reported the results from clear speech, setting a starting point for the entire dissertation study and the following extension studies. The next paper will report findings from comparisons of the data for clear speech with another set of data for fast speech. In addition, the same experiment using the fast speech stimuli were administered to the same number of Korean listeners to confirm the notion that JP listeners' difficulty in identifying word-final nasals is due to the negative influence of L1 phonology. The report of the Korean study will follow the dissertation study. Furthermore, supported by a Grant-in-Aid for Scientific Research, or KAKENHI, a new set of follow-up studies using the same experimental paradigm with the stimulus materials from new recordings by multiple speakers of AE are in preparation to establish a series of studies, the accumulated findings of which would make a contribution to the area of cross-language speech perception.

Notes
*The present study is written based on my dissertation study submitted to the Ph.D. program in Speech-Language-Hearing Sciences at the Graduate Center of the City University of New York. I would like to thank the members of the supervisory committee of the dissertation, Dr. Winifred Strange, Dr. Klara Marton, Dr. Valerie Shafer, Dr. Lisa Davidson, and Dr. Douglas Whalen. This material is based upon work supported by the National Science Foundation under Grant No. BCS-1023192.

Appendix
Stimulus Sentence List

Target Words (word-final minimal triplets: 54 words)			
contrast type	vowel	minimal triplet stimuli	Adverb
/p/-/t/-/k/	/□/	sip-sit-sick lip-lit-lick	positively
	/æ/	sap-sat-sack rap-rat-rack	
	/□ or /□	shop-shot-shock hop-hot-hock	
/b/-/d/-/g/	/□/	rib-rid-rig bib-bid-big	
	/æ/	tab-tad-tag lab-lad-lag	
	/□ or /□	cob-cod-cog dub-dud-dug	tauntingly
/m/-/n/-/ˌ/	/□/	dim-din-ding Kim-kin-king	
	/æ/	ram-ran-rang bam-ban-bang	
	/□ or /□	sum-sun-sung rum-run-rung	cautiously
Fillers (word-initial minimal triplets: 24 words)			
contrast type		minimal triplet stimuli	
/p/-/t/-/k/		pick-tick-kick puff-tough-cuff pan-tan-can	
/b/-/d/-/g/		bet-debt-get bun-done-gun bait-date-gate	
/m/-/n/		mock-knock-(dock) mitt-knit-(bit) map-nap-(gap)	

References
Amanuma, Yasushi, Kazuo Otsubo and Osamu Mizutani. 1983. *Nihongo onseigaku* [Japanese phonetics]. Tokyo: Kuroshio Shuppan.

Aoyama, Katsura. 2003. Perception of syllable-initial and syllable-final nasals in English by Korean and Japanese speakers. *Second Language Research* 19.251–265

Bernstein, Jared. 2009. Proficiency instrumentation for cross language perception studies. *Journal of the Acoustical Society of America* 125.2753-2753.

Brysbaert, Marc and Boris New. 2009. Moving beyond Kučera and Francis: a critical evaluation of current word frequency norms and the introduction of a new and improved word frequency measure for American English. *Behavior Research Methods* 41.977-990.

Cutler, Anne and Takashi Otake. 1998. Assimilation of place in Japanese and Dutch. *Proceedings of the Fifth International Conference on Spoken Language Processing* 1751-1754.

Cutler, Anne and Takashi Otake. 1994. Mora or phoneme? Further evidence for language-specific listening. *Journal of Memory and Language* 33.824-844.

Flege, James Emil and Serena Liu. 2001. The effect of experience on adults' acquisition of a second language. *Studies in Second Language Acquisition* 23.527-552.

Flege, James Emil. 1989. The perception of /t/ and /d/ by native and Chinese listeners. *Journal of the Acoustical Society of America* 84.1639-1652.

Flege, James Emil and Chipin Wang. 1989. Native-language phonotactic constraints affect how well Chinese subjects perceive the word-final English /t/ - /d/ contrast. *Journal of Phonetics* 17.299-315.

Gaskell, Gareth M. and William Marslen-Wilson. 2001. Lexical ambiguity resolution and spoken word recognition: Bridging the gap. *Journal of Memory and Language* 44.325–349.

Gay, Thomas. 1981. Mechanisms in the control of speech rate. *Phonetica* 38.148-158.

Gow Jr., David W. 2002. Does English coronal place assimilation create lexical ambiguity? *Journal of Experimental Psychology: Human Perception and Performance* 28.163–179.

Gow Jr., David W. 2003. Feature parsing: Feature cue mapping in spoken word recognition. *Perception and Psychophysics* 65.575–590.

Householder Jr., Fred W. 1956. Unreleased PTK in American English. *For Roman Jakobson: Essays on the occasion of his sixtieth birthday, 11 October 1956,* ed. by M. Halle, H. G. Lunt, H. McLean and C. H. Van Schooneveld, 235-244. The Hague: Mouton.

Manuel, Sharon Y. 1995. Speakers nasalize /ð/ after /n/ but listeners still hear /ð/. *Journal of Phonetics* 23.453-476.

Manuel, Sharon Y., Stefanie Shattuck-Hufnagel, Marie. K. Huffman, Kenneth N. Stevens, Rolf Carlson, and Sheri Hunnicutt. 1992. Studies of vowel and consonant reduction. *ICSLP-1992* 943-946.

Nakajo, Osamu. 1990. *Nihongo no onin to akusento.* Tokyo: Keisō shobō.

Nolan, Francis. 1992. The descriptive role of segments: evidence from assimilation. *Papers in laboratory phonology II: Gesture, segment, prosody,* ed. by G. J. Docherty and D. R. Ladd, 261–280. Cambridge: CUP.

Otake, Takashi, Giyoo Hatano, Anne Cutler and Jacques Mehler. 1993. Mora or syllable? Speech segmentation in Japanese. *Journal of Memory and Language* 32.258-278.

Otake, Takashi, Kiyoko Yoneyama, Anne Cutler and Arie van der Lugt. 1996. The representation of Japanese moraic nasals. *Journal of the Acoustical Society of America* 100.3831-3842.

Sumner, Meghan and Arthur G. Samuel. 2005. Perception and representation of regular variation: the case of final /t/. *Journal of Memory and Language* 52.322-338.

Vance, Timothy J. 1987. *An introduction to Japanese Phonology.* New York: State University of New York Press.

Warren, Paul and William Marslen-Wilson. 1987. Continuous uptake of acoustic cues in spoken word recognition. *Perception & Psychophysics* 41.262-275.

Warren, Paul and William Marslen-Wilson. 1988. Cues to lexical choice: Discriminating place and voice. *Perception & Psychophysics* 43.21-30.

The Universal Nature of Substantive Features?

Keren Rice
University of Toronto

ABSTRACT. There has long been debate about the role of substance in phonology, with controversy about whether features are innate or emergent, and whether phonological substantive markedness hierarchies exist. In this paper, I address this debate, considering two issues. While in general there has been a move in linguistics to reduce what is considered to be innate (e.g., Mielke 2008), recent work on features (Duanmu 2016) and on markedness (de Lacy 2006; de Lacy and Kingston 2013), among others, asserts the need for substantive universals in phonology, with both features and markedness hierarchies being universal. I examine their arguments from an empirical perspective, concluding that in both cases aspects of phonological activity remain unaccounted for if a particular set of substantive features is universal, with universal markedness relations between features. I outline a model of phonology that incorporates general concepts such categorization, asymmetries, activity, and complexity.

1. Introduction

There has long been debate about the role of substance in phonology, with controversy about whether features are universal and innate or emergent based on exposure to a language and about whether phonological substantive markedness hierarchies exist. In this paper, I address this debate, focusing on two major issues, what I call categorization and predictability. In terms of categorization, I examine recent work on features by Duanmu (2016). In terms of predictability, I focus on work by de Lacy (2006) and de Lacy and Kingston (2013). I draw on empirical evidence to support the view that substantive features and hierarchies are not innate, but emerge through acquisition of a language, and can vary from language to language.

This perspective on substance, while addressed in work such as Anderson (1981), has been a topic of much discussion in recent years, including in work by Mielke (2005, 2008), Menn and Vihman (2011), Dresher (2014), Krekoski (2016) and many others. Dresher (2014:166), for instance, writes that "[t]here is a growing consensus that phonological features are not innate, but rather emerge in the course of acquisition", while Menn and Vihman note that:

> We have argued that they [features] are the result of an intricate interplay between the auditory-acoustic input signal (with its variations across speakers and noise conditions as well as across languages and cultures), the child's developing cognitive capacity (which induces system, yet also retains cumulative auditory statistical information about input tokens – not raw, but as perceived – plus multisensory statistical information about output tokens), and articulatory capacities, which also develop over time. Yes, of course they are inherent (biologically grounded, as opposed to arbitrary) – but as emergents of this complex chaotic system, not as pre-experiential cognitive givens. We claim that they become part of a mental grammar as they are discovered by the speaker, becoming more and more fully realized as they come to be more stably represented in production. There may be theoretical elegance in holding otherwise, but there is (at least so far) no good evidence for it.
>
> Menn and Vihman 2011:284)

McMurray, Cole, and Munson (2011:230) also conclude that features are an emergent property of real-time perceptual processes.

While the non-innatist view has perhaps become prevalent in recent years, the universalist view continues. These two hypotheses are compared in (1).

(1) Hypotheses compared

Hypothesis A: innate, universal substantive features	Hypothesis B: emergent features
Distinctive features are substantive, innate, universal	Features emerge through exposure to language
Distinctive features "must be determined absolutely, within general linguistic theory, and independently of the grammar of any particular language" (Chomsky and Halle 1968:164)	
"Things happen because of features." (Mielke 2013:166)	"Features happen because of things." (Mielke 2013:167)
e.g., de Lacy and Kingston 2013; Duanmu 2016; Kiparsky 2008; Staroverov 2014	e.g., Dresher 2014; Krekoski 2016; McMurray *et al.* 2011; Menn and Vihman 2011; Mielke 2005, 2008

The major focus of this paper concerns whether there is universal substantive content using Mielke's terms, do things happen because of features, or do features happen because of things?

2. Categorization of sounds

Let me begin with an analogy to categorization in 'real' life. When my children were young, they would go trick-or-treating at Halloween, and come home and categorize their collection in various ways – by size, by shape, by colour, by content, and more. There seemed to be no particular reason for choosing one way of sorting the treats over another. I call this the categorization problem – how does one know what categories to sort things into? Work that assumes that features are innate essentially deals with the categorization problem, assuming that the features needed to categorize sounds are given, and the limited set of sounds and inventories of sounds follows from this.

In a recent book, Duanmu (2016) provides rich discussion of features, and his work can be used to illustrate the categorization problem in phonology. He develops a theory of features, arguing that there is a minimal set of distinctive features that account for the segmental contrasts found in phonological inventories, and these features define the categories that are important to phonology. His analysis rests on three basic concepts, universality, contrast, and economy. In particular, he proposes three principles, the Principle of Contrast, Maxima First, and Known Feature First. These are summarized in (2).

(2) *The Principle of Contrast*

If two sounds A and B can contrast in any language, they must be distinguished by at least one feature.

If two sounds A and B never contrast in any language, they need not be distinguished by a feature.

Maxima First

First, search through all languages in order to determine the maximal number of contrasts in each phonetic dimension. When all dimensions have been examined, we obtain a maximal feature system.

Then interpret each sound of a language in terms of the maximal feature system.

Known Feature First

Unless evidence requires otherwise, use known features first before introducing a new feature (or a new feature combination) to represent a contrast.

Economy plays a major role, with as few features introduced as possible to capture contrasts within languages.

Duanmu's goal is not to deal with categorization, but rather to define a "feature system that is minimally sufficient to distinguish all consonants and vowels in the world's languages" (2016:ix), nevertheless his work provides a good example of the categorization problem.

An example of the type of reanalysis proposed by Duanmu to meet his goal of establishing a feature set that is minimally sufficient to distinguish all sounds can be seen in his treatment of vowel height. One vowel system that he examines, drawing on inventories from UPSID and P-base, is that of Dan, a Mande language. Bearth and Zemp (1967: 19-21) give the vowel inventory in (3).

(3) Dan vowel inventory (Bearth and Zemp 1967:19-21)

	Front	Central	Back
Close	i	ɨ	u
Mid close	e	ɘ	o
Mid open	ɛ	ə	ɔ
Open	æ	a	ɒ

Duanmu (2016:59) revises this inventory. Following his principles, he proposes that no language has more than two heights, and thus height contrasts can be captured with a single feature. He proposes that Dan has the inventory in (4), where pairs separated by a comma differ in [ATR].

(4) Dan vowel inventory (Duanmu 2016:59)

	-back	+back	
		-round	+round
+high	i, e	ɨ, ɘ	u. o
-high	ɛ, æ	ə, a	ɔ, ɒ

Similarly, Duanmu proposes that Woisika (Timor-Alor-Pantar) is not to be organized as proposed by Stokhof (1979:59), as in (5), but rather as in (6) (Duanmu 2016:61). Duanmu excludes the vowels [ae] and [ao] based on frequency (note that [û] has the same frequency as [ae] but is not excluded), and treats pairs in a cell as differing by [ATR].

(5) Woisika vowel inventory (Stokhof 1979:59)

	Front		Central		Back	
	Lax	Tense	Lax	Tense	Lax	Tense
High	i	î			u	û
Mid	e				o	ô
Low	ae		a	â	Ao	

(6) Woisika vowel inventory (Duanmu 2016:16)

	-back	+back	
	-round	-round	+round
+high	î, i		û, u
-high	ê, e	â, a	ô, o

Such reconceptualization is perhaps reasonable in these cases, with a universally given feature set serving to define categories. I next offer some cases in which this type of approach is perhaps less well grounded, namely languages in which we see phonological activity that groups sounds in ways unexpected under Duanmu's feature set. While in the candy categorizing example that I began with there is no evidence from the candy as to which way might be reasonable to sort it, this is not the case in language – the patterning of sounds, or phonological activity, provides evidence for categorizing those sounds.

A brief comment on what I mean by phonological activity is in order. Based on Clements (2001), a feature is active if it plays a role in phonological computation, meaning that it is required to express phonological regularities including static phonotactic patterns and patterns of alternation.

Consider a language with phonological activity involving vowel height, Shona (Bantu; Odden 2015, based on Fortune 1955 and Beckman 1997). Shona has the vowel system in (7).

(7)　　i　e　a　o　u

In Duanmu's feature theory, the following representations are expected:

(8) Vowel features, Duanmu's features

	-back	+back	
		-round	+round
+high	i		u
-high	e	a	o

Shona also has a system of vowel harmony, usually analyzed as high vowel suffixes lowering to mid in the presence of a mid vowel, as illustrated in (9).

(9)　　Verb　　　　Verb+applicative

　　　ip-a　　　　ip-[i]r-a　　　'be evil'
　　　rum-a　　　rum-[i]r-a　　'bite'
　　　per-a　　　per-[e]r-a　　'end'
　　　son-a　　　son-[e]r-a　　'sew'
　　　vav-a　　　vav-[i]r-a　　'itch'

The following question arises. If /a/ is the same height as /e, o/, why does it pattern with /i, u/ in harmony? If [a] is [+low] in this system, then the non-low vowels trigger the alternation. While the Similar examples can be adduced from many other languages. Mielke's slogan, given in (1), is that in theories invoking innate features, things happen because of features. In this case, the features do not allow the appropriate things to happen.

Duanmu's pursuit of a single universal feature set that categorizes sounds has implications for languages with similar inventories. We expect that if languages have the same inventory, there would be highly restricted variation in patterning of the sounds. As has been well-documented by Dresher (2009) and others, phonological activity reveals that inventories that appear on the surface to be the same are not necessarily so when patterning is considered. In the following I compare two Pama-Nyungan languages of Australia, both of which are said to have a three vowel inventory. The analyses are based on work by D'Arcy (2003).

To begin, given the features proposed by Duanmu, a three-vowel inventory would be expected to have the following features.

(10)　Three vowel inventory: Duanmu's features

	-back	+back	
		-round	+round
+high	i		u
-high		a	

In Warlpiri (Nash 1980), the vowel /u/ is a harmony target and /i/ and harmony trigger, with /a/ outside the domain of harmony, as illustrated in the following forms. See Nash (1980) for details of harmony.

(11) Warlpiri vowel harmony (Nash 1980:86)
/-juku/ 'still': -juku after /a, u/, -jikki after /i/
   a. after /a/   wanti-ja-j[**u**]k[**u**]   'fell-still'
   b. after /u/   ya-nu-j[**u**]k[**u**]   'went-still'
   c. after /i/   wanti-mi-j[**i**]k[**i**]   'fall-still'

A possible analysis of this is that there is assimilation of place within the high vowels, with /u/ assimilating to a preceding /i/. As a non-high vowel, /a/ does not participate in harmony. This patterning is well accounted for by Duanmu's analysis.

Nyangumarta (northern dialect; based on Sharp 2004) exhibits a rather different pattern, again with a three-vowel surface inventory. Nyangumarta has alternating suffixes with /a/, represented as 'V' by Sharp. See Sharp (2004) for detailed discussion.

(12) Nyangumarta (northern dialect) vowel harmony
Alternating suffixes: /a/ assimilates to /i, u/
   a. -nga locative
      after /i/   pirti-ngV   pirti-ng[**i**]   'hole, locative' p. 63
      after /u/   paru-ngV   -aru-ng[**u**]   'spinifex, locative' p. 63
      after /a/   ngurra-ngV   ngurra-ng[**a**]   'camp, locative' p. 63
   b. -rna non-future
      after /i/   yirri-rnV   yirri-rn[**i**]   'see, non-future' p. 64
      after /u/   kalku-rnV   kalku-rn[**u**]   'keep, non-future' p. 64
      after /a/   wirla-rnV   wirla-rn[**a**]   'hit, non-future' p. 65

There are also suffixes with /u/ and /i/, and these are invariant.

(13) Invariant suffixes
   a. -lku potential
      yirri-lku-rnV   yirri-lk[**u**]-rnu   'I might see it' p. 67
      see-potential-1SG.SUBJ
      kalku-lku-rnV   kalku-lk[**u**]-rnu   'I might keep it' p. 67
      wirla-lku-rnV   wirla-lk[**u**]-rnu   'I might hit it' p. 67
   b. -li first person dual inclusive
      yirri-rnV-li   yirri-rna-l[**i**]   'we two saw it' p. 68
      see-NONFUTURE-1DU.INC.SUBJ
      kalku-rnV-li   kalku-rna-l[**i**]   'we two kept it' p. 68

D'Arcy proposes that this is a three-place system, with /a/ assimilating to the frontness of /i/ and the backness of /u/. The two systems are compared in the diagram in (14), with the vowels in Walpiri differing in height and place phonologically but those in the northern dialect of Nyangurarta differing solely by place.

(14) Analyses

Language	vowels	activity	phonological analysis
Warlpiri	i a u	u: target i: trigger	i u a
Nyangumarta	i a u	a: target i, u: triggers	i a u

These languages provide evidence of what features are important based on phonological activity, and suggest that there are problems with a universal categorization if activity is to be accounted for. The vowel /a/ patterns in three distinct ways. In Shona, it must be distinguished from /e, o/ since it patterns with /i, u/ rather than with /e, o/ - the problem is one of miscategorization since /a/ does not in fact pattern together with /e, o/ in harmony, and if a feature [low] were available, the patterning could straightforwardly be accounted for. In Walpiri, the vowel /a/ simply patterns as if it were non-high (or the vowels /i, u/ pattern as if they were non-low), as expected by Duanmu's features. In Nyangumarta, the /a/ patterns as if it is the same height as /i, u/. The problem is one of too many features: introducing the feature [high] obscures an otherwise straightforward analysis. These examples serve to show that while the sounds in the three languages considered are all represented with the same vowel symbol, they in fact pattern rather differently. Thus categorizing the vowels as the same creates a problem in accounting for their varying phonological activity. (See Mielke 2016 and Rice 2017 for more discussion of Duanmu 2016).

Given Duanmu's features, we must ask, in a model with a small set of features determined by contrast, how phonological activity is to be accounted for. This question is addressed by Clements (2001:77-78), who proposes that there are three levels of feature specification, the lexical level, the phonological level, and the phonetic level, and he defines these as follows:

(15)   Levels of feature specification (Clements 2001:77-78)
    a. Lexical level: distinctiveness
        A feature or feature value is present in the lexicon if and only if it is distinctive.
    b. Phonological level: feature activity
        A feature or feature value is present at a given phonological level if is required for the statement of phonological patterns (phonotactic patterns, alternations) at that level.
    c. Phonetic level: pronounceability
        Feature values are present in the phonetics if required to account for relevant aspects of phonetic realization.

At the lexical level, essentially the level that Duanmu is concerned with, what matters is distinctiveness – a feature from a universal feature set is present in a language if it is distinctive in that language. At the phonological level, phonological activity is important, and features are added as necessary to account for this patterning. Finally, at the phonetic level, pronounceability enters in, with features added for phonetic realization. One mightt ask what the evidence is for the set of features at the lexical level, the level that is generally used to argue for a universal feature set. As Dresher (2009:236) points out, referring to the lexical level, "… it is difficult to prove or disprove any proposed set of contrastive features for a particular language."

What can we conclude about categorization in language? It is quite different from categorizing Halloween candy. Without phonological activity, sounds can be categorized in various ways; however, activity points to what sounds group together, and to the features that are needed to account for the activity. Activity yields feature classes that are unexpected given Duanmu's feature set (and other feature sets tested by Mielke 2008). Activity rather suggests a model where features are not universal. They are inherent in the sense that they are based largely on what is possible articulatorily and perceptually, but not in the sense of fixed limited substance. Rather than things happening because of features, features happen because of things.

3. Markedness and predictability

In section 2, I essentially followed Mielke (2005, 2008) in showing that phonological activity suggests that a level of lexical distinctiveness defined over a set of universal features is problematic when it comes to alternations. In this section I examine markedness and the notion of universal markedness hierarchies. Markedness is a topic that has been hotly debated in the literature; see, for example, work by Hume (2011) and Rice (2003, 2007) for recent perspectives on markedness.

The principle of markedness is simple. Expressed in terms of Optimality Theory, markedness suggests that, in the absence of faithfulness (and competing hierarchies), markedness is "decisive in selecting the output form" (de Lacy 2006:110). Markedness in phonology is often expressed in terms of substantive feature hierarchies, with certain features more marked and other features less marked with respect to each other. The unmarked features appear in emergence-of-the-unmarked environments. In this section I briefly examine markedness and place of articulation, suggesting that in fact things are less constrained than might be expected.

I began the previous section with Halloween candy, and begin this one with lego blocks. If there is just a single lego present, and you request a lego, you will get that single one. Suppose there are two legos, of the same size and shape but different colours. In this case, if you request a lego, it is unlikely that you can predict which one you will be given – the choice will probably be essentially random (although there might be individual preferences). Markedness theory rests on the assumption that if there are two features on the same hierarchy and the environment is unmarked, the choice of feature should be predictable – the unmarked one is selected. (See de Lacy 2006 for detailed discussion of diagnostics for unmarked.)

In this section I respond to very interesting work by de Lacy and Kingston (2013) on markedness. In a discussion of phonological substance, they examine dorsal consonants in particular. Dorsal place of articulation is considered to be more marked than labial, coronal, and laryngeal places of articulation phonologically; see de Lacy (2006) for detailed discussion. de Lacy and Kingston (2013:288 and following) argue that the markedness of dorsals is not expected on phonetic grounds, and thus the failure of dorsals to occur in unmarked environments is due to its phonological status. They state that "the lack of certain sound patterns is due to the phonological component's inability to generate them; we will call this 'synchronic explanation" and further suggest that "synchronic neutralization to and epenthesis of [k] (and dorsals generally) is unattested, yet is desirable for Performance reasons and thus expected."

I will examine two places of articulation, dorsal and coronal. Given a substantive markedness hierarchy where dorsals are more marked than coronals (e.g. Lombardi 2002; de Lacy 2006), one would expect to find coronals in unmarked environments but not dorsals. One process in which the unmarked is expected is epenthesis, and thus epenthetic coronals are expected, but not epenthetic dorsals. However, both have been argued for in the literature. Axininca Campa (Arawakan) is perhaps the best-known case of coronal epenthesis. The data below is taken from Morley (2015a:9). (Morley (2015a:8) questions whether there is truly evidence for epenthesis of consonants other than laryngeals. She concludes that "It turns out that both Axininca Campa and the Altaic language Buryat provide considerably more, and considerably more consistent, evidence for epenthesis than do most of the other languages of the sample."

(16)　　Axininca t-epenthesis
　　　　i-N-koma-i　　　iŋkoma[t]i　　　'he will paddle'
　　　　i-N-koma-aa-i　　iŋkoma[t]aa[t]i　'he will paddle again'
　　　　i-N-koma-ako-i　iŋkoma[t]ako[t]i　'he will paddle for'

Surprisingly, given the place markedness hierarchy, epenthetic dorsals are also reported, as in a second case examined by Morley (2015a:12), Buryat (Mongolic).

(17) Buryat g-epenthesis

ʃere:-ai	ʃere:[**g**]ai	'of the table'
cf. mal-al	malai	'of the cattle'
noxoi-a:r	noxoi[**g**]o:r	'by means of the dog'
cf. mal-a:r	mala:r	'by means of cattle'

Staroverov (2014:145-146) examines epenthesis in Halh Mongolian (Mongolic), arguing that this language too exhibits dorsal epenthesis.

Similar findings arise in an examination of neutralization, another emergence-of-the-unmarked context. I compare neutralization to coronal, an expected neutralization, with neutralization to dorsal, an unexpected neutralization given the markedness hierarchy. Neutralization to coronal is expected; some examples are given in (18) and (19).

(18) Saami: Word-final consonants neutralize to coronal (Odden 2005:244)

nominative sg.	essive	
ahhku[b]-in	ahhku[t]	'grandchild of woman'
tʃuoivva[g]-in	tʃuoivva[t]	'yellow-brown reindeer'

Basque (Hualde 1991:13) is similar in showing neutralization to coronal in certain environments. There is a coronal-dorsal contrast in morpheme-final position, with neutralization to coronal syllable-finally.

(19) Basque: Syllable-final consonants neutralize to coronal (Hualde 1991:13)

| o[g]i 'bread' | o[t]-apur | 'bread crumb' |
| i[d]i 'ox' | i[t]-zan | 'ox driver' |

However, neutralization to dorsal also occurs. In Manam (Austronesian; Lichtenberk 1983), only nasal consonants are possible word-finally; these neutralize to [m] or [ŋ], in free variation, with [ŋ] more frequent, as illustrated in (20).

(20) Manam: word-final neutralization to labial or dorsal (Lichtenberk 1983:30-31)

da/ŋ/ 'water'	*da[m],* da[**ŋ**]	'water'
	cf. mata-da[ŋ]-igu	'my tears'
	eye-water-1SG.ADNOMINAL	
ze/m/ 'chew'	*bua u-ze[m],* bua u-ze[**ŋ**]	'I chewed betel nuts'
	betel nut 1SG.REALIS-chew	
	cf. búa ú-ze[m]-i	'I chewed a betel nut'
	betel nut 1SG.REALIS-chew-3SG.OBJECT	
/aʔn/ 'eat'	*udi go-ʔá[m],* udi go-ʔá[**ŋ**]	'eat the bananas!'
	banana 2SG.IRREALIS-eat	
	cf. údi gó-ʔa[n]-i	'eat the banana!'
	banana 2SG.IRREALIS-eat-3SG.OBJECT	

Cuban Spanish too shows neutralization to dorsal in syllable final position (Guitart 1976).

(21) Cuban Spanish (syllable final position) (Guitart 1976:48)

/konsep/	konsé[**k**]to	'concept'
	cf. konse[β]ír	'to conceive'
/sub/	su[**ɣ**]liŋwál	'sublingual'
	cf. su[β]arrendado	'subleased'
/ad/	a[**ɣ**]mitir	'to admit'

Tlachichiko Tepehua (Totonacan; Watters 1980) also has neutralization to dorsal in syllable-final position.

(22)   Tlachichiko Tepehua (Totonacan; Watters 1980:98) (syllable-final position)
        p, t → k at the end of a syllable

talitsúku[t]i	'animal'	talitsukú[k]na	'animals'
hóʔa[t]i	'man'	hoʔá[k]na	'men'
qasmá[t]a	'he hears it'	qasmá[k]ɬi	'he heard it'
ká[p]a	'he forgets it'	kaw[k]ɬi	'he forgot it'
ʃá[p]a	'he pants'	ʃáw[k]ɬi	'he panted'

Note that in loanwords as well, [k] is found syllable finally: *Huehuetla* (place name) is realized as *wewe[k]la*, and *septiembre* 'September' as *se[k]tiembre*.

Carib (also called Kari'nja; Cariban; Hoff 1968) shows similar patterning, with active neutralization of stops in syllable-final position to [x]. Ecuador Quichua (Quchuan; Orr 1962:65) is reported to have only dorsals stops word finally (the word-final inventory is k, g, m, n, s, l, y), as in examples including *pusa[k]* 'eight', *sini[k]* 'porcupine'). (The syllable-final consonants also include ts and tʃ, found only before k; geminates do not occur; Orr 1962:67). In loanwords, too, dorsals appear syllable-finally where coronals are present in the source language: *pi[g]ru* 'Pedro' (Orr 1962:73).

It thus appears that the predictions of the substantive place of articulation hierarchy are not supported. The hierarchy predicts cross-linguistic uniformity in epenthesis and neutralization positions. However, dorsals are possible as both epenthetic consonants and as the output of neutralization, not just coronals, something that is not expected given a substantive hierarchy. This type of cross-linguistic variation is not expected (nor is similar language-internal variation, not illustrated here).

4. The start of an account

I have illustrated two types of variation, one where what is considered to be the same sound patterns differently in different languages, illustrated in section 2 with the patterning of the vowel /a/ in three languages, and a second , discussed in section 3, where unexpected epenthesis and neutralization are found, given a universal substantive place of articulation hierarchy. Why is such variation possible? Here I briefly outline a possible account, focusing on the markedness cases.

In early discussion of markedness, Trubetzkoy notes (1969:81): "the opposition member that is permitted in the position of neutralization is *unmarked* from the standpoint of the respective phonemic system, while the opposing member is *marked."* It is interesting to note that Trubetzkoy does not refer universal unmarkedness, but rather to markedness with respect to the particular phonemic system.

Battistella (1990:27), writing on semantic markedness, notes that "Indeterminateness refers to the semantic criterion that marked elements are characteristically specific and determinate in meaning while the opposed unmarked elements are characteristically indeterminate, a factor that follows from the definition of semantic markedness as having both a general meaning and a meaning opposite from that of the marked term." He (1990:4) further comments on the notion of opposition and how the poles of an opposition are defined, writing that "... whenever we have an opposition between two things, one of those things – the unmarked one – will be more broadly defined." Notice the importance of an opposition in this statement. What is the content of the unmarked in the absence of an opposition? Battistella uses the term 'indeterminate.' In his definition, markedness is relevant under conditions of contrast. In the absence of an opposition (a contrast), the possibility arises that markedness is simply indeterminate from the perspective of phonology. Given the absence of a contrast, what actually happens is constrained in various ways – factors including articulation, perception, information content, complexity, language history, and social variables matter, and there are probably additional factors as well that play important roles in determining what happens in the absence of a contrast, but the substance is not determinate by the phonology. It is possible to make educated guesses, but the hierarchy does not in fact have predictive value. Just as categorization is problematic given phonological activity, so is predictability – there are statistical tendencies, but the variation that is found is striking.

Features play an important role in phonological theory, so we might ask what remains of phonology if we remove substantive features as being universal and innate, and see them as emergent. Phonology consists of abstract notions such as asymmetries, contrast, complexity, and activity. Critical to phonology is the notion of contrast, and how contrast is determined through phonological activity; see for instance work by Dresher (2009, 2014), Hall (2007, 2011), Krekoski (2016), Oxford (2015) and others. Phonological activity guides the understanding of what the contrasts are in a language, and thus what the necessary features are in that language.

Suppose that there is not activity in a language to help determine what the feature classes are? Krekoski (2016), in an examination of tonal systems in Chinese languages, argues that in that situation, phonetic factors are important. Following from this, he proposes that systems with more phonological activity are more likely to be less phonetically natural than those with less activity, where phonetic naturalness will shine through, a very intriguing hypothesis that requires further careful study.

5. Conclusion

To conclude, I have argued, following others such as Mielke, that substantive features are not universal in the sense that there is a given set of them that is assigned simply by establishing contrasts. Rather, the key to what features are needed comes through understanding phonological activity, or patterning, and how activity reveals what sounds pattern as a class within a particular language. There are many similarities between languages, not unexpectedly, given articulatory, auditory, and acoustic aspects of speech. But the variation between (and within) languages shows that how sounds pattern in particular languages can vary in many ways. The variation is not unlimited, but more than expected with Duanmu's features and with the fixed substantive markedness hierarchies. The number of features required remains small, and related to the contrasts and activity present in a particular language. Speakers, through coming to understand the contrasts and phonological activity of their language, determine what features must be constructed.

I end with a quote from Sapir (1921) about what he calls the genius of a language:

> For it must be obvious … that there is such a thing as a basic plan, a certain cut, to each language. This type or plan or structural "genius" of the language is something much more fundamental, much more pervasive, than any single feature of it that we can mention, nor can we gain an adequate idea of its nature by a mere recital of the sundry facts that make up the grammar of the language.
>
> Sapir (1921:120)

Each language has its genius that defines it. How the sounds pattern is one of the things that must be discovered as part of trying to understand the genius of a language, and that patterning provides insight into the features and feature classes that are important in that language.

Notes

This work was supported by the Canada Research Chair in Linguistics and Aboriginal Studies. Thank you to all those who have participated in the phonology research group at the University of Toronto over the years for stimulating discussion and ideas that have led to this work – there are many of you.

References

Anderson, Stephen R. 1981. What phonology isn't 'natural.' *Linguistic Inquiry* 12.493-539.

Battistella, Edwin. 1990. *Markedness: the evaluative superstructure of language*. Albany: State University of New York Press.

Bearth, Thomas and Hugo Zemp. 1967. The phonology of Dan (Santa). *Journal of African languages* 6.9-29.

Beckman, Jill. 1997. Positional faithfulness, positional neutralisation, and Shona vowel harmony. *Phonology* 14.1–46.

Chomsky, A. Noam and Morris Halle. 1968. *The sound pattern of English*. New York: Harper & Row.

Clements, G.N. 2001. Representational economy in constraint-based phonology. *Distinctive feature theory*, ed. by T. Alan Hall, 71-146. Berlin: Mouton de Gruyter.

D'Arcy, Alexandra. 2004. Unconditional neutrality: Vowel harmony in a two-place model. *Toronto Working Papers in Linguistics* 23.1–46.

de Lacy, Paul. 2006. *Markedness: reduction and preservation in phonology*. Cambridge: Cambridge University Press.

de Lacy, Paul and John Kingston. 2013. Synchronic explanation. *Natural Language and Linguistic Theory*. 31.287-355.

Dresher, B. Elan. 2009. *The contrastive hierarchy in phonology*. Cambridge: Cambridge University Press.

Dresher, B. Elan. 2014. The arch not the stones: universal feature theory without universal features. *Nordlyd* 41.165-181.

Duanmu, San. 2016. *A theory of phonological features*. Oxford: Oxford University Press.

Fortune, George. 1955. *An analytical grammar of Shona*. Capetown & New York: Longmans, Green.

Guitart, Jorge M. 1976. *Markedness and a Cuban dialect of Spanish*. Washington, D.C.: Georgetown University Press.

Hall, Daniel Currie. 2007. *The role and representation of contrast in phonological theory*. Doctoral dissertation, University of Toronto.

Hall, Daniel Currie. 2011. Phonological contrast and its phonetic enhancement: dispersedness without dispersion. *Phonology* 28.1.1-54.

Hoff, Bernd. 1968. *The Carib language*. The Hague: Martinus Nijhof.

Hualde, José Ignacio. 1991. *Basque phonology*. London: Routledge.

Hume, Elizabeth. 2011. Markedness. *The Blackwell companion to phonology*. ed. by Marc Van Oostendorp, Colin Ewen, Elizabeth Hume and Keren Rice, 79-106. Oxford: Wiley-Blackwell.

Krekoski, Ross. 2016. *Contrast and complexity in Chinese tonal systems*. Ph.D. dissertation. University of Toronto.

Lichtenberk, Frank. 1983. *A grammar of Manam*. Honolulu: University of Hawaii Press.

Lombardi, Linda 2002. Coronal epenthesis and markedness. *Phonology* 19.219–251.

McMurray, Bob, Jennifer S. Cole, and Cheyenne Munson. 2011. Features as an emergent product of perceptual parsing: Evidence from V-V coarticulation. *Where do phonological features come from? Cognitive, physical and developmental bases of distinctive speech categories*, ed. by G.N. Clements and R. Ridouane. 197-236. Amsterdam: John Benjamins.

Menn, Lise and Marilyn Vihman. 2011. Features in child phonology: inherent, emergent, or artefacts of analysis? *Where do features come from?* ed. by G.N. Clements and Rachid Ridouane. 261-301. Amsterdam: Benjamins.

Mielke, Jeff. 2005. Ambivalence and ambiguity in laterals and nasals. *Phonology* 22.169-203.

Mielke, Jeff. 2008. *The emergence of distinctive features*. Oxford: Oxford University Press.

Mielke, Jeff. 2013. Phonologization and the typology of feature behavior. *Origins of sound change: Approaches to phonologization*. ed. by Alan C.L. Yu. 165-180. Oxford: Oxford University Press.

Mielke, Jeff. 2016. Review of San Duanmu, A theory of phonological features. *Language* 93.477-481.

Morley, Rebecca. 2015a. Deletion or epenthesis? On the falisifiability of phonological universals. *Lingua* 154.1-26.

Morley, Rebecca. 2015b. Can phonological universals be emergent? Modeling the space of sound change, lexical distribution, and hypothesis selection. *Language* 91.e40-e70.

Nash, David. 1980. *Topics in Walpiri grammar*. Ph.D. dissertation, MIT.

Odden, David. 2005. *Introducing phonology*. Cambridge introductions to language and linguistics. Cambridge: Cambridge University Press.

Odden, David. 2015. Bantu phonology. *Oxford handbooks online*. Available at http://www.oxfordhandbooks.com/view/10.1093/oxfordhb/9780199935345.001.0001/oxfordhb-9780199935345-e-59

Orr, Carolyn. 1962. Ecuador Quichua phonology. *Studies in Ecuadorian Indian languages* 1, ed. by Benjamin Elson, 60-77. Norman: Summer Institute of Linguistics of the University of Oklahoma.

Oxford, Will. 2015. Patterns of contrast in phonological change: Evidence from Algonquian vowel systems. *Language* 91.308–357.

Rice, Keren. 2003. Featural markedness in phonology: Variation. *The second Glot International state-of-the-article book: The latest in linguistics*. ed. by Lisa Cheng and Rint Sybesma. 387–427. Berlin: Mouton de Gruyter.

Rice, Keren. 2007. Markedness in phonology. *The Cambridge handbook of phonology*. ed. by Paul de Lacy. 79-97. Cambridge: Cambridge University Press.

Rice, Keren. 2017. Review of San Duanmu, *A theory of phonological features*. *Folia Linguistica*. 51.289-300.

Sapir, Edward. 1921. *Language: An introduction to the study of speech*. New York: Harcourt, Brace and Company.

Sharp, Janet. 2004. *Nyangumarta: a language of the Pilbara region of Western Australia*. Canberra: Pacific Linguistics.

Staroverov, Peter. 2014. *Splitting theory and consonant epenthesis*. Ph.D. dissertation, Rutgers University.

Stokhof, W.A.L. 1979. *Woisika II: Phonemics*. Canberra: Australian National University.

Trubetzkoy, N. 1969. *Principles of phonology*. Berkeley: University of California Press.

Watters, James K. 1980. Aspects of Tlachichilco Tepehua (Totonacan) phonology. *SIL-Mexico Workpapers* 4.85-129.

発表要旨 / ABSTRACTS

Acquisition of English Prosody by Korean EFL Learners

Hyebae Yoo
Incheon National University

English pronunciation has been emphasized in education over several decades, while traditional accuracy-based pronunciation has been avoided in Korea. In this atmosphere, the relative importance of suprasegmentals in language acquisition has received more attention, and efforts have been made to enhance suprasegmental learning.

A recent longitudinal study (Yoo 2016) on Korean EFL students' prosody analyzed acoustically the English pronunciation of Korean cohorts of 2000 and 2012 to investigate their accent improvement over a decade. Group 2012 who had received elementary English education outperformed Group 2000 who had not had exposure to English until junior high school in the ratios of stress-timing, intensity, speech rate, and pitch change. The question arising from the research was whether this improvement in suprasegmental features contributed to an improvement in comprehensibility by native speakers of English. Does improved prosody result in greater comprehensibility? This study seeks to answer this question by examining the effects of suprasegmental features on the comprehensibility judgment of EFL learners' pronunciation. Previous studies that supported the role of suprasegmentals (Anderson-Hsieh et al. 1992; Trofimovich and Baker 2006; Kang 2010) would predict a positive result. While studies have been conducted on native speakers' judgments of the comprehensibility of foreign accented speech (Kang 2010; Yom 2011; Lee 2013), the findings of these studies were cross-sectional and did not demonstrate changes over time.

The participants of this study were divided into three groups: 19 (male 10, female 9) Korean students who entered university in 2000 (hereafter Group 2000), 19 (male 10, female 9) Korean students who entered university in 2012 (hereafter Group 2012), and 10 native English speakers, used as a rater group (NE). The Korean groups were further divided by gender, such as 2000M (male) and 2000F (female). The raters comprised ten native English speakers, eight American and two Canadian, with American English accents.

The recordings used for the native speakers' judgment task and their acoustic measurements were extracted from the corpus collected for Yoo (2016). The recordings were measured and calculated in the three acoustic correlates of stress (pitch, duration, and intensity), pitch range, and speech rate. As for the correlates of stress, the mean ratios of stressed to unstressed vowels were calculated for pitch, duration, and intensity: For example, duration ratio was calculated in the following way: the average duration of stressed vowels in each clause or sentence was divided by the average duration of unstressed vowels in the same sentence. Pitch range was calculated by subtracting the lowest from the highest F0 in a clause or sentence. Speech rate was measured by the number of syllables per second for each sentence.

Comprehensibility judgment ratings revealed that Korean students have improved their comprehensibility significantly over a decade in all areas of segmental, suprasegmental, and general comprehensibility. As the purpose of English pronunciation education is to improve comprehensibility, this improvement can be seen as a success for English education.

A close look at the data showed gender differences in many respects. First, the comprehensibility of the female group of 2012 was much higher than that of the male group of 2012 (4.87 vs 3.89), whereas the gender difference was not as large for Group 2000 (3.71 vs 3.53). This gap for Group 2012 can be seen as the result of a greater improvement for female students than for male (1.16vs0.36).

— 133 —

Second, female students have improved suprasegmentals (1.10) more than segmentals (1.02), whereas male students showed improvement of 0.36 for suprasegmentals and 0.38 for segmentals. The gender difference can be regarded as evidence for the more prominent role of suprasegmentals in comprehensibility.

Another purpose of this study was to examine the relative importance of segmentals and suprasegmentals on comprehensibility, since there is little agreement (Sereno et al. 2016; Park and Park 2014). This study supports the pre-eminence of suprasegmentals over segmentals based on coefficients of a regression analysis; the general comprehensibility turned out to be more correlational with suprasegmentals (β=.556) than segmentals (β=.363).

Finally, this study investigated the relative impact of five suprasegmental features – pitch ratio, duration ratio, loudness ratio, pitch range, and speech rate – on comprehensibility. According to the stepwise multiple regression, the relative contribution of the suprasegmental factors to comprehensibility judgment is as follows: speech rate > duration ratio > pitch range > loudness ratio > pitch ratio. This result supports the superiority of speech rate in perception (Munro and Derwing 2001; Kang 2010; Trofimovich and Baker 2006) and rejects the view that prosodic factors such as sentence stress, intonation, and rhythm are more important than speech rate (Warren *et al.* 2009).

In conclusion, this study provides evidence for the relative role of prosodic features that are derived not merely from a cross-sectional method. This study not only sheds light on the development in abilities of Korean EFL students over decades, but also upon the influence of prosodic features in comprehensibility in general.

References

Anderson-Hsieh, Janet, Ruth Johnson and Kenneth Koehler. 1992. The relationship between native speaker judgments of non-native production and deviance in segmentals, prosody, and syllable structure. *Language Learning* 42.529-555.

Kang, Okim. 2010. Relative salience of suprasegmental features on judgments of L2 comprehensibility and accentedness. *System* 38.301-315.

Lee, Joo-Kyeong. 2013. The role of prosody in the perception of foreign accent and comprehensibility: Prosody-corrected-L2 speech vs. prosody-distorted-L1 speech. *Korean Journal of Linguistics* 39.155-179.

Munro, Murray J. and Tracey M. Derwing. 2001. Modeling perceptions of the accentedness and comprehensibility of L2 speech: The role of speaking rate. *Studies of Second Language Acquisition* 23.451-468.

Park, Chang-Won and Sayhyon Park. 2014. Comprehensibility of advanced Korean high school students' English pronunciation. *New Korean Journal of English Language and Literature* 56.163-185.

Sereno, Joan, Lynne Lammers and Allard Jongman. 2016. The relative contribution of segments and intonation to the perception of foreign-accented speech. *Applied Psycholinguistics* 37.303–322

Trofimovich, Pavel and Wendy Baker. 2006. Learning second language suprasegmentals: Effect of L2 experience on prosody and fluency characteristics of L2 speech. *Studies in Second Language Acquisition* 28.1-30.

Warren, Paul, Irina Elgort and David Crabbe. 2009. Comprehensibility and prosody ratings for pronunciation software development. *Language Learning and Technology* 13.87-102.

Yom, Mun Sil. 2011. The correlation between Korean English acoustic features and the comprehensibility for native listeners. *The Journal of Studies in Language* 27.287-305.

Yoo, Hyebae. 2016. An acoustic analysis of Korean EFL learners' English prosody: A longitudinal study. *Studies in Phonetics, Phonology and Morphology* 22.55-75.

ルクセンブルク語の音韻記述

The Phonology of Luxembourgish

西出佳代

Kayo Nishide

神戸大学

Kobe University

1. はじめに

　ルクセンブルク語は、ドイツ語西モーゼルフランケン方言に分類される西ゲルマン語で、1984年言語法によってルクセンブルク大公国の「国語」に昇格した比較的新しい言語である。発表者は、研究領域としても新しいルクセンブルク語研究の基盤作り、すなわち言語記述を長期的な目標としており、学位申請論文ではまず同言語の音韻記述を行った（西出 2015）。記述の対象としたのは、4つに大別されるルクセンブルク語の内部方言のうち、首都圏で話されるルクセンブルク語中央方言である。本発表では、その中から共時的なトピックに関する研究成果をいくつか紹介した。

2. 母音体系

　本研究では、2011年に行った録音調査の音響解析結果をもとに、数少ないルクセンブルク語の母音体系の記述のうち音響音声学的な観点から分析を試みた Keiser-Besch (1976) の研究を取り上げ修正を施した。単母音では、強勢を伴う中舌母音の音素 /ɐ̆/ を新たに設定し、半広前舌母音についてはより適切な IPA /æ/ を提示し、狭母音 /i/, /u/ の異音を整理した。二重母音はその音質の記述を修正した。

(1) Keiser-Besch (1976) によるルクセンブルク語の母音体系

　　11 個の単母音：/iː/, /ɪ/, /uː/, /ʊ/, /e/, /ɛ/, /ə/, /o/, /ɔ/, /aː/, /ɑ/

　　8 個の二重母音：/ɑɪ/, /ɛɪ/, /ɑʊ/, /ɛʊ/, /əɪ/, /ɪə/, /ɔʊ/, /ʊə/

(2) 本研究のルクセンブルク語の母音体系

　　13 個の単母音：/iː/, /i/, /uː/, /u/, /eː/, /ɛ/, /ɐ̆/, /ə/, /æ/, /oː/, /ɔ/, /aː/, /ɑ/

　　8 個の二重母音：/ɑɪ/, /æɪ/, /ʊ/, /æʊ/, /ɛɪ/, /ɪə/, /ɐ̆ʊ/, /ʊə/

3. 形態素境界における音韻現象

3.1 境界を明示する現象：名詞句初頭における歯茎閉鎖音

　ルクセンブルク語には、標準ドイツ語と同様、形態素境界を明示する現象の一種と考えられる形態素末における子音の無声化（final devoicing）が観察される。

(3) a. gudden_{M.NOM.} [gudən] "good" – gutt_{F.NOM.} [gʊt] "good"

　　b. Bierger [bɪəzɐ] "mountains" – Bierg [bɪəɕ] "mountain"

　ルクセンブルク語においては、さらにもう一つの境界を明示する現象、すなわち名詞句の初頭における複雑な子音群（consonant cluster）が観察される。特に歯茎閉鎖音 [d], [t] の重子音が特徴的であり、前置詞末尾に挿入された歯茎音（ënner-t [ënɐt] "under"）および接語的定冠詞（d' [t] "the_{F/N/PL}"）が、歯茎閉鎖音 [d]/[t] から始まる名詞に先行する場合がある（Dänn [dæn] "fir tree", Tania [taːnɪa] "Tania"（人名））。2011年の調査によって、ルクセンブルク語におけるこのような複雑な子音群は、調音的、聴覚

的及び音響音声学的に明確に区別されることが明らかとなった。

 (4) a. ënner*t d'D*änn [ënɐt̚ ˈdæn] "under the fir tree"

   b. nief*t d'T*ania [nɪəft̚ ˈtaːnɪa] "next to the Tania"

3.2 境界をあいまいにする現象

一方、境界を曖昧にする現象として、以下の 2 つの現象が挙げられる。

3.2.1 コーダにおける子音の有声化

母音で始まる後続の要素との間での再音節化に伴い、複合語の内部 (5a) 及び語間 (5b) において先行する形態素末の子音（群）が有声化を起こす。ただし、語幹と屈折語尾の間では有声化しない。

 (5) a. Te*xt*-analys [tækst] [ɑnɑlyːs] > [tægzdɑnɑlyːs] "text analysis"

   b. Ueb*st* a Geméis [ʊəpst] [ɑ] [gəmɛɪs] > [ʊəbzdɑgəmɛɪs] "fruit and vegetables"

3.2.2 /ʀ/ の母音化の阻害

音節末尾の /ʀ/ は原則として母音化されるが（Bi*r* [biːɐ] "pear"）、母音で始まる後続の要素との間での再音節化に伴い、この母音化が阻害される。この現象は、子音の有声化 (3.2.1) と同様、複合語の内部 (6a) と語間 (6b) で起こる他、語幹と屈折語尾の間でも起こる (6c)。

 (6) a. vi*r* [fiɐ] "in front of" – vi*r*un [fi.ʀʊn] "before"

   b. me*r* [mɐ] "me_DAT" – [...] huet me*r* erzielt [...] [hʊət mɐʀɐtsɪəlt] "(he) has explained to me [...]"

   c. léie*r*t [lɛɪɐt] "learns" – léie*r*en [lɛɪ.ʀən] "to learn"

3.3 その他の現象 – n の脱落

音節末尾の [n] は、その後ろにポーズが置かれない限り、母音や特定の子音（[t], [d], [ts], [n], [h]）の前という環境以外で脱落する。Gilles (2006) は、末尾の [n] を韻律外分節 "extraprosodisches Element" とし、これが後続の音節に連結される再音節化が起こらない限り、表層において脱落すると説明した（Stray Erasure）。[t], [d], [ts], [n], [h] と末尾の [n] は部分的重子音を形成することによって保たれる。

 (7) a. gudde_ Wäin [gudəvæɪn] "good wine"

   b. en Auto [ənɑʊtoː] "a car"

   c. de*n* Téi [dəntɛɪ] "the tea"

4. まとめ

本発表では、音韻研究の基礎となる音素記述の中から母音体系の記述に焦点を当て、先行研究の問題点を指摘し、独自の調査結果から先行研究の記述に大幅な修正を加えた（第 2 節）。また音韻現象については、形態素境界における現象をいくつか取り上げ、特徴を整理した（第 3 節）。本研究によって、ルクセンブルク語は CV 構造を好む傾向があること (3.2, 3.3)、ただし独立形態素初頭の歯茎閉鎖音 /d/, /t/ が関与する場合のみ例外的に境界を明示する傾向があることが明らかとなった (3.1, 3.3)。

参照文献

Gilles, Peter. 2006. Phonologie der *n*-Tilgung im Moselfränkischen ('Eifler Regel'). *Perspektiven einer lInguistischen Luxemburgistik. Studien zu Diachronie und* Synchronie, ed. by Moulin, Claudine and Damaris Nübling, 29-68. Heidelberg: Universitätsverlag Winter.

Keiser-Besch, Denise. 1976. Étude descriptive et analytique du vocalisme luxembourgeois. *Bulletin linguistique, étymologique et toponymique*, 91-100.

西出佳代 2015 『ルクセンブルク語の音韻記述』札幌：北海道大学出版社.

Various Contextual Factors Under Way for C Insertion in Korean Reduplication

Youngran An
KC University

ABSTRACT. Among the other factors concerning the insertion of consonants in Korean reduplication, this paper deals with the contextual factors, focusing mainly on the relationships between inserted consonants and their surrounding sounds. The findings particularly point to the inserted consonants being affected by both the preceding consonants and the following vowels. The inserted consonants were also found to have the tendency of identity avoidance in general and identity preference in specific instances.

Keywords: consonant insertion, reduplication, Korean, context, identity avoidance, identity preference

A type of total reduplication in Korean has a consonant inserted (CI) in the reduplicant, e.g., oson-**t**oson 'on good terms,' oŋki-**ʧ**oŋki 'densely,' ulak-**p**ulak 'roughly.' The choice of CIs is not random; rather, there is a tendency to insert a C which is dissimilar from existing base Cs (Figure 1).

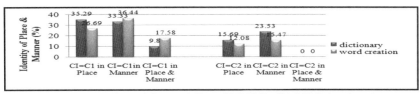

Figure 1 *Relationship of CIs and Cs in $V_1C_1V_2C_2$-CV$_1$C$_1$V$_2$C$_2$ in place/manner*

This tendency to prefer a non-identical or dissimilar C from existing Cs has been attested in many other languages; e.g., Turkish emphatic reduplication prefers to choose /p/ unless a labial C, including /p/, already exists in the base, kara 'dark' → ka**p**kara 'pitch black,' belli 'clear' → be**s**belli 'obvious' (Wedel 1999; Yu 1999).

Regarding pairs of CI and C_1, in $V_1C_1V_2C_2$-CV$_1$C$_1$V$_2$C$_2$, sharing the place of articulation, for the dictionary data, O/E values showed that pair <p, labial> was underrepresented at a marginally significant level; <ʧ, palatal> was underrepresented, but not at a significant level; and <ʧ, alveolar> (both, coronals) were significantly underrepresented. For the experimental responses, O/E values showed that <p, labial> was significantly underrepresented; <t, alveolar> was neither significantly underrepresented nor significantly overrepresented; and <ʧ, alveolar> was significantly underrepresented. There was no significant underrepresentation for pairs of CI and C_1 sharing the manner of articulation. For pairs of CI and C_2 in either place or manner, there was no significant underrepresentation. These results indicate that place is more relevant to identity avoidance than manner.

The data from the Korean reduplication with CIs are similar to the other languages in terms of the strong tendency to avoid similarity among Cs; however, the Korean reduplication also shows another tendency, a tendency to insert an identical C to an existing base C. Figure 1 shows that there is no identical pair of CI and C_2, whereas there are some identical pairs of CI and C_1. It was found that if the vowels in the base are identical already, then a CI yet to be chosen is more likely to be the one identical to the existing first C in the base (VC$_1$VC$_2$-CVC$_1$VC$_2$). Peruvian Aymara allows only one ejective/aspirated stop per morpheme, unless the ejectives/aspirated stops are identical, [k'ink'u] 'clay,' [pʰuspʰu] 'boiled beans' (McEachern 1999; Zuraw 2002). In Sundanese two /r/'s in onsets of adjacent syllables cannot be dissimilated (Suzuki 1999; Zuraw

2002). When the ejectives/aspirated stops and the rhotics were identical, they were followed by identical vowels more frequently than non-identical Cs would be.

The tendency to prefer identical CV strings was confirmed in the experimental data of word creation in which the participants were asked to create the most natural reduplicated form with a nonce base form of VCVC by inserting a C in the reduplicant (N=55, 15 stimuli). It was more likely to have identical Vs in the cases in which CI and C_i are identical (78.31%), than in the control cases (41.13%). The same tendency was also found in the reduplication data from the dictionary (80% vs. 41.3%; MEB 2006) and in the corpus (100% vs. 50%; CJS 2007). The results from the behavioral experiments also imply that Korean speakers tend to group C_i and V, rather than V and C_2, as a unit in a syllable of C_iVC_2, contrary to prediction that V and C_2 will form a sub-syllabic unit on the basis of the traditional syllable structure, onset + rime (Y. Lee 2006; Chen *et al.* 2005).

It was also found that there is some relationship between the two consonants across a border of syllables, in $V_iC_iV_2C_2$-$\underline{CV_iC_iV_2C_2}$. This C_2-C relationship could be determined by the constraint that regulates acceptable syllable contacts, Syllable Contact Law (SYLLCON), which has been attested as one of the critical constraints in Korean, e.g., n-epenthesis (/ʧom+jak/ → [ʧom.**n**jak] 'mothball'), nasalization (/naᵗ+mal/ → [nan.mal] 'word'), and lateralization (/kon+lan/ → [kol.lan] 'difficulty') (Davis and Shin 1999; Kang 2001, 2005; M. Lee 2006; Sohn 2008; *inter alia*). The inserted consonants in reduplication were in general chosen to avert rising sonority across a syllable boundary. SYLLCON was respected in 98.28% of the dictionary data (58 words with the form of V.CVC-$\underline{CV.CVC}$), and 97.67% of the responses in the experiment (word creation, N=55, 817 tokens).

The diverse factors appear to influence the choice behavior of CIs in the reduplication, and the interaction among these contextual factors call for more investigation.

References

Chen, Train-Min, Gary S. Dell and Jenn-Yeu Chen. 2005. A cross-linguistic study of phonological units: syllables emerge from the statistics of Mandarin Chinese, but not from the statistics of English. *Proceedings of the 26th annual meeting of the Cognitive Science Society*, ed. by Kenneth Forbus, Dedre Gentner and Terry Regier, 216–220. The Cognitive Science Society.

CJS (= 21ˢᵗ Century Sejong Project). 2007. *Sejong balanced corpus*. The National Institute of the Korean Language.

Davis, Stuart and Seung-Hoon Shin. 1999. The syllable contact constraint in Korean: an optimality-theoretic analysis. *Journal of East Asian Linguistics* 8.285–312.

Kang, Eungyeong. 2001. Edge-integrity and the syllable structure in Korean. *Language, information, and computation: Proceedings of the 16th Pacific Asia Conference.* ed. by Ik-Hwan Lee, Yong-Beom Kim, Key-Sun Choi and Minhaeng Lee, 135–146. The Korean Society for Language and Information.

Kang, Eungyeong. 2005. Consonant copy in Korean. *Studies in Phonetics, Phonology and Morphology* 11(2).3–20.

Lee, Minkyung. 2006. Gyeongsang Korean /n/-insertion revisited. *Studies in Phonetics, Phonology and Morphology* 12(3).623–641.

Lee, Yongeun. 2006. *Sub-syllabic constituency in Korean and English*. Ph.D. dissertation, Northwestern University.

MacEachern, Margaret. 1999. *Laryngeal cooccurrence restrictions*. New York: Garland.

MEB (= Minjung Editorial Bureau). 2006. *Essence Korean dictionary*. Phacwu, Korea: Minjung.

Sohn, Hyang-Sook. 2008. Phonological contrast and coda saliency of sonorant assimilation in Korean. *Journal of East Asian Linguistics* 17.33–59.

Suzuki, Keiichiro. 1999. Identity avoidance vs. identity preference: the case of Sundanese. Paper presented at the 73rd Annual Meeting of the Linguistic Society of America, Los Angeles.

Wedel, Andrew. 1999. Turkish emphatic reduplication. Manuscript. Linguistics Research Center: Phonology at Santa Cruz.

Yu, Alan. 1999. Dissimilation and allomorphy: The case of Turkish emphatic reduplication. Manuscript. University of California, Berkeley.

Zuraw, Kie. 2002. Aggressive reduplication. *Phonology* 19.395–439.

日本音韻論学会

2017 年度の主な活動

2017 年

5 月 30 日　　Newsletter 第 21 巻第 1 号(通算 60 号)の発行
　　　　　　　(新執行部・理事就任のお知らせ、春期研究発表会のプログラ
　　　　　　　ム、音韻論フォーラム 2017 の発表募集など)

6 月 17 日　　韓国音韻・形態論学会に太田聡氏を派遣

6 月 23 日　　2017 年度春期研究発表会、第 41 回理事会、第 21 回会員総会
　　　　　　　の開催 (於、慶応義塾大学 日吉キャンパス)

7 月 28 日　　Newsletter 第 21 巻第 2 号(通算 61 号)の発行
　　　　　　　(春期研究発表会・会員総会報告、『音韻研究』第 21 号の論文
　　　　　　　募集、音韻論フォーラム 2017 プログラムなど)

8 月 23 日　　音韻論フォーラム 2017、第 42 回理事会の開催
　　〜25 日　(於、首都大学東京 南大沢キャンパス)

12 月 12 日　Newsletter 第 21 巻第 3 号(通算 62 号)の発行
　　　　　　　(音韻論フォーラム 2017 報告、2018 年度春期研究発表会予告
　　　　　　　と発表募集、音韻論フォーラム 2018 予告など)

2018 年

3 月 31 日　　『音韻研究』第 21 号発行

以上
日本音韻論学会事務局

日本音韻論学会会則

第1章　名称、所在地、目的、会員

第1条　本会の名称は、日本音韻論学会（The Phonological Society of Japan）とする。

第2条　本会の所在地は、事務局長の所在地とする。

第3条　本会の目的は、音韻研究の発展に寄与することとする。
　　2　第1項の目的を達成するために、次の事業を行う。
　　　（1）研究発表会及び総会等の会を開催する。
　　　（2）機関誌及び会報等を発行する。
　　　（3）その他本会の目的にかなう事業を行う。

第4条　本会の会員は、通常会員、学生会員、維持会員及び賛助会員からなる。
　　2　通常会員は、本会の趣旨に賛同し、会費等に関する所定の手続きを経て本会に登録された個人とする。
　　3　学生会員は、本会の趣旨に賛同し、会費等に関する所定の手続きを経て本会に登録された学生とする。
　　4　維持会員は、本会の趣旨に賛同し、本会に財政援助を供し、理事会の承認を経て本会に登録された個人とする。
　　5　賛助会員は、本会の趣旨に賛同し、本会に財政援助を供し、理事会の承認を経て本会に登録された個人及び団体とする。

第2章　役員等

第5条　本会は、第3条の事業を遂行するために、次の役員を置く。
　　　（1）会長　　　　　　1名
　　　（2）副会長　　　　　1名
　　　（3）理事　　　　　　若干名
　　　（4）監事　　　　　　1名
　　　（5）事務局長　　　　1名
　　2　役員は、通常会員もしくは維持会員であることを必要とする。
　　3　役員の任期は、1期を継続4年とし、事務局長を除いて引き続き同一役に再任するこ

とはできない。

  (2) 役員に欠員が生じた場合の補欠の役員の任期は、前任者の残任期間とする。ただし、残任期間が一年に満たない場合は、第3項の規定にかかわらず、引き続き再任することができる。

4 役員の年齢は、就任時に65歳を超えていてはならない。

5 第1項に規定された役員以外に、顧問を若干名置くことができる。

第6条 会長は、理事会が選出する。

2 会長は、本会を代表し、その業務を統轄し、会議の議長となる。

3 会長は、副会長及び事務局長の候補者を選出し、理事会の承認を経て業務を委嘱する。

4 会長は、理事会に対して、当該年度の事業計画案と予算計画案を提出する。

5 会長は、理事会の承認を経て、本会の業務を第5条の役員以外の通常会員もしくは持会員に委嘱することができる。

第7条 副会長は、会長を補佐し、会長が職務を果たすことができない場合、会長の代行となる。

第8条 理事は、総会の承認を経て、会長が委嘱する。

2 理事の改選は、ほぼ半数とする。

3 理事は、正副会長及び事務局長と併せて、理事会を構成する。

  (1) 理事会の招集は、通常、毎年1回会長が行う。

  (2) 理事会は、委任状を含めて、理事会構成員の過半数の出席がなければ開催することができない。

  (3) 理事会の職務は、本会の事業計画、予算計画、役員選出等に関し、本会の重要事項を審議決定することにある。

  (4) 理事会での議決は、出席者の過半数で決める。可否同数の場合は、議長が決める。

  (5) 理事会は、理事会構成員以外の者に理事会に出席することを求め、意見や説明を聴取することができる。

  (6) 緊急時などの場合、会長は、理事会構成員に郵便その他の通信手段でもって審議と決議を求めることができる。

  (7) 理事会は、その構成員の過半数の同意があれば、文書でもって会長に理事会開催を要請することができる。

  (8) 理事会には、本会の会員であれば誰であっても、文書でもって議案を提出することができる。

第9条 監事は、理事会の議決を経て、会長が委嘱する。

2 監事は、事業計画と予算計画の適切な執行を監督し、確認する。

第10条 事務局長の職務には、次の事項を含む。

　(1) 議事要旨を記録保存する。

　(2) 総会において年次報告を行う。

　(3) 会員名簿及び会費を管理する。

　(4) 会員その他に必要な諸連絡を行う。

　(5) その他、本会の管理運営に関する事務一切を総轄する。

2　事務局長は、理事会の承認を経て、事務局員を若干名任命することができる。

第11条 顧問は、本会に功労のあった個人その他で、理事会において承認されたものとする。

2　顧問には、特に任期規定を設けないものとする。

3　顧問には、会費納入の義務はない。

4　顧問は、理事会に対して相談役をつとめ、必要に応じて意見を述べることができる。

第3章　総会、研究発表会など

第12条 総会の招集は、通常、毎年1回、会長が行う。

2　総会の構成員は、通常会員、学生会員、維持会員及び賛助会員とする。

3　総会は、出席者があれば成立するものとする。

4　総会では、理事選出案を審議議決する。

5　その他、理事会審議決定事項や事務局業務などの報告を受ける。

第13条 研究発表会は、少なくとも年1回は、総会に合わせて開催する。

2　研究発表会の開催場所、日時、規模、その他は理事会の決定に従う。

第4章　会計

第14条 本会の経費は、会費、補助金、寄付金等をもって当てる。

2　本会の会計年度は、4月1日に始まり、翌年3月31日に終わる。

3　本会の予算案は、理事会の議決を経て定め、総会に報告する。

4　本会の決算書は、当該年度終了後約1ヶ月以内に作成し、監事の監査と理事会の承認を経た後、総会に報告する。

第15条 本会の会計に係わる振替口座および預貯金口座の住所は、事務局会計担当者の居所とする。

第 5 章　会則の細則と変更など

第 16 条　本会則を施行するために必要な細則は、理事会の承認を経て、会長が定める。

第 17 条　本会の会則の変更は、理事会の議決により行い、これを総会に報告する。

第 6 章　雑則

第 18 条　本会設立に際して、理事の半数は、任期を引き続き 6 年とする。
　　2　設立に先んじて生じる諸問題の解決は、音韻論研究会の役員に一任する。

附　　則

本会則は、1997 年 5 月 23 日開催の総会での承認を経て施行し、同年 4 月 1 日より適用する。
本会則は、1998 年 11 月 6 日開催の理事会にて変更が議決され、同年同日より適用する。
本会則は、2006 年 8 月 23 日開催の理事会にて変更が議決され、同年同日より適用する。

『音韻研究』一般投稿規定　（2012 年 8 月 20 日制定）

1.　一般投稿論文の投稿資格は会員のみとする。ただし、共著の場合は筆頭著者が会員であればよい。

2.　同一著者による論文の掲載は、各号で 2 編以内とし、このうち筆頭著者としては 1 編とする。

3.　投稿は随時受け付けるが、各号の投稿の締め切りを発行日 （3 月 31 日）の前年 10 月 20 日とする。

4. 投稿は未公刊の完全原稿に限る。

5. 他誌に応募中の原稿は投稿できない。

6.　論文の執筆は、原則として最新の「執筆要項」に従うこととする。

7.　論文の採否は、編集委員が決定する。

8. 印刷上の体裁については、編集委員が決定する。

9. 原稿料は支払われない。

以上。

『音韻研究』執筆要領

1. **使用言語**：日本語または英語（米スペリング）。執筆言語が母語でない場合、ネイティブチェックをかけてから提出する。編集および査読者は言語に関して責任を負わない。

2. **基本設定**：**A4**
   マージン：上下左右 2.5 cm。
   日本語：40 行　両端そろえ。
   英語：シングルスペース　両端そろえ。

3. **フォント**：MS 明朝。最新の Times New Roman。発音記号は Windows Vista, 7, Mac OS X に付属の Times New Roman の IPA 記号を使用。その他のフォントはファイルに埋め込み、使用フォント名と文字を編集者に連絡する。

4. **文字サイズ**：本文　**10 pt** 日本語　**12 pt** 英語、その他の部分についてはサンプル参照。

5. **ページ数**：標準 **8** ページ、必ず**偶数**で。超過は 4 ページまで。招待講演者無料。投稿者は 2 頁まで¥10,000、4 頁まで¥30,000。

6. **ページスタイル**：詳細は別頁サンプル参照

- 段落頭：和文は全角 1 文字空け、英文はインデント 1/4 インチ(6.3 mm)。

- 例番号：(...)でくくる。和文の場合は、例番号の前を全角一文字分空ける。英文の場合は、インデント 1/4 インチ(6.3 mm) 空ける。

- 注：文末注。自動脚注機能は使用せず手動で番号をふる。番号は文中も注の冒頭も、1, 2, 3, ... のように上付きにする。注の本文は番号のあと、半角 1 文字空けて始める。ただし、できるだけ注は避けること。**日本語、英語ともに 10 pt**。

- 引用：短い引用語句はイタリック(ローマ字)、または「 」(日本語)。引用を 1 段落にするときは、両端インデント 12.5 mm にする。和文は一重「 」で前後をくくる。英文は引用符なし。最後の行に出典を(Author Year:pages)のように記す。

- 参照文献リスト：別頁の Reference Style を参照。

- 図、表：タイトルに太字や斜体字を用いない。黒色以外の色は使わない。黒色以外を用いた場合、印字結果について編集は責任を負わない。

- 和文の丸括弧は、MS 明朝半角を使用。

Style Sheet for *Phonological Studies*

1. Write in English or in Japanese only.　Follow US spelling conventions. If you are not a native speaker of the language used in your paper, it should be checked by a native speaker before submission.

2. **Basic settings:** A4 size paper.
   Single-spaced justified.
   1 inch (25.4 mm) margin on all sides.

3. **Fonts:** Times New Roman, which also contains all standard IPA symbols. (WinXP's TNR font doesn't contain IPA; therefore WinXP is not recommended for phonetic symbol users.) Embed any other exotic fonts in the file and report their use to the editor.

4. **Font size:** 12 pt for body text.
   Refer to the sample page for others.

5. **Number of pages:** normally 8 pages. If the number of pages is less than 8, make it an even number. Up to 4 additional pages are allowed at the author's expense: ¥10,000 for 2 pages, or ¥30,000 for 4 pages. (Free of charge for invited speakers.)

6. **Page format** (also refer to the sample)**:**

- Indent 1/4 inches or 6.3 mm at the beginning of a paragraph.

- Parenthesize example numbers as in (1), (23). Indent these 1/4 inch or 6.3 mm.

- Avoid notes as much as possible but if unavoidable: Use 10 pt endnotes; superscript the numbers as in 1, 2, 3; do not use automatic numbering but number notes manually; put one space between the number and the text.

- Italicize short cited words or phrases.
  A long quoted paragraph should be indented on both sides with no quotation marks.
  Give the source information as in:
  (Author Year:pages) following the quoted text.

- Reference Style: refer to the Reference Style Sample.

- Do not use boldface or italics in the titles of figures and tables. Do not use colors other than black: the journal cannot be responsible for how other colors will appear in print.

Citation and Reference Style Guide:

The Basics: Follow the style of *Language*. 漢字かな表記で記述する際は『言語研究』に従う。

Quick tips:
- Use small letters throughout for article and book titles except the first letters of the first words of the main title and subtitle.
- Use en-dashes '–' (not hyphens '-') between page numbers.

♦ **Journal articles**

Use a period before page numbers, with no space in between.

> Embick, David and Alec Marantz. 2008. Architecture and blocking. *Linguistic Inquiry* 39.1–53.
>
> 小林賢次 1968 「否定表現の変遷」『国語学』15.5–62.
>
> 服部四郎 1976 「上代日本語の母音体系と母音調和」『言語』5(6).2–14.
> (月刊言語のように毎号ページ数が1からふられるものは号数をカッコ内に記す。巻を通して通し番号のページが付いているときは号数を省略。)

♦ **Books**

Italicize the title.

> Anderson, Stephen R. 2005. *Aspects of the theory of clitics.* Oxford: Oxford University Press.
>
> de Lacy, Paul. 2006. *Markedness: Reduction and preservation in phonology.* Cambridge: Cambridge University Press.
>
> Inkelas, Sharon and Draga Zec. 1990. *The phonology-syntax connection.* Chicago: Chicago University Press and Stanford, CA: CSLI Publications.
>
> 柴谷方良 1978 『日本語の分析』東京：大修館書店.

♦ **Edited book section**

Use a comma before page numbers.

Embed the book name. Always use "ed. by" not "eds. by" nor "(eds.)"

> Daniel, Michael. 2005. Understanding inclusives. *Clusivity,* ed. by Llena Filimonova, 3–48. Amsterdam: John Benjamins.
>
> Gibson, Edward. 2000. The dependency locality theory. *Image, language, brain,* ed. by Alec Marantz, Yasushi Miyashita and Wayne O'Neil, 95–126. Cambridge, MA: MIT Press.
>
> 山口佳紀 1987 「各活用形の機能」山口明徳（編）『国文法講座2』1–36. 東京：明治書院.

Or list the book name separately to save space when there are a lot of citations from one book using "(ed.)" or "(eds.)" abbreviation, as in:

Casali, Roderic F. 2011. Hiatus resolution. In van Oostendorp, Ewen, Hume and Rice. 2011, 1434–1460.

van Oostendorp, Marc, Colin J. Ewen, Elizabeth Hume and Keren Rice (eds.) 2011. *Blackwell companion to phonology*. Malden, MA: Wiley-Blackwell.

◆ **Dissertation:**

See the example below.

Inkelas, Sharon. 1989. *Prosodic constituency in the lexicon.* Ph.D. dissertation, Stanford University.

南西太郎 2005 「南西語音韻論研究」博士論文, 南西大学.

◆ **Online URLs:**

Add to the end with an underscore or in a monospaced font.

Kiparsky, Paul. 2010. .... Online: http://www.stanford.edu/~kiparskuy/Papers/....xxx.pdf.

　　　　　　　　　　　　Online: Rutgers Optimality Archive, ROA-340.

　　　　　　　　　　　　Online: University of California eScholarship.

　　　　　　　　　　　　Online: `http://www.praat.org/`.

（日本語も同様）

◆ **Miscellaneous:**

➢ Indent 1/4 inch or 6.3 mm for the second and following lines of a reference entry (i.e., hanging indent).

➢ For US cities, the abbreviated state name <u>may be</u> added for disambiguation.

　　　　Cambridge, MA: MIT Press
　　　　Cambridge: Cambridge University Press
　　　　Stanford, CA: Stanford University Press

　　Also acceptable:
　　　　New York: Routledge
　　　　Chicago: University of Chicago Press

➢ 日本語：スペース、数字、ピリオドは半角。

➢ かぎカッコ『』「」の前後にはスペースを入れない。

➢ 1項目が2行以上に渡る場合、2行目以降は6.3 mmのぶら下げインデントを設ける。

➢ 英語と日本語のリファレンスはローマ字順に混在させる。

➢ 日本語で執筆の場合の丸括弧は、<u>MS明朝半角</u>を使用する。

➢ 図のラベル（日本語）：MS明朝（例：図1　・・・の分布）

➢ 　　　　　　　（English）：italics（ex.　*Figure 1　The distribution of ...*）

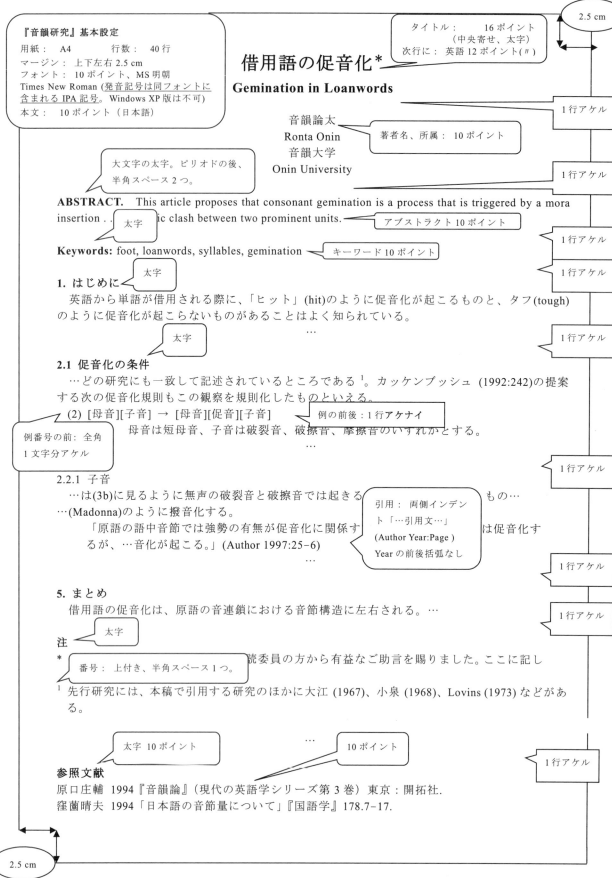

『音韻研究』基本設定
用紙： A4　　　　行数： 40 行
マージン： 上下左右 2.5 cm
フォント： 10 ポイント、MS 明朝
Times New Roman (発音記号は同フォントに含まれる IPA 記号。Windows XP 版は不可)
本文： 10 ポイント（日本語）

タイトル：　　16 ポイント
（中央寄せ、太字）
次行に： 英語 12 ポイント(〃)

2.5 cm

借用語の促音化*
Gemination in Loanwords

1 行アケル

音韻論太
Ronta Onin
音韻大学
Onin University

著者名、所属： 10 ポイント

1 行アケル

大文字の太字。ピリオドの後、半角スペース 2 つ。

ABSTRACT.　　This article proposes that consonant gemination is a process that is triggered by a mora insertion . . . ic clash between two prominent units.

太字

アブストラクト 10 ポイント

1 行アケル

Keywords: foot, loanwords, syllables, gemination

キーワード 10 ポイント

1 行アケル

1. はじめに

太字

　英語から単語が借用される際に、「ヒット」(hit)のように促音化が起こるものと、タフ(tough)のように促音化が起こらないものがあることはよく知られている。
…

1 行アケル

2.1 促音化の条件

太字

　…どの研究にも一致して記述されているところである[1]。カッケンブッシュ (1992:242)の提案する次の促音化規則もこの観察を規則化したものといえる。
　(2) [母音][子音] → [母音][促音][子音]
　　　　　母音は短母音、子音は破裂音、破擦音、摩擦音のいずれかとする。
　　　　　…

例の前後：1 行アケナイ

例番号の前： 全角 1 文字分アケル

1 行アケル

2.2.1 子音

　…は(3b)に見るように無声の破裂音と破擦音では起き〇〇〇〇〇もの…
…(Madonna)のように撥音化する。
　　「原語の語中音節では強勢の有無が促音化に関係す〇〇〇〇〇は促音化するが、…音化が起こる。」(Author 1997:25−6)
　　　　　…

引用： 両側インデント「…引用文…」
(Author Year:Page)
Year の前後括弧なし

1 行アケル

5. まとめ

　借用語の促音化は、原語の音連鎖における音節構造に左右される。…

1 行アケル

注

太字

*〇〇〇〇〇〇〇読委員の方から有益なご助言を賜りました。ここに記し

番号： 上付き、半角スペース 1 つ。

[1] 先行研究には、本稿で引用する研究のほかに大江 (1967)、小泉 (1968)、Lovins (1973) などがある。

太字 10 ポイント

… 10 ポイント

1 行アケル

参照文献
原口庄輔 1994『音韻論』（現代の英語学シリーズ第 3 巻）東京：開拓社.
窪薗晴夫 1994「日本語の音節量について」『国語学』178.7−17.

2.5 cm

Page settings: A4 Single space 1 inch (25.4 mm) margin on all sides. Times New Roman (12 pt: Use IPA symbols in this font installed with Windows 7, Vista, Mac OS X.)

1 inch margin

Rules vs. Constraints in Phonology*

Title: 16 pt bold-faced centered

blank 16 pt

Name & Affiliation: 12 pt centered

Koichi Tateishi
Kyoto University of Foreign Studies

blank 12 pt

bold-faced, capitalized, two spaces before text

ABSTRACT. This paper argues that, for the Optimality Theory to be successful as a plausible theory of Universal Grammar, it must incorporate all of the so-called post-Spell-Out syntax. . . .

bold-faced 10pt

10 pt for Abstract and Keywords (both text and heading)

Keywords: minimalist, procrastinate, move α, stress

blank

1. Introduction

bold-faced 12 pt

Generative linguists have always dreamed of constructing a system grammar that can elegantly explain why children . . . achieve

Quote: indented by 1/2 inch (12.5 mm) on both sides (Author Year:Page)

Indent 1/4 inch (6.3 mm).

> However, this success in the syntactic . . . has left unsolved many once important problems. . . . This is one of the characteristics of the Extended Standard Theory. (Tateishi 1992:121–22)

blank

2.1 Minimalist program

. . . In English, Infl lowers into a verb position, while in French, a verb raises to Infl.[1]

(3) a. Jean [$_{Infl}$ embrasse$_i$ + Infl] souvent [$_{VP}$t$_i$ Marie.]
    b. John [$_{Infl}$t$_i$] often [kisses + Infl$_i$ Mary.]

Indent 1/4 inch (6.3 mm). Set a 6 pt line space before and after examples, tables and figures.

. . . (e.g., Chomsky 1994, 1995), attributes the cross-linguistic . . . the . . . ch are "pronounced" or "Spell-Out."

Enclose commas and periods in the quotation marks.

Plain (non-bold) section number from the 3rd level and below

. . .

Use a semicolon to give items from different authors. Write out 'and' in in-text citations. Don't parenthesize years.

blank

3.1.1 Procrastinate

Procrastinate is actually irrelevant to phonology (McBright 2005; Onin and Onin 2012) and this is significant (t=0.14, p=0.009, n=32).

. . .

Use APA style for results of statistical tests.

blank

bold-faced

The note number: superscripted [1,] [2, 3,] . . . One space before text.

Notes

* I would like to thank everybody. Write acknowledgements here.
[1] Infl for Pollock is a combination of T(ense) and AGR(eement).
[2] Prince and Smolensky (1993:25) argue that the Arabic pattern can be explained by the interaction of . . . and . . . .

Notes: 10 pt

blank

References list: 10 pt

12 pt bold-faced

References

Gibson, Edward. 2000. The dependency locality theory. *Image, language, brain,* ed. by Alec Marantz, Yasushi Miyashita and Wayne O'Neil, 95–126. Cambridge, MA: MIT Press.
Yip, . . . s. *Phonology* 6.149–174.. . .

Indent 1/4 inch (6.3 mm).

1 inch margin

編集後記

　『音韻研究』第 21 号をお届けします。本号には、「日本音韻学会 2017 年春季研究発表会」と「音韻論フォーラム 2017」において発表された論文、及び本誌への一般投稿論文の中から査読を経た 10 編の研究論文、同研究発表会とフォーラムでの博士論文講演を含む招待講演論文 4 編、発表要旨 3 編、合計 17 編が収録されています。

　編集に際しまして、多くの方々にご協力とお力添えをいただきました。別掲の査読委員の方々には、詳細な査読をいただきました。また、開拓社の川田賢氏からは、出版に関してご助言をいただきました。みなさまに厚く御礼申し上げます。

　　2018 年 3 月 31 日

2017 年度　　編集担当理事
アーウィン　マーク
岩井　康雄

2017年度査読委員一覧

伊藤智ゆき （東京外国語大学）

岡崎正男 （茨城大学）

小川晋史 （熊本県立大学）

桑本裕二 （公立鳥取環境大学）

佐野真一郎 （慶応義塾大学）

ジスク　マシュー （山形大学）

高山知明 （金沢大学）

竹安大 （福岡大学）

時崎久夫 （札幌大学）

那須川訓也 （東北学院大学）

ポッペ　クレメンス （早稲田大学）

六川雅彦 （南山大学）

山根典子 （広島大学）

米山聖子 （大東文化大学）

ラブリューヌ　ローランス　（Université Bordeaux Montaigne）

【あいうえお音順】

音韻研究 2018 第21号

Phonological Studies

編集者　日本音韻論学会　　会長　田中伸一
発行者　武村哲司

2018 年 3 月 31 日　第 1 版第 1 刷発行©

発行所　　株式会社　開拓社　　113-0023　東京都文京区向丘 1-5-2
電話 (03) 5842-8900 (代表)
振替 00160-8-39587

印刷　日之出印刷株式会社　　ISBN978-4-7589-2021-6　C3380